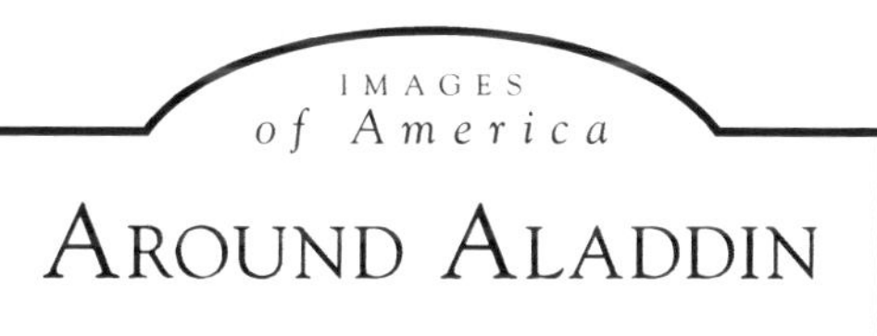
IMAGES
of America
AROUND ALADDIN

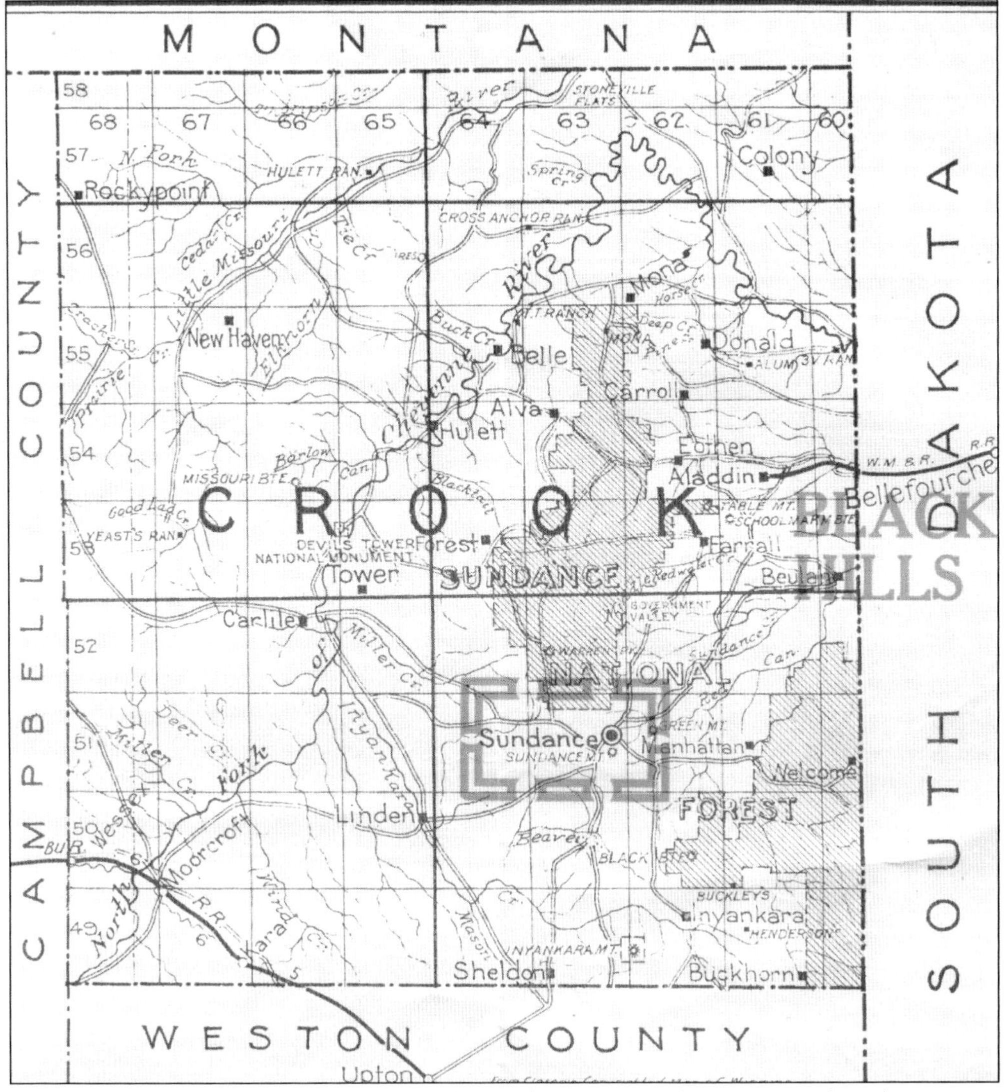

This map shows Crook County, located in the northeast corner of Wyoming. When the map was printed there were many small communities in the northeast portion of the county. Aladdin is the only one of these communities to thrive and survive to this day. The post offices and villages of Forks, Donald, Eothen, and Mona that have faded into the past continue to contribute to the rich history and stories in this corner of the state. The map shows the rivers and streams and geographical landmarks important to the area. Also illustrated is the Wyoming Valley Railroad crossing into South Dakota. (Courtesy of the Crook County Museum.)

ON THE COVER: Pictured is a view of Aladdin in the early 1900s looking east from the hill behind the store down Hay Creek through the Aladdin Valley. (Courtesy of the Crook County Museum.)

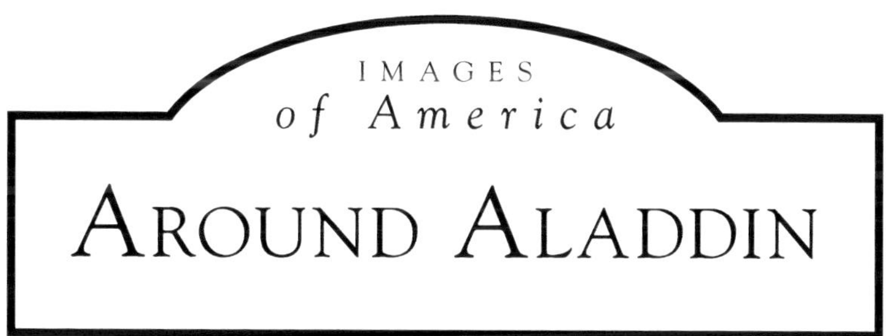

Pam Thompson

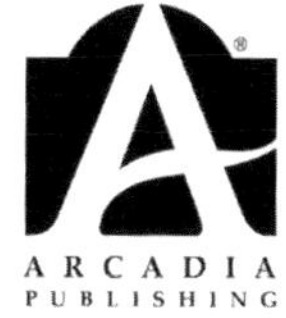

ISBN 978-14671-1548-3

Published by Arcadia Publishing
Charleston, South Carolina

Printed in the United States of America

Library of Congress Control Number: 2016931815

For all general information, please contact Arcadia Publishing:
Telephone 843-853-2070
Fax 843-853-0044
E-mail sales@arcadiapublishing.com
For customer service and orders:
Toll-Free 1-888-313-2665

Visit us on the Internet at www.arcadiapublishing.com

This book is dedicated to Peggy Nelson for her devotion to the history and stories of the Aladdin community, and also to Claudice Pearson for her careful identification and recording of history in pictures.

Contents

ACKNOWLEDGMENTS

This undertaking would not have been possible without the encouragement and support of so many friends and family. Thanks to the members of the Crook County Historical Society for recording so much of the history of Crook County almost 30 years ago, the Crook County Museum District, the Crook County Museum and museum director Rocky Courchaine, the Crook County Library, and Roberta Sago, director of the Case Library at Black Hills State University, who made their records and books available to me including the Watson Parker Collection. I will always remember the many friends and neighbors surrounding Aladdin who were eager to share their memories with me. There are so many who have shared their stories, memories, and pictures to make this book possible, and there are just as many who did not get their memories and stories onto these few pages. Everyone has a great number of stories to share, and there is just not enough time or pages to fit them all into one book. I welcomed and appreciated all the people who offered any help they could. These wonderful people include Dr. Warren Wilson, Chester and Evelyn Hejde and cousin Donabell Ross, Judy and Alan Cowardin for letting me use the information from Margaret Carr's books, Susan Rice for sharing her aunt Peggy's notebooks and showing me where buildings used to be, Chuck Pearson for letting me use the pictures in his mother's photo albums, Judy Brengle and the Aladdin Store, Cindy Brengle, Margaret Ellsbury, Antoinette Curren, Keith McDonald, and Steve Sick for letting me keep his Sanborn map for more than a few days. John Whalen deserves a special thank you for the afternoons he spent telling me great stories. I thank every one of you, especially those of you whose names escape me from time to time. A special thank you goes to my husband, Hugh Thompson, for his patience and tolerance. And to Earl, who didn't get all the ear rubs he wanted. And of course I need to thank the editors at Arcadia for not giving up on me and this project. Thank you all.

Introduction

Aladdin is the lowest settlement in Wyoming at 3,749 feet. A basin just eight miles to the north of town is the lowest point in the state at 3,125 feet above sea level where the Belle Fourche River crosses out of Wyoming into South Dakota. The area is rich in fossil remains, from petrified tree branches to lizard footprints.

The discovery of coal and the building of a railroad established Aladdin. There was much interest in the coalfields, which were known at the time as "coal lands," in Township 54 of the new Crook County in the northeast corner of Wyoming. The numerous goldmines and reduction mills in the Lead-Deadwood area of South Dakota were eager to find a nearby supply of coal. Timber was too valuable to burn, as it was being harvested for mine timbers and buildings.

On April 13, 1882, an official survey was made. There were three companies that established claims in the area where coal was discovered. The companies established their own towns or communities. Aladdin belonged to the California Company. Bakertown was the town for the Hay Creek Company. The third coal company was the Philadelphia Company, but the company ownership of the town of Barrett has never been completely established.

As coal mining progressed, a townsite was surveyed and platted, and company houses were built for miners and their families. These houses were square in shape. Sheds, root cellars, and outhouses accompanied each home. There were about 20 houses on the south side of Hay Creek. Other buildings and businesses began to pop up as the small communities began to show signs of growing pains. Some of these buildings were schools, hotels, saloons, a barbershop, a Methodist-Episcopal church, a dance hall or two, and a pest house, a crude type of isolation ward where people with communicable diseases were taken. This building sat across Hay Creek just east of the store. Pest houses were common in communities not only in the West but throughout the country.

To meet the demands of the busy community, the company commissary became a general store. It sold clothing, groceries, and other supplies needed by the people living there and also those living in the nearby countryside. Aladdin served as the hub of commerce in the early years.

The coal mine employed immigrant miners from Italy, Sweden, and Scotland, plus many other countries. The mining was difficult and dangerous. Most miners were paid 75¢ per mined ton.

Hauling coal and freight by oxen kept pace with the growing community and its needs for a few years. As more mines in the Black Hills were worked, the need for coal grew, as did the need for goods to reach the inhabitants of the new and growing settlements, and faster transportation was needed. At first, the coal from quickly opened mines was hauled to the mills. After a time, it was hauled to Belle Fourche, South Dakota, by ox teams to be loaded onto trains. Within 10 years, the demand exceeded this means of shipping's capacity. The three companies combined to build a railroad between the mines and the train station. The new railroad followed a survey that was first made by the Chicago & North Western Railroad Company. This new railroad would travel westward from Belle Fourche into Wyoming and the coal mining district, connecting the coal mine with the Chicago & North Western, which would then move the coal farther along the line.

The Wyoming & Missouri Valley Railroad filed papers of incorporation on June 24, 1897, and construction began in the spring of 1899. Aladdin served as the end of the line for all things hauled into this end of Wyoming. Watson Parker noted of this part of Northeast Wyoming that it was not as isolated and uninhabited as it appeared at first glance. At the peak of coal production, there were around 500 people living in the Aladdin Valley. The Wyoming & Missouri Valley Railroad and the people who settled and worked along Hay Creek in the Aladdin Valley helped start what in this modern age is Wyoming's most important industry.

Coal production around Aladdin may have tapered off, but 90 miles to the west, the coal industry of neighboring Campbell County supplies 40 percent of the nation's coal from 13 mines of the top 20 coal producers in the state of Wyoming. In 2011, these 13 mines produced a combined total of over 426 million tons of coal. The coal in one of today's hopper cars is probably a bit more than what was carried by an entire Wyoming & Missouri Valley coal train, and the coal in an average 100-car shipment today is most likely greater than all the coal ever shipped out of the Aladdin Valley by train or wagon.

One

The Coal

The earliest working coalfields in Wyoming were small banks of naturally exposed outcroppings of coal uncovered by erosion. The first discovery of coal was probably in the Wyoming Brakes southeast of present-day Aladdin. It had been mined by early settlers, who for protection lived in a nearby stockade. Coal was discovered at the north end of the Black Hills on Hay Creek between 1875 and 1880.

The coal along Hay Creek was in two beds in the lower part of the Lakota Sandstone Foundation. The prominent escarpment that flanks the encircling outer rim of the Black Hills is produced by the massive hard sandstone of the Lakota and Dakota Formations. The weathering of the soft shale beneath enhances the relief and the sandstone outcrops in the high cliffs. The Lakota Sandstone is usually 150 to 300 feet thick and is composed of coarse-grained massive and cross-bedded sandstone with thin partings of shale. At or near the base there is a formation with an erratic bed of bituminous coal. The Lakota Sandstone is conspicuous on Hay Creek around Aladdin, where with the Dakota Sandstone it makes prominent cliffs. Here the Lakota is thinner than in other places in Wyoming, averaging less than 100 feet. To the west and south of Aladdin, the Lakota is somewhat thicker. On the south fork of Hay Creek, in a section measured by Professor Walter P. Jenny, the Lakota measured 75 feet. The Lakota Sandstone Formation in which the coal is found is poorly exposed near the valley as it caps the middle and south forks of Hay Creek near Barrett, Bakertown, and Aladdin.

Coal was not the only ore to be found in these mines. Gold, copper, and uranium were also found in the fossil formation. Coal mining was greatest from 1898 to 1902, when 150 to 200 men were employed and 10,000 long tons of coal were shipped. Peak production was in 1901, when 40,000 tons of coal were mined and shipped out. One Black Hills newspaper stated that this discovery of coal would run 1,000 miles for 100 years.

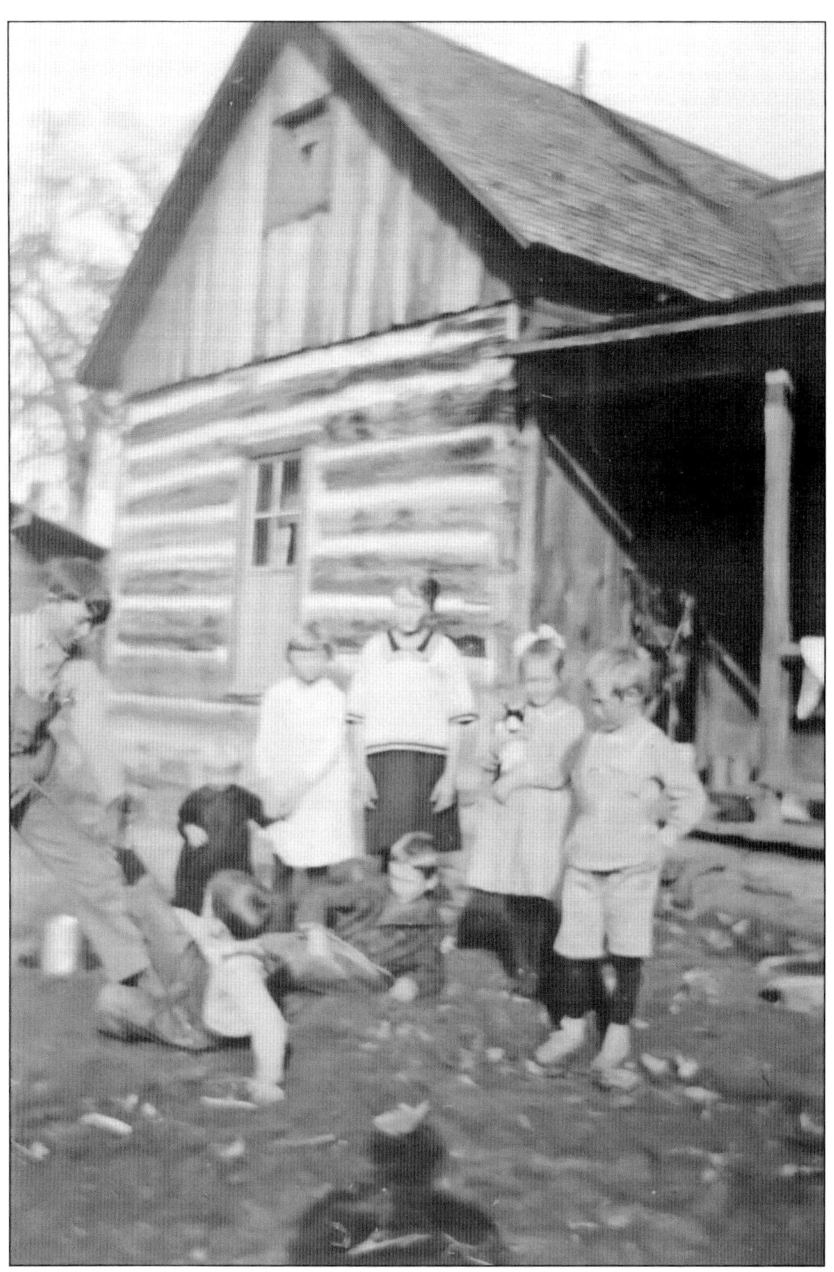

The coal land along Hay Creek was officially surveyed in April 1882. By this time, there already had been about 2,000 tons of coal mined, but that coal had not been put on the market. Often the early settlers simply took buckets or barrels to these coal banks and gathered up any loose coal they could carry away. When it was possible to use a team and wagon close to a good outcropping, a sizeable load could be hauled at one time. A lump of coal would provide a longer-lasting source of warmth than wood cut from the nearby forests and was considerably less work. At the time coal was being mined, it was said that good coal burned so hot it made the stove top rattle. Pictured here in front of the Pearson log cabin, the five Hassenbuler kids and E.J. Linsay enjoy the sunshine with Frank and Mary Pearson, knowing that their home will be warm and cozy when they go inside. (Courtesy of Chuck Pearson.)

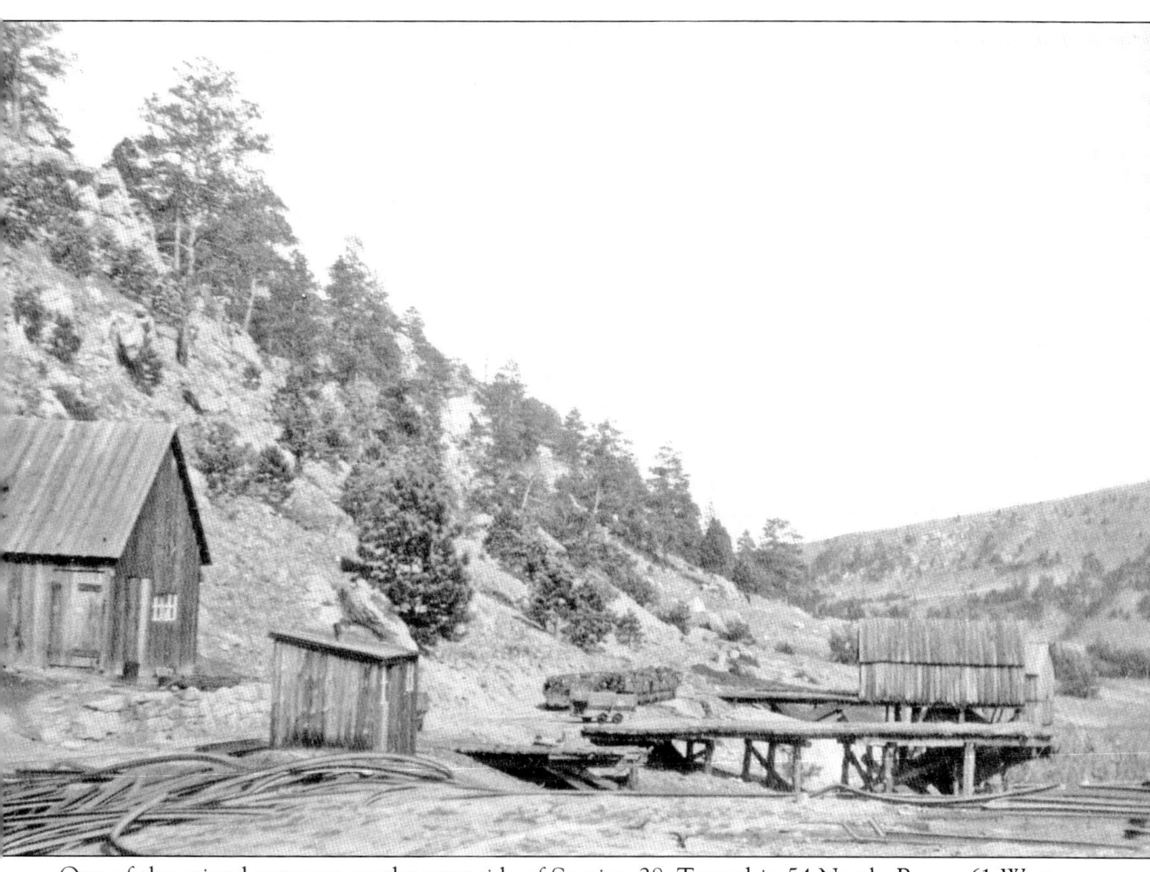

One of the mined outcrops on the west side of Section 28, Township 54 North, Range 61 West shows to have been 300 feet long. Within a half-mile of the Aladdin Valley along the base of the bluff, seven entries and prospect holes were driven into the coal bed. All are now caved in, so the coal bed itself cannot be seen. The dump, mine tracks, and cable used for hauling ore out of the mine show that a workable coal bed must have been found here. Mine reports state that this coal bed was about five feet thick, but complete abandonment suggests the coal may not have been of a satisfactory quality. This is the Stillwell Mine, owned by a San Francisco company. The Lakota Formation, which contains the coal layers, can be seen in the background as it runs down the Aladdin Valley. The formation could also produce a trace of gold and good-quality moonshine. It has been said that in the winter months when passersby saw a column of steam going up, they knew it was not coffee but a still. The earnings from moonshine were considerably more than the wages for working in a coal mine. (Courtesy of the Crook County Museum.)

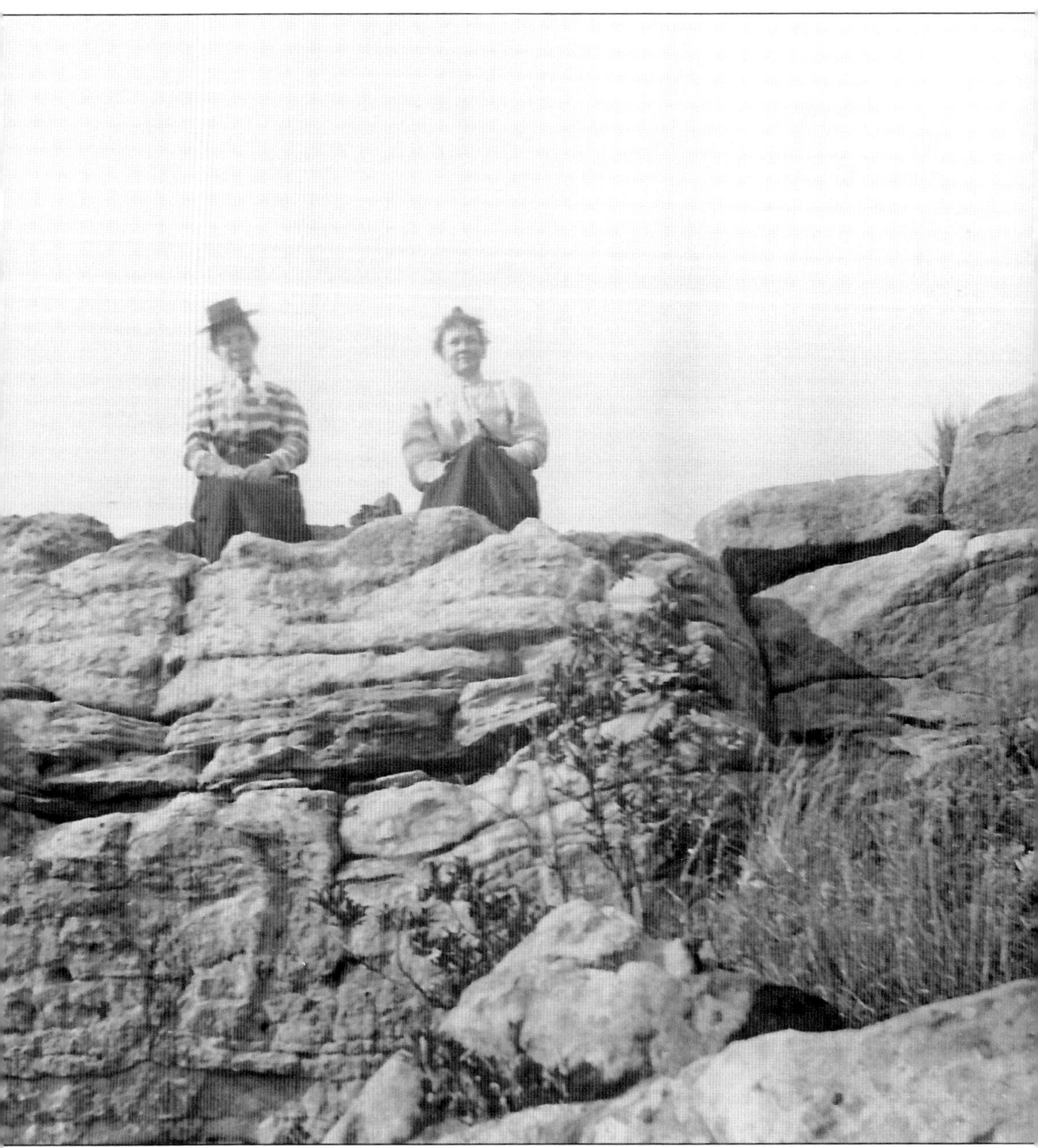

Here sit two adventurous young ladies atop the Lakota Formation above the mines at Aladdin. The Lakota Formation is a sequence of rock of the early Cretaceous Period in western North America. The area that is now Crook County was once covered by a prehistoric ocean, as seen by the sea plant, shellfish, and shark fossils found in the area. These fossils date back 110 million years. The formation consists of interfingering deposits of palatal and fluvial sandstone, siltstone, and claystone exposed on the floor and lower slopes of the valleys. This makes up the main cross-bedded thick masses of sandstones interlaced with shale, fire clay, and local coal beds. Generally, the Lakota supports a fairly dense growth of pine trees, which contrasts with the grassy slopes. (Courtesy of Tom Robinson.)

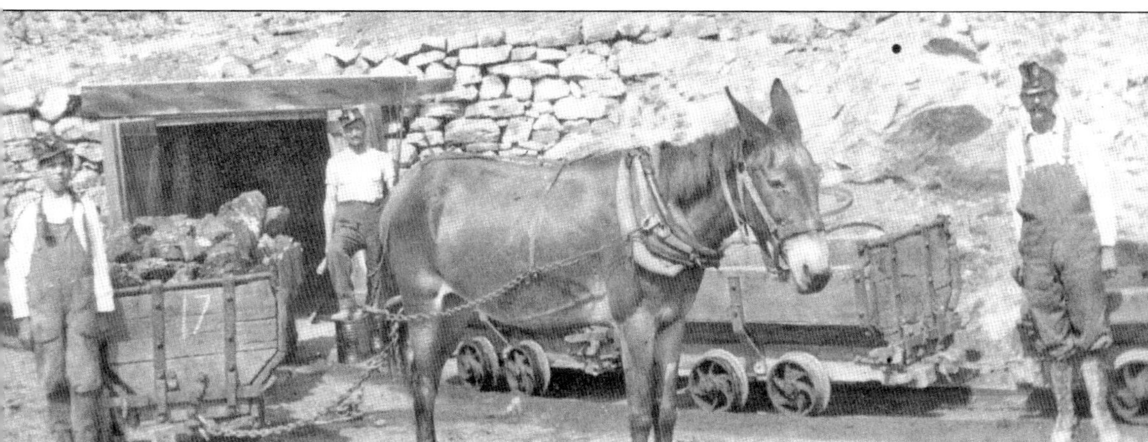

This is the entrance to the mine at Bakertown. George the mule and his ore car were used to bring the coal or the coal miners to the mine entrance. Pictured with George are Frank Gervasi (far right) and his son Joseph Gervasi (far left). Standing by the mine entrance is John De Francesh. For 10 years, Frank was the manager for the mine at Bakertown, known as the Stilwell Coal Company. At the same time, he operated a saloon with his brother-in-law, Louis Graif. Later, Frank would the buy Bakertown Township. In its heyday, it had a saloon, a pool hall, a hotel, and a dance hall. There he engaged in farming and ranching. It was a happy day when in 1902 he received his first citizenship papers. He filed on a homestead in October 1906 and received his final citizenship papers on April 30, 1912. The American flag never failed to fly over his home every Fourth of July. To Frank Gervasi, it was the most important day of the year. (Courtesy of the Aladdin Store.)

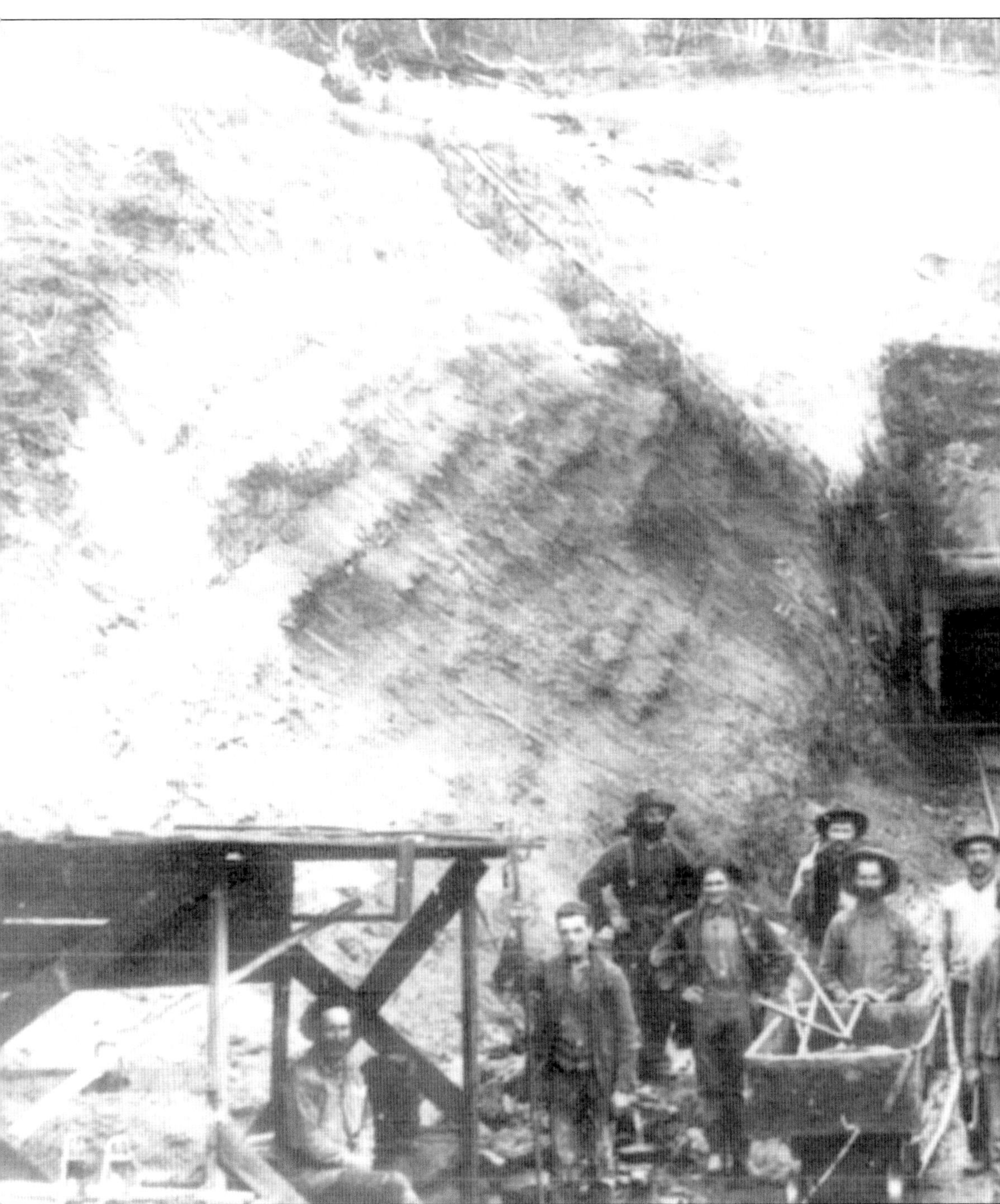

This mine was on the Geis family ranch along Oak Creek. It was blown shut many years ago to keep curious young boys from going too far inside. At the peak of mining, 500 people lived in the Aladdin Valley. Most of these families had one or two members working in one of the coal mines in the valley. Many of the miners were from Italy, Sweden, and Scotland. The homeland of each and every miner working in Wyoming is listed in all reports the mines were expected to submit to the state mine inspector. All accidents, with the name of the injured or deceased,

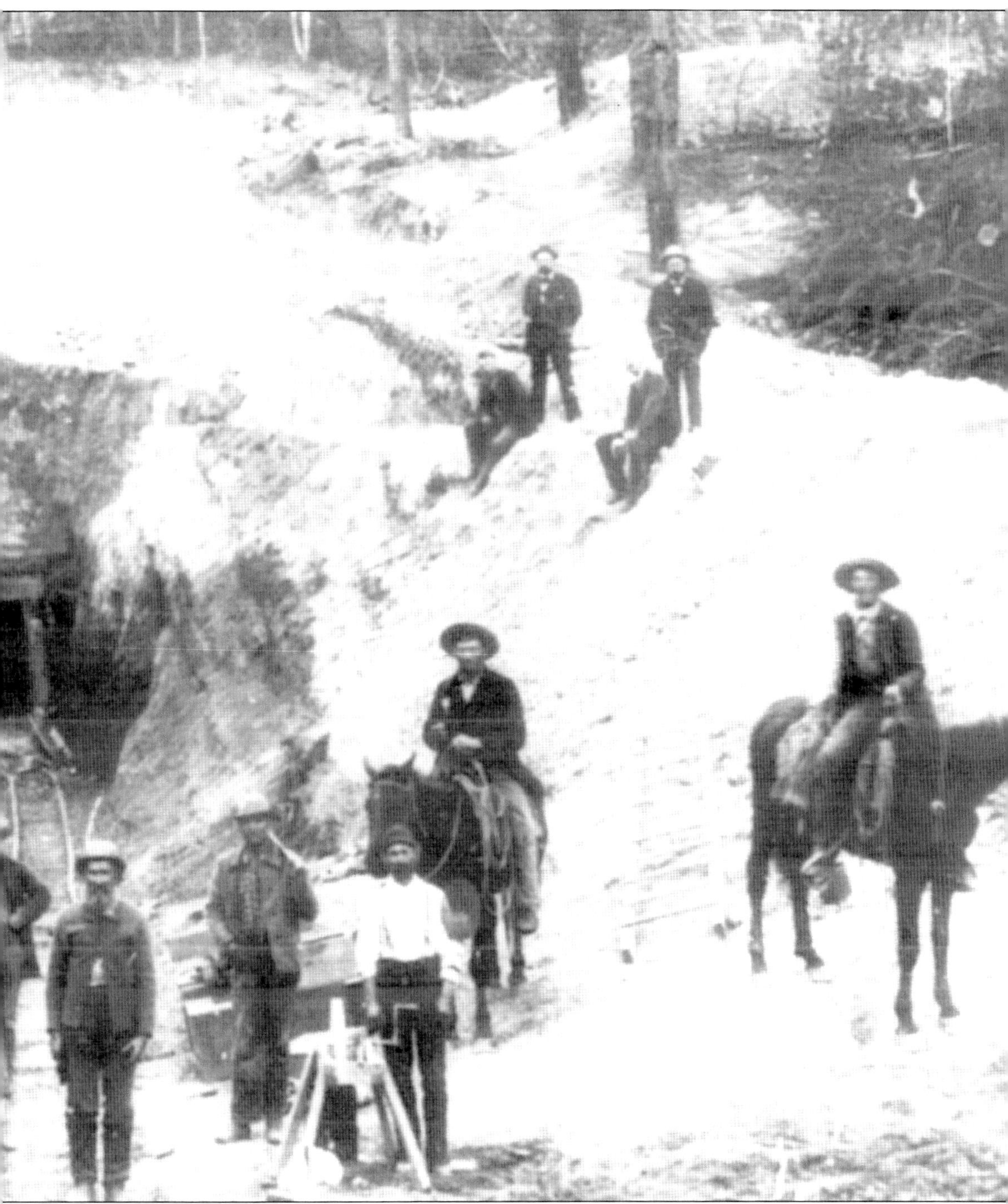

were also recorded with the Wyoming State Mine Office. Working in these mines was difficult and dangerous. The danger from a collapse of the tunnel was very real, and the threat of the coal catching fire was always with them. One such coal fire is said to have burned for 15 years. The miners earned 75¢ for each ton of coal mined. The names of these miners have passed from the memory of those who stayed in the valley long after the coal ran out. (Courtesy of the Crook County Museum.)

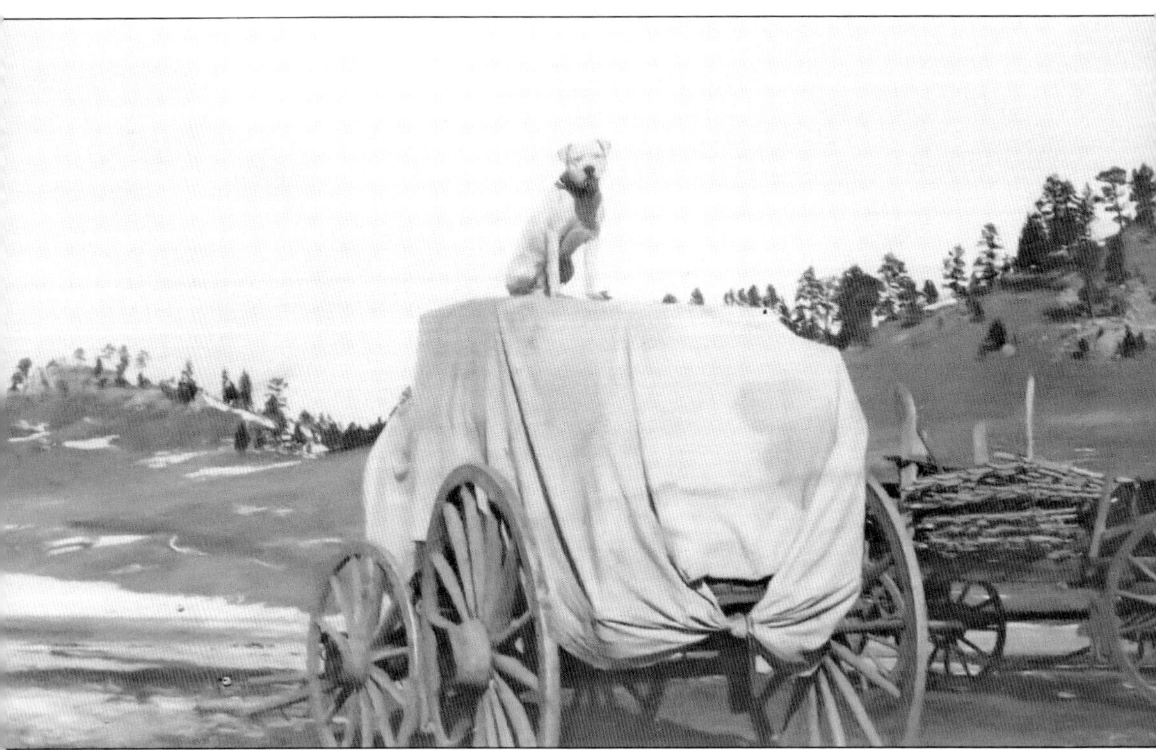

Here sits Spot on his favorite perch for freight train duty. For the first few years, the coal companies hauled their coal to the gold smelters in the mining towns of Lead and Deadwood, South Dakota, by freight wagons. These wagon teams would travel south to Beulah, Wyoming, and into South Dakota along Sand Creek Canyon to reach the mines and smelters. As the railroads reached farther west, the coal companies found they could haul the coal by wagon to Belle Fourche, South Dakota, along a gentler grade. At Belle Fourche, the coal would be loaded onto trains that would continue up into the Black Hills or back onto wagons to continue to more isolated mining operations. It was not long before the demand for coal from Hay Creek was more than wagons could haul. (Courtesy of Chuck Pearson.)

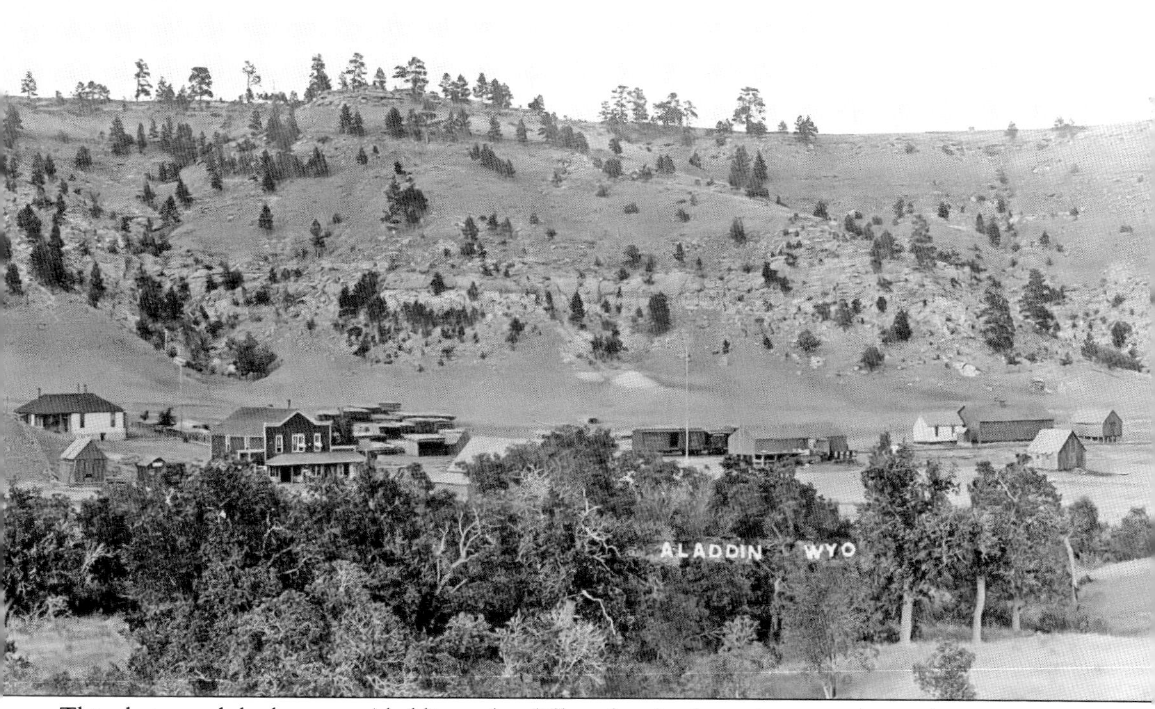

This photograph looks across Aladdin to the cliffs and rocks above the town. A semi-bituminous, black coal resembling the soft coal of the East is found on the eastern border of the county. These rocks consist of massive ochre-yellow sandstone weathering to a yellowish brown on the surface, underlain with gray drab clay shales with local thin layers of coal and plant remains. Coal mined at Larrabee and Young was seen to be 10 to 20 feet and at Barrett as 2 to 16 feet along with gray shales, sandy shales, and plant remains. At 20 to 30 feet, the formation became soft gray sandstone with carbonized plant remains. This information was furnished by the 1889 Sundance Board of Trade report for the commercial, industrial, and transportation interests of Wyoming. (Courtesy of the Crook County Museum.)

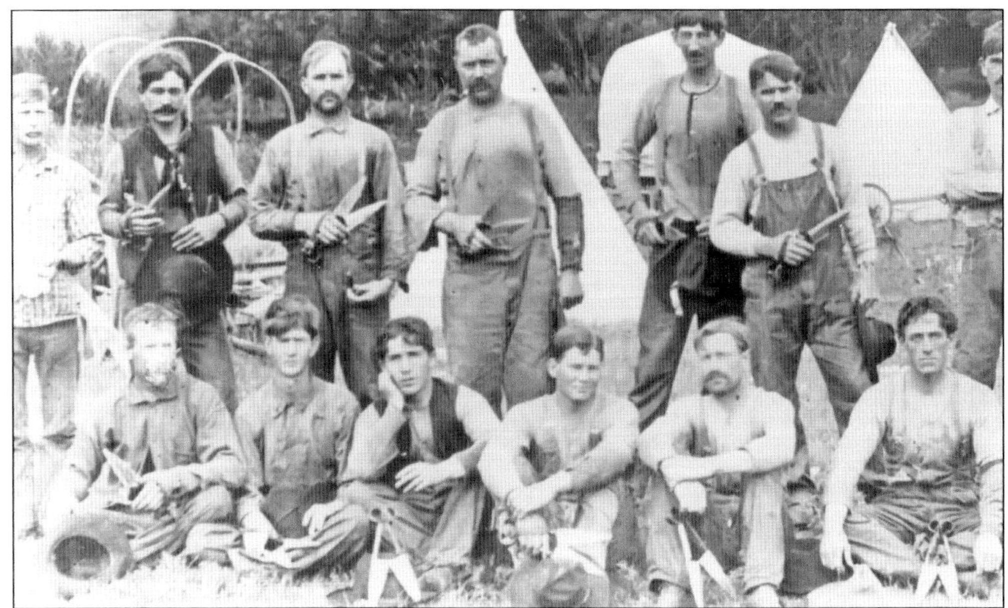

Many miners found it necessary to hold two or more jobs. During the winter, Walt Marchant drove a mule that pulled ore cars from the mine. At the age of 16, he learned to shear sheep; come spring, he put together a shearing crew. He also established a ranch that is still in his family. Pictured here in the early 1900s at the H.G. Ware ranch are, from left to right, (first row) Duff Mewhirter, Vaughn Ackerman, Guy Prickett, Walt Marchant, Guy Mewhirter, and a Prickett brother; (second row) Mick (cook for the Ware ranch), Ed DeFord, George Grenier, Louis Strand, Clint Walker, Jim Jolley, and Sherman DeFord. (Courtesy of Chuck Pearson.)

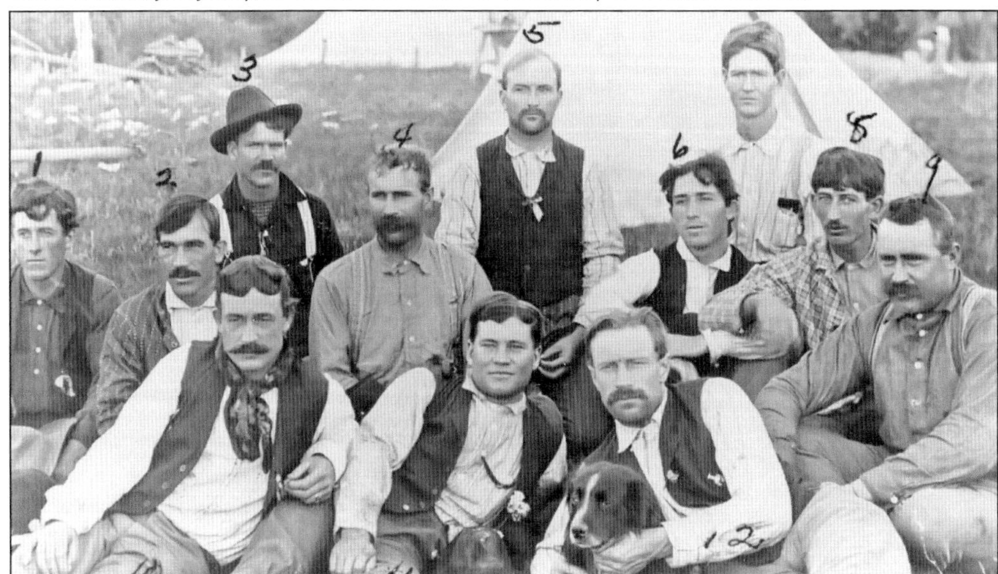

In 1907, Ed DeFord was in the sheep business. He had a crew that sheared with manual blades; they became very good and could shear at a fast pace. This was important because they were paid by the number of sheep sheared. From left to right are Vaughn Ackerman, Sherman DeFord, unidentified, Duff Mewhirter, George Grenier, Guy Prickett, Clint Walker, Jim Jolley, Louis Strand, Ed DeFord, Walt Marchant, Guy Mewhirter, and Earl the dog. (Courtesy of the Crook County Museum.)

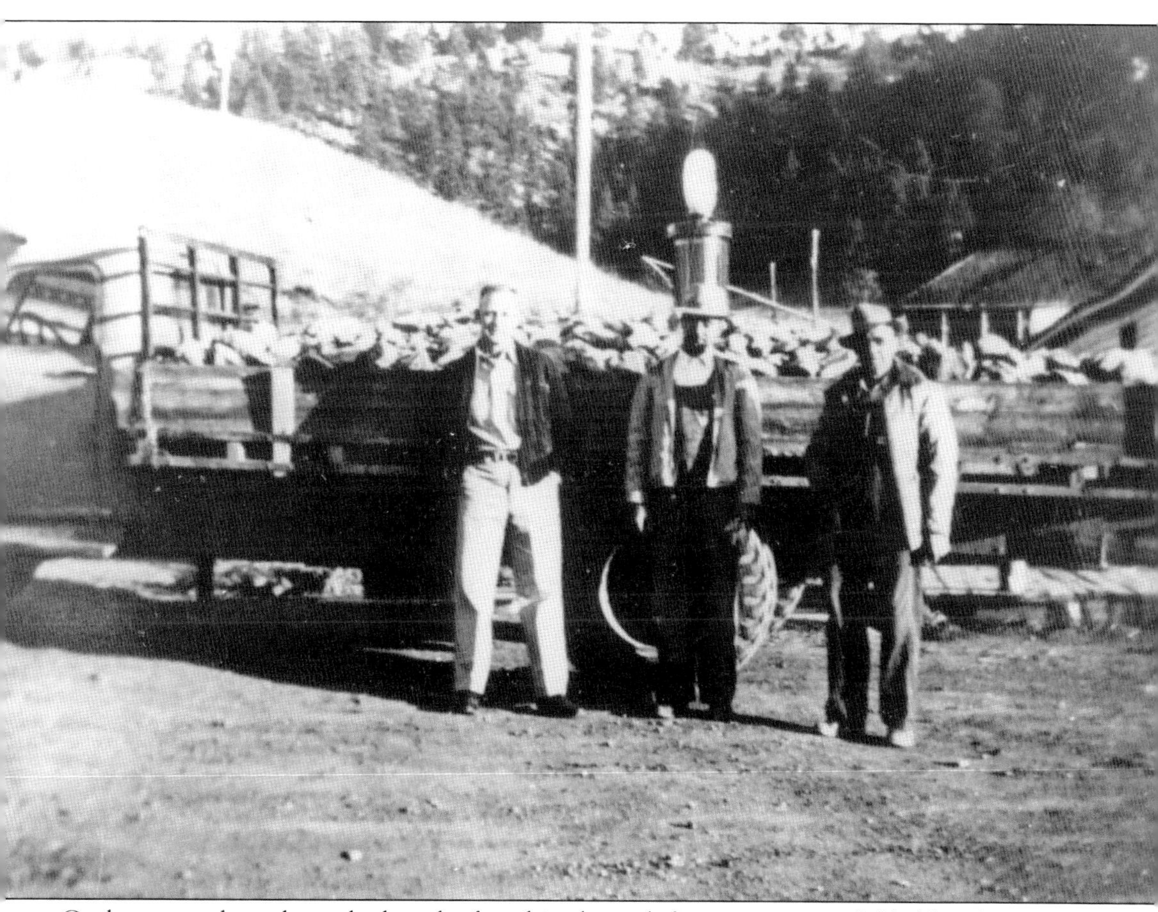

Coal was not the only ore body to be found in the rock formations around Aladdin. Copper, gold, silver, and uranium could be discovered at any time in any place. On January 16, 1914, the *Crook County Monitor* ran the headline "Discovery of Fabulously Rich Gold Ore Made Near Aladdin." The newspaper told of the latest gold discovery at Eothen, four miles from Aladdin. This discovery stirred up considerable excitement. Pictured here from left to right are Verle Wagner, Tony Stedellie, and Paul Heetland as they stopped at the Aladdin Store before they hauled a truckload of uranium to Edgemont, South Dakota, to be processed. Tony was said to walk everywhere he went. (Courtesy of Chuck Pearson.)

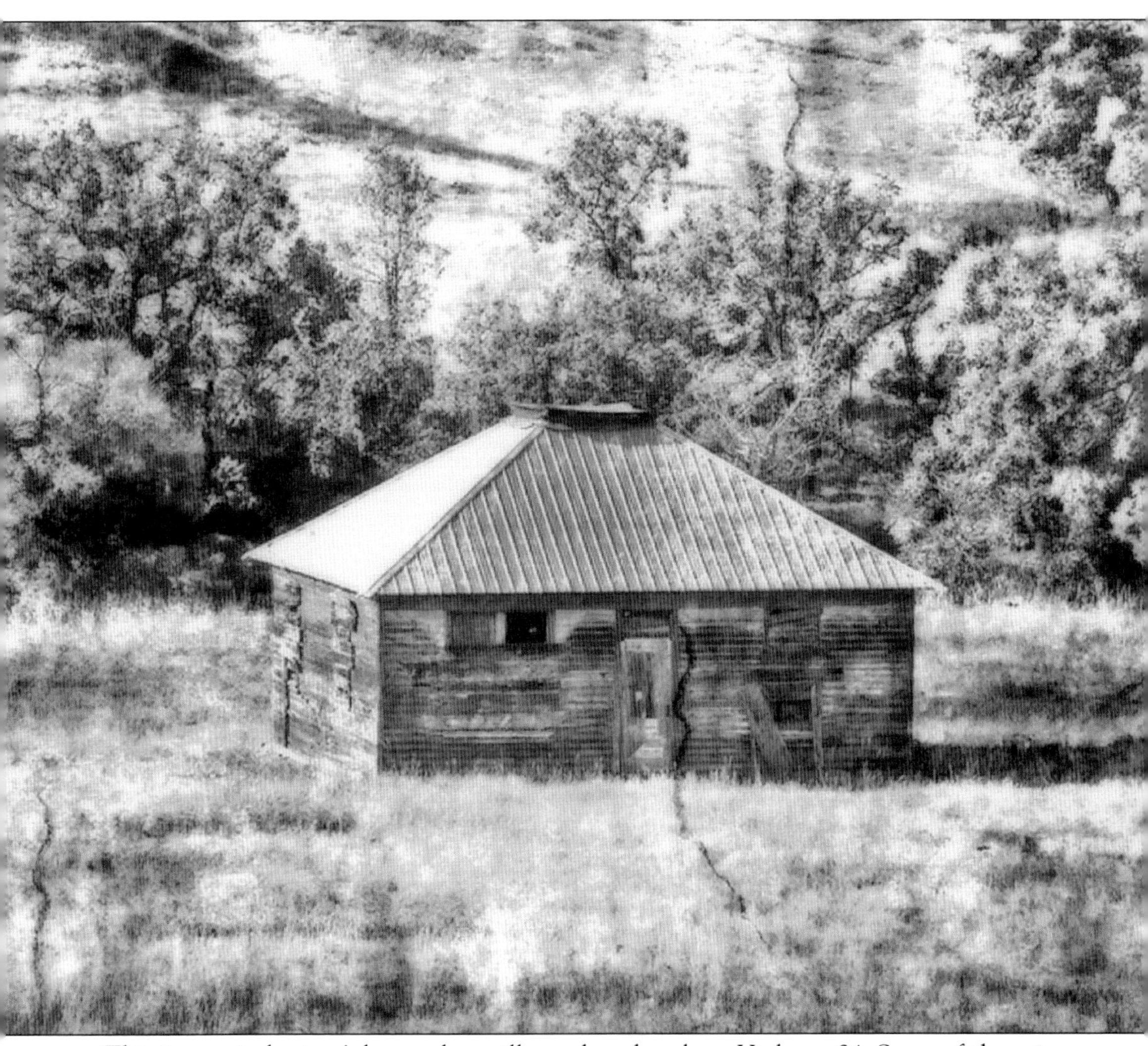

This is a typical miner's house that still stands today along Highway 24. Some of the miners built their own houses, while others lived in houses that the mine company built. The small, square houses could hold a family or several unmarried miners. Coal miners were often European immigrants seeking a better life. These hard-working men faced many dangers in the early Wyoming coal mines. Explosions from the extremely volatile coal dust were common and often fatal. Mining coal was a systematic and laborious process. The Wyoming coal mine inspector reported in 1899 that the Aladdin Mine No. 1 had an average of 35 miners, but at the time of the report, 80 were employed. The capacity of the mine was 160 tons per day. This mine had natural ventilation. There had been one non-fatal accident during the year. (Courtesy of the Crook County Museum.)

Two

The Tipple

A tipple is a structure used for sorting and loading coal into railroad cars, wagons, and even pick-up trucks. There were tipples in use at most of the mines along Hay Creek in the late 1800s and early 1900s. The tipple now called the Aladdin Tipple was built in 1898 as part of the coal mining operations at Bakertown and the Stillwell mine in the Aladdin area north of Hay Creek. Most coal mines in the area had tipples to make sorting and loading easier and more efficient. The Aladdin Tipple is believed to be one of the last, if not the last, wooden tipples standing west of the Missouri River.

When the coal was pulled out of the mine tunnels by mules, donkeys, or men, it was dumped into the tipple to be sorted as it rolled down the hillside. Gravity did most of the work. A chute operator had little to do to encourage the pieces of coal to continue rolling on down the chute. Timbers for this structure came from the forests in the Bear Lodge Mountains, some 10 to 15 miles to the west of the coal mines. John Pearson and his sawmill at Eothen supplied the timber needed to complete the building of this tipple.

The tipple may lean a bit with age, its timbers may be cracked and worn, and the catwalk may sway in the breeze, but people still take time to admire and wonder how this strange wooden thing worked and how it has stood for so very long. The Aladdin Tipple has long since been out of work, but for over 100 years, it has stood as a sentinel over the valley.

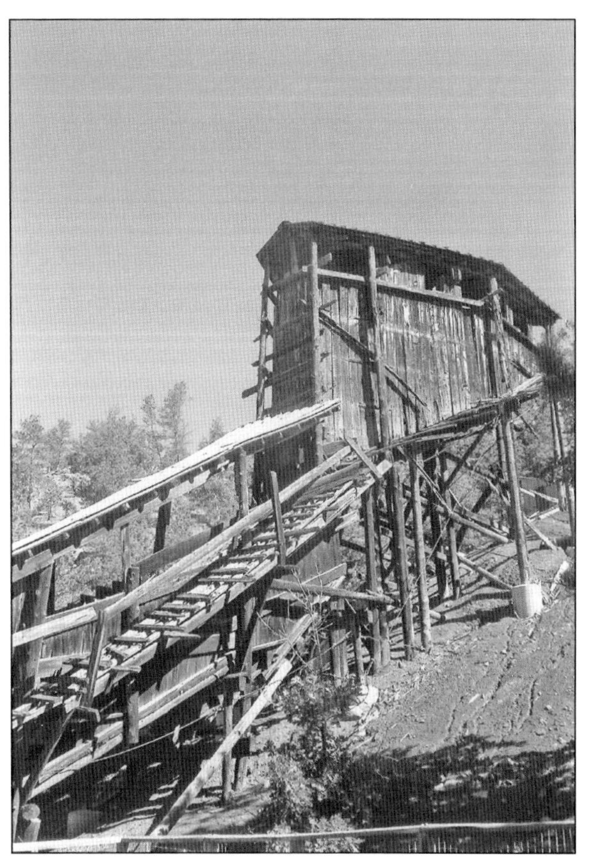

The Aladdin Tipple consists of two parts, the coal bin and the chute. The coal bin is at the upper end of the tipple, at the entrance to the mine. The timber and rails that connected the tipple to the mine entrance have long since gone away. When the ore car full of coal reached the surface, it would be tipped, and the coal would run into a gable-roofed structure and stored until the sorting and loading process took place. When the door at the bottom of the bin was opened, the tapered funnel shape of the bin floor would gravity-feed the coal into the chute system. The remaining part of the wooden catwalk still clings to the right side of the chute. A miner or the manager of the tipple would walk up and down the catwalk with a large wooden rake-like tool to help the coal along as it tumbled down to find the right-sized slot before it could be loaded into the waiting wagons or railroad cars. (Left, courtesy of Hugh Thompson; below, courtesy of Black Hills State University, Case Library, Watson Parker Collection.)

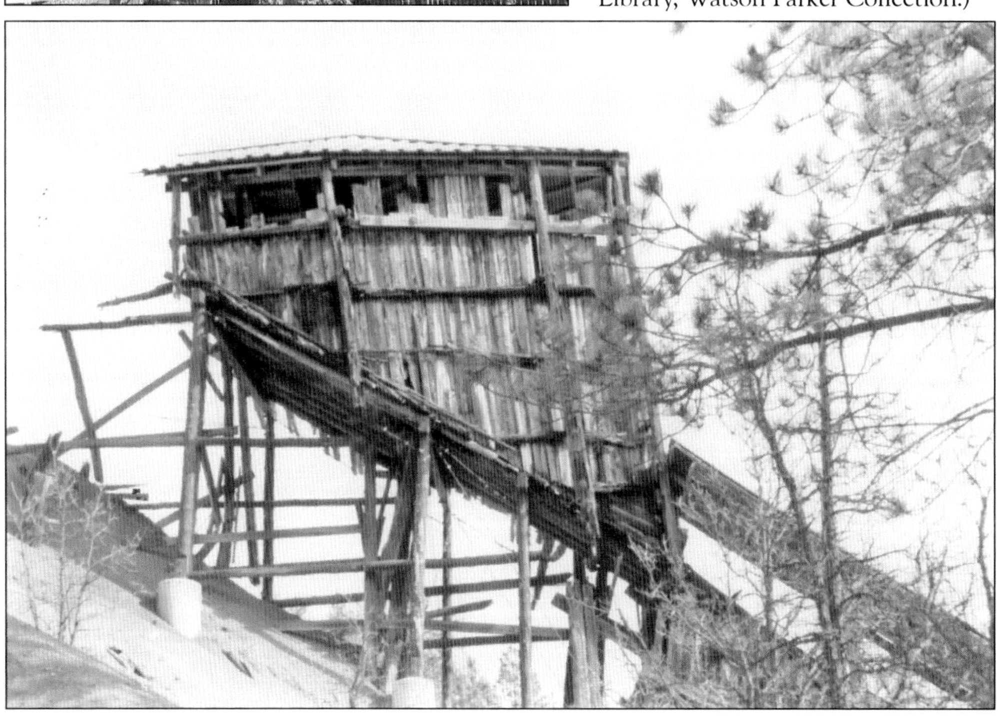

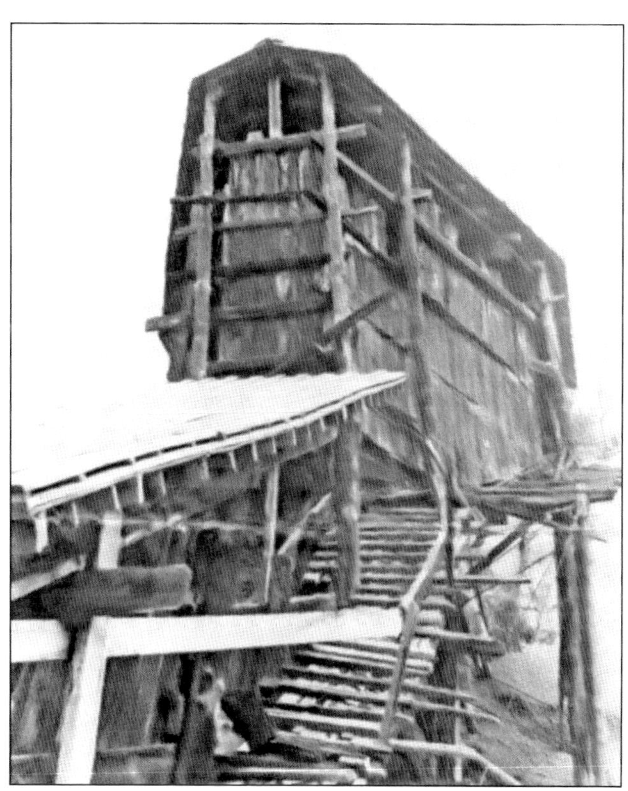

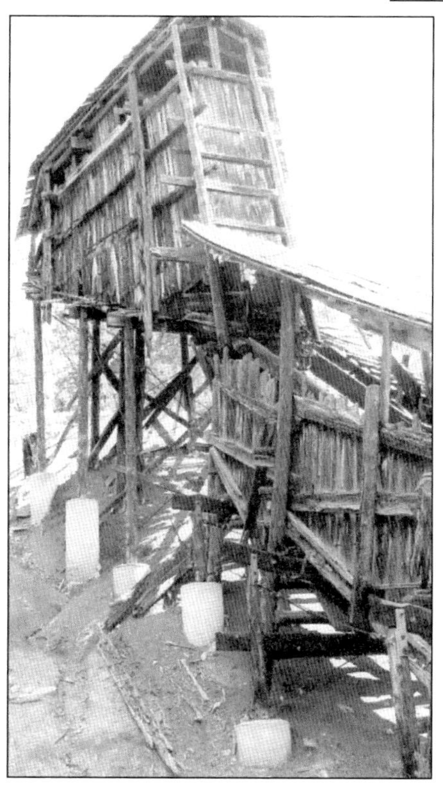

The chute system was constructed in such a manner as to allow three sizes of coal to be sorted as it traveled with gravity down the slope of the tipple and the hillside. The three sizes were nut, egg, and lump. The nut size was the size of a walnut, the egg size was the size of an average egg, and the lump size was anything larger. There were three passages in the chutes, one for each size of coal. The coal would them be dumped into the waiting wagons or train cars depending on the size and what it was needed for. Coal for household use could be almost any size, but most housewives would not want to try to load big clunkers into their stoves. Coal to be used in the smelting process and for fueling locomotives would have had to meet a size requirement that would give the most efficient energy. (Above, courtesy of Hugh Thompson; left, courtesy of Black Hills State University, Case Library, Watson Parker Collection.)

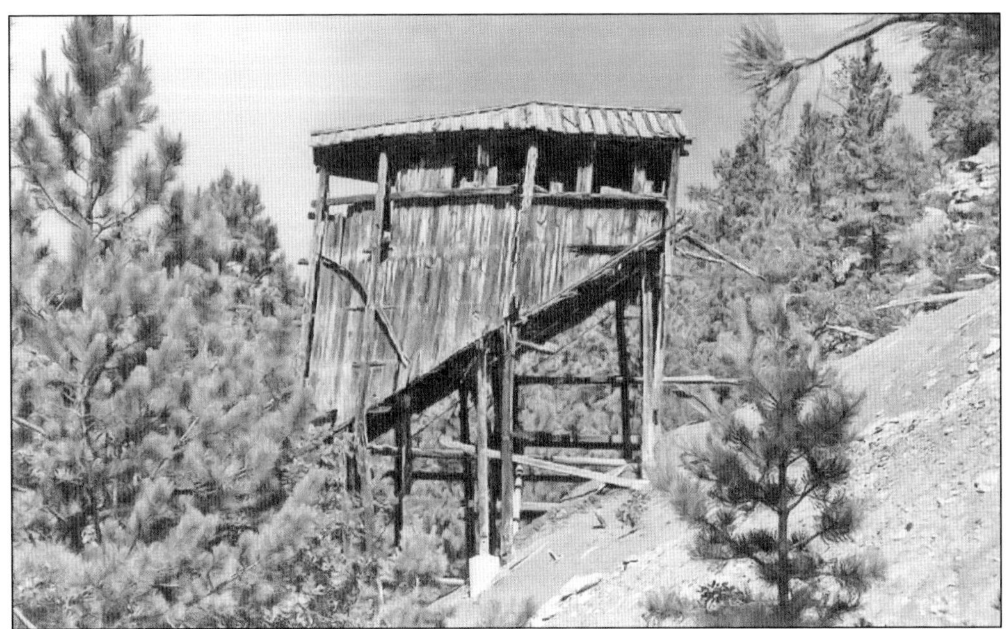

The coal that had already dropped through the right-sized screens onto the different chutes would then be delivered into railcars under the structure. Years of sediment carried down the slope of the hillside because of erosion has now almost completely filled the space that was originally created for loading the coal into waiting cars and wagons. The shifting of loose shale from the Lakota Formation, upon which the tipple sits, has not only filled in the road bed and loading spaces built into the structure but is also in the process of causing permanent damage to the structure itself. When the tipple was in constant use, this normal erosion would have been controlled by the coal mine company, and the damage would have been minimal. (Above, courtesy of Hugh Thompson; below, courtesy of Black Hills State University, Case Library, Watson Parker Collection.)

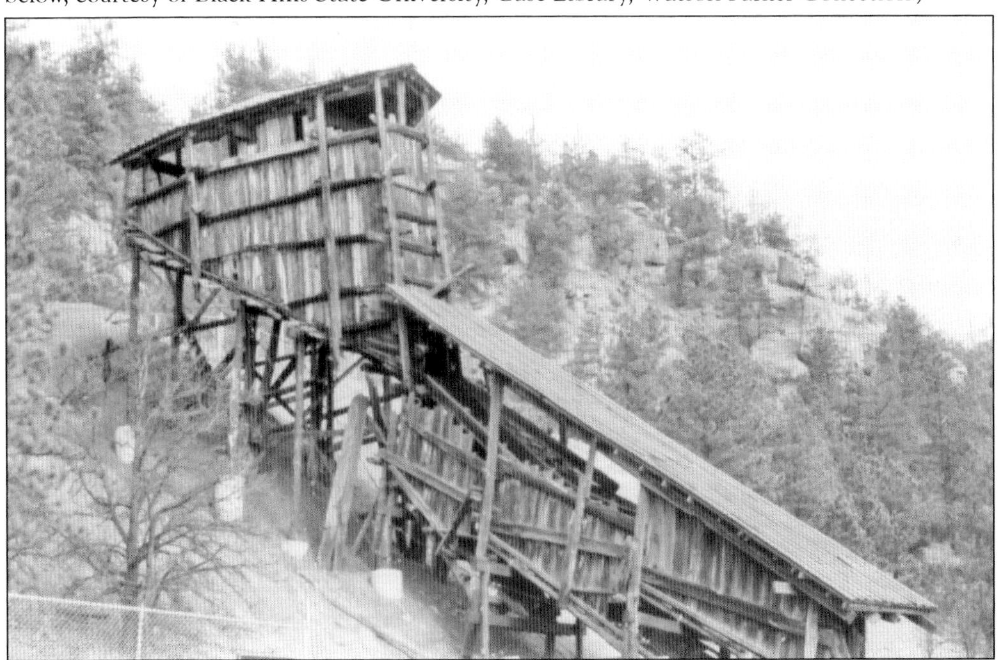

The historic Aladdin Tipple was first looked at for mitigation by the Wyoming Abandoned Mine Land division in May 1990 at the request of many of the residents of the Aladdin area. That investigation indicated that the dilapidated wooden structure posed a significant physical hazard to people wanting to explore the site of both the tipple and the mine itself. There was also a well-developed local call to preserve the tipple for posterity. Because of the efforts made by the residents of the Aladdin Valley, a two-phase restoration project was developed and put into place by the Abandoned Mine Land office. This restoration project officially began in October 1991. The first phase involved stabilization of the tipple structure itself with timber supports and cement reinforcements. This first phase was completed in just three months. The second phase involved the development of interpretative features, a parking area, and a security fence. This two-month-long phase was completed in June 1992. (Right, courtesy of Hugh Thompson; below, courtesy of Black Hills State University, Case Library, Watson Parker Collection.)

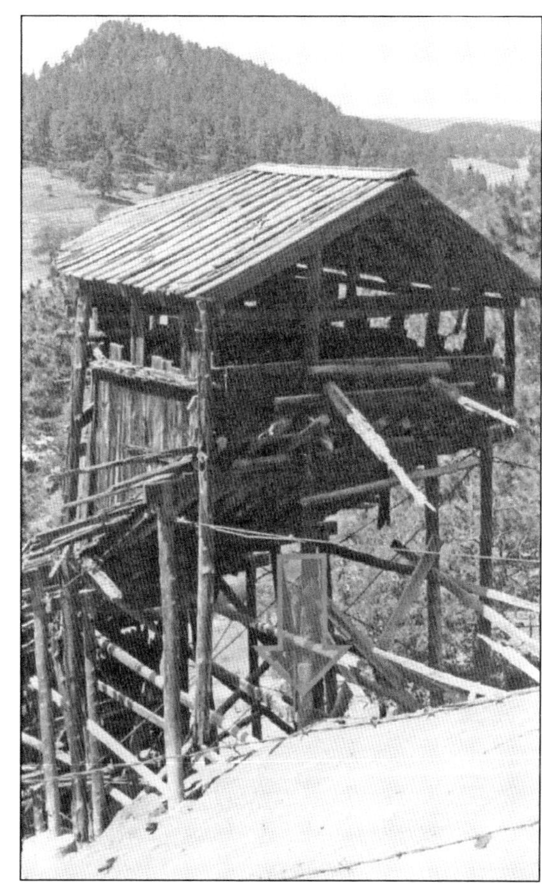

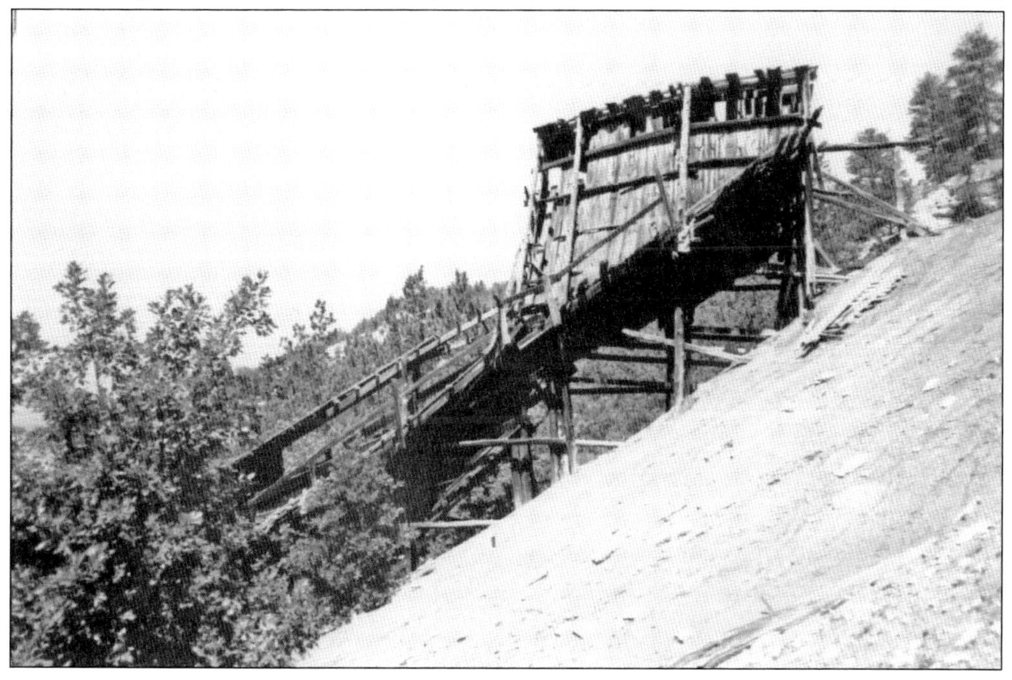

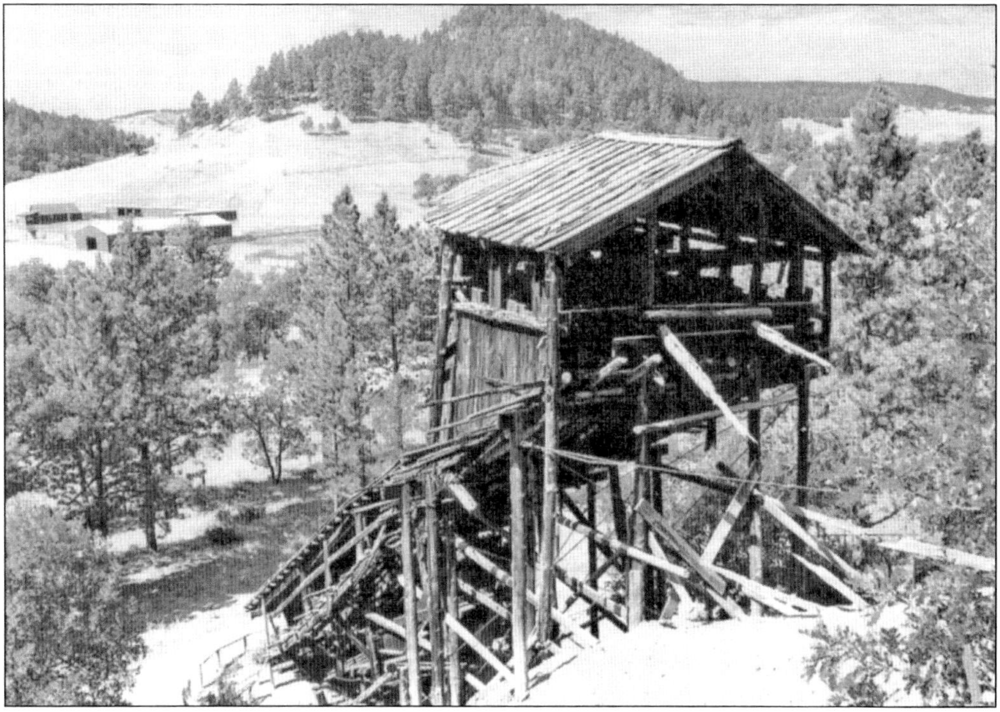

A reevaluation of the Aladdin Tipple in October 2011 concluded that the structure was extremely unsafe and threatened to totally collapse. This could endanger the visitors who enjoy the hike to the mine entrance. A controlled collapse was found to be the best and most efficient means to preserve the nature of the coal bin and chute. Placement on the ground would leave the possibility of future maintenance and repair. Unfortunately, the complete integrity of the structure would be lost. (Courtesy of the State of Wyoming.)

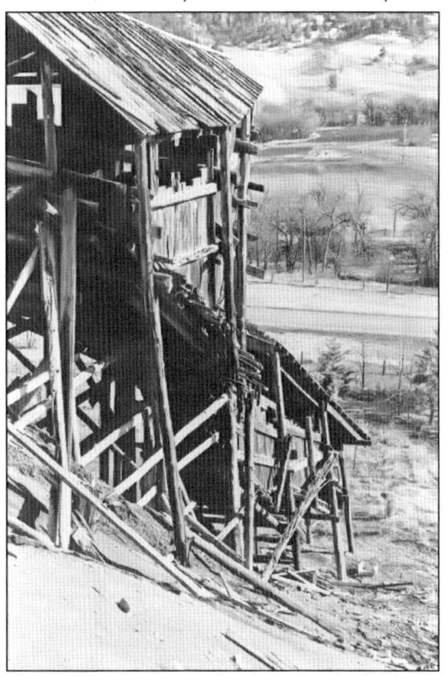

In the 21 years since the completion of the Aladdin Tipple stabilization, the wooden structure has been subjected to the normal deterioration of time and Wyoming weather. In addition, the steep, barren hillside where the tipple is located has suffered from considerable erosion. Many of the log supports have rotted, causing the structure to once again twist and tilt. This shifting of the structure has caused numerous support beams to crack or break. Erosion has removed substantial material, exposing many of the concrete pier foundations anchoring the primary support timbers. These exposed piers have the potential to overturn and cause the loss of all support and the collapse of the structure. (Courtesy of Black Hills State University, Case Library, Watson Parker Collection.)

Three

The Railroad

It has been said that the railroad made Aladdin; if that is so, then the coal of the Aladdin Valley made the railroad.

For the first few years after the discovery of coal in the valley, the coal companies were able to use teams and wagons to haul their coal to the smelters in Lead and Deadwood, South Dakota. These wagons would haul the coal south to Beulah and continue up Sand Creek Canyon to reach the South Dakota gold mines. But soon, the demand was more than the wagons could haul, and with more mines being worked, faster transportation was needed.

After Chicago & North Western Railroad changed its plans for a railroad from Belle Fourche through Aladdin and on west for a more southerly route that would go through what today is Moorcroft, the three mining companies in the area formed a company whose sole purpose was to furnish rail service. The Wyoming & Missouri Valley Railroad was incorporated on January 24, 1895. Construction was started in the summer of 1897 following the Chicago & North Western Railroad survey for the 18-mile standard-gauge line between Belle Fourche and Aladdin. Work on the railroad was brought to a halt by Wyoming's very harsh winters and the growing lack of finances.

In the spring of 1898, M.S. and J.L. Kemmerer acquired a controlling interest in the railroad. With their money to back the construction and with the determination of the miners and the neighbors along the Aladdin Valley, the railroad was completed in eight months and opened in February 1899. The train that first day consisted of one locomotive and two cars.

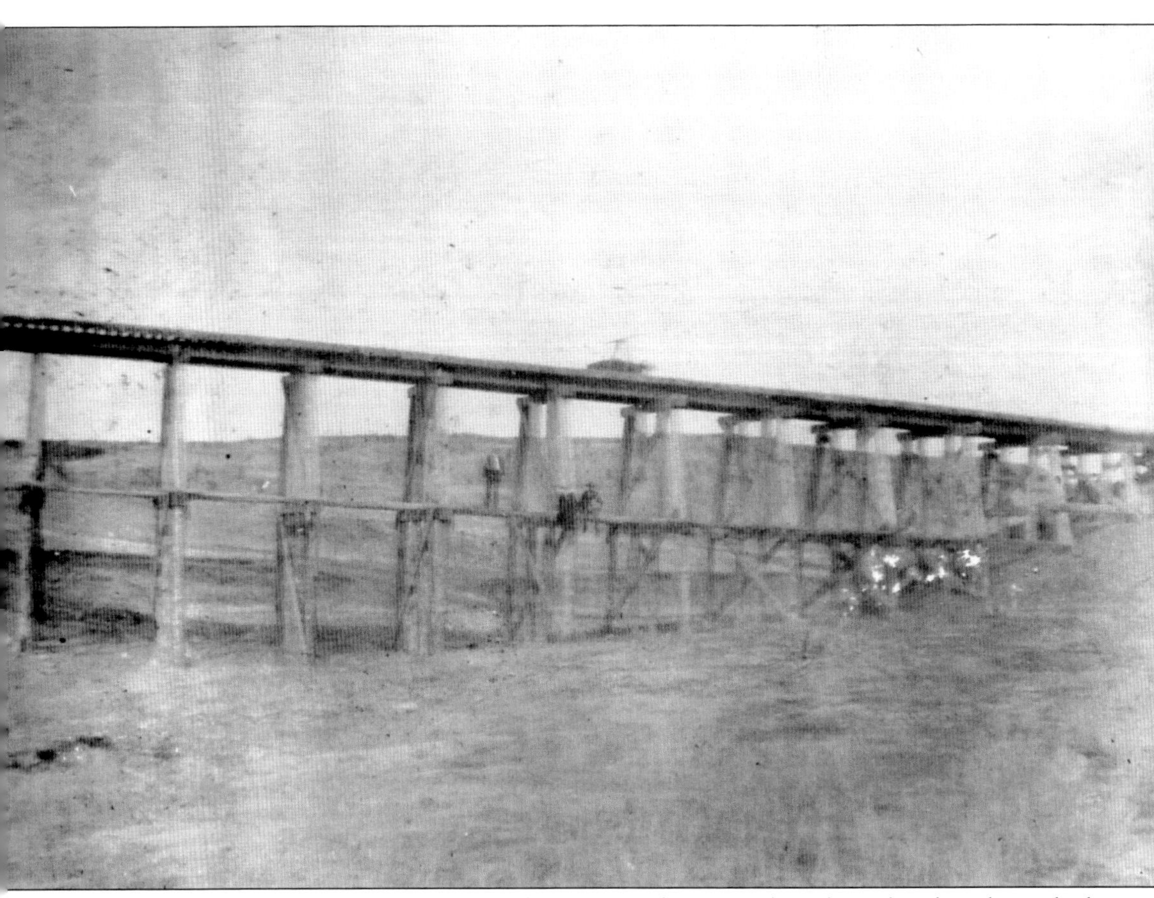

This very old photograph shows the bridge over Sand Draw. When the railroad track was laid, there were 28 bridges along the route. George Harris is said to have graded the roadbed following the survey made by the Chicago & North Western Railroad Company. The track was standard gauge. Because it was downhill from the mines to Belle Fourche, a small engine was all that was needed. A used 4-4-0 locomotive and a passenger car were bought from a Pennsylvania company. Coal cars and other equipment were provided by the Chicago & North Western Railroad. A flatcar and a handcar were included for maintenance of the track. (Courtesy of Tom Robinson.)

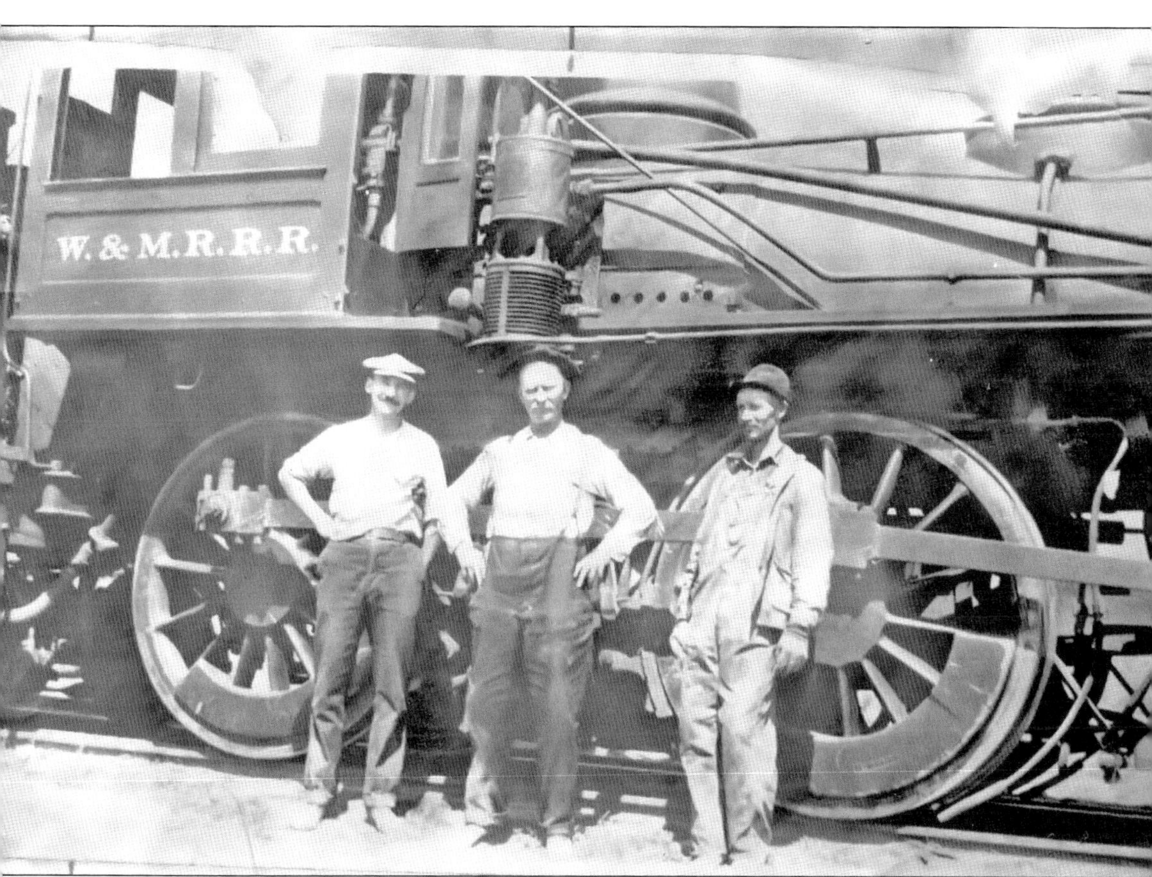

From left to right are Fred Mann, Bill Morrison, and Frank Houtz. Morrison was the engineer for the Wyoming & Missouri Valley Railroad from 1902 until 1920. Mann operated the railroad agency. Charlie Dayton was the conductor. A few years later, Houtz would become the engineer. He was also a blacksmith and made many branding irons still in use today. In the early days, the engineer and the fireman could trade jobs. When the fireman got tired, he could be the engineer and drive the train for a while. The fireman also had the job of opening and closing all gates as the train passed through. (Courtesy of the Crook County Museum.)

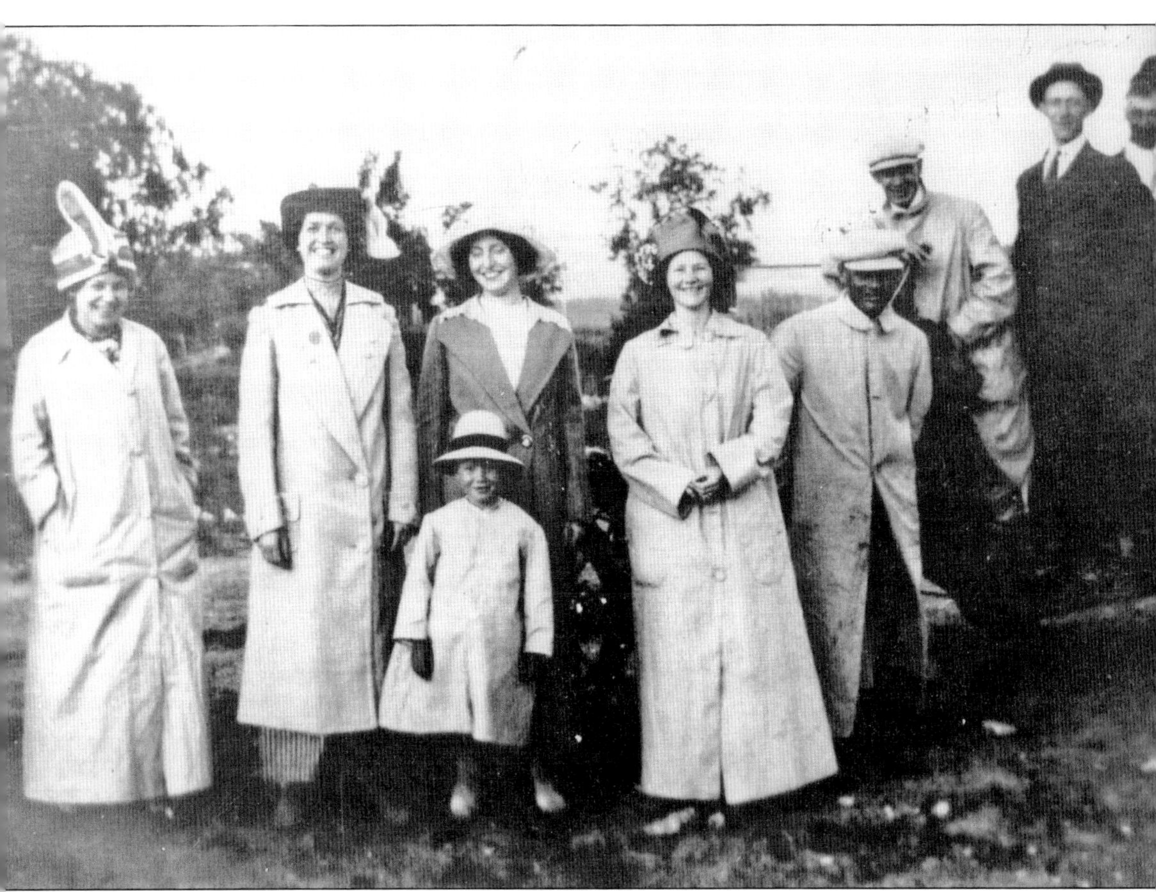

Pictured here dressed for travel are, from left to right, Perice Mann, Myrtle Tracy, Olga Hejde, Minnie Tracy, Fred Tracy, Henry Tracy, Irven Hejde, and Fred Mann. In front is little Walter Tracy. Fred Mann was the manager of the railroad. Henry Tracy was an insurance agent, and Fred Tracy managed a nearby farm. At times, Henry and Fred Tracy and Irven Hejde each either worked in the Wyoming Mercantile or owned it. A little motorcar, called a Dinky, was used to take groups like this on Sunday afternoon excursions. They could ride the car down to a favorite picnic spot or continue into town for shopping, dinner, or dancing. With Walter along, they might be going to take in the Butte County Fair. The long duster coats will protect them from the wind, weather, and lots of bugs! (Courtesy of Chuck Pearson.)

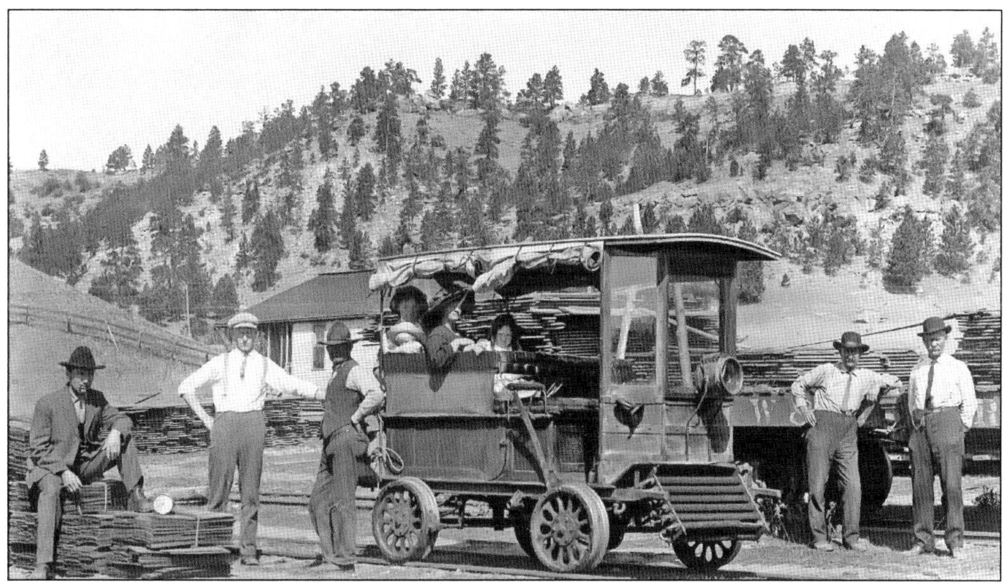

Here is the Dinky, the motorcar taking passengers to Belle Fourche. On the left, sitting on a stack of shingles, is Matt Whalen. Standing next to him are Irvin Hejde and Bert Derrickson. Inside the car are Christina Derrickson, Margaret Derrickson, Elydia Pearson, and Cecil Pearson. Elydia and her son Cecil were from Eothen. The Derricksons lived north of Aladdin near Donald. To the right are conductor Charlie Dayton and engineer Bill Morrison. The motorcar was used often after there was not as much coal to be shipped and the train did not run as often. This looks like a shopping trip. (Courtesy of Chuck Pearson.)

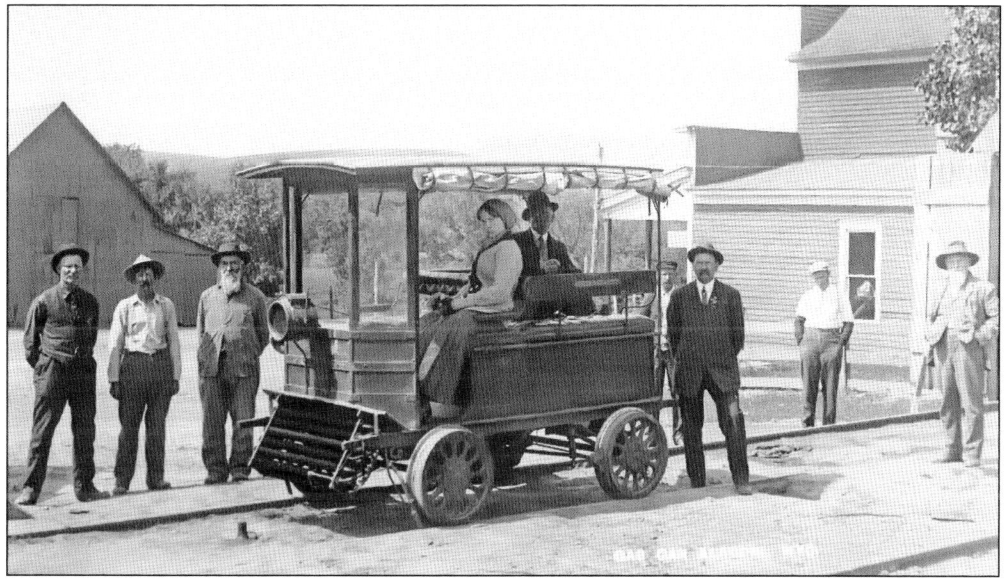

The Dinky is pulled up close to the store. The railroad tracks go right behind the store. The barn in the background would be sitting right in the middle of State Highway 111 today. The car came complete with side curtains, which are rolled up out of the way in the picture. Standing around the motorcar are, from left to right, Charlie Daton, Frank Gervasi, C.C. Ripley, Bill Morrison, Irven Hejde, and Charlie Sumac. Seated in the care are Elydia Pearson and her husband, Frank Pearson. (Courtesy of the Crook County Museum.)

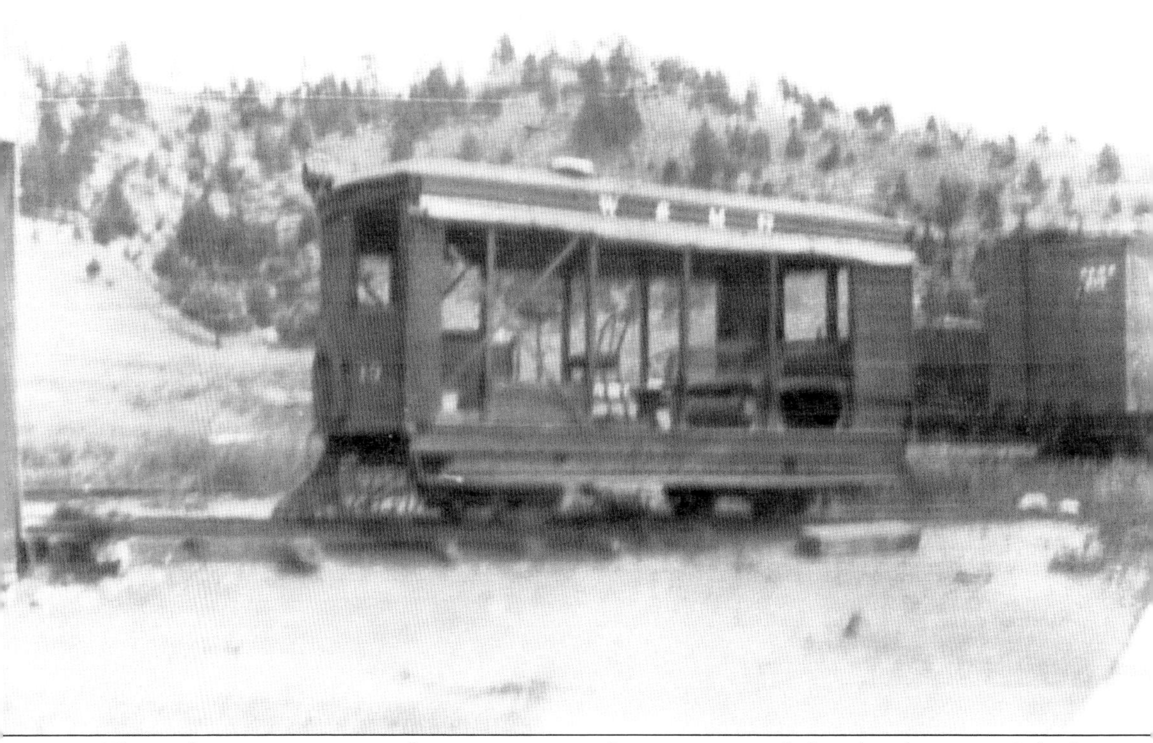

This is the same train car without passengers, side curtains, or side benches for sitting. It looks like the Dinky has come to the end of its days. When Phillis Anderson Lanning came to Crook County to teach, she traveled by train to Belle Fourche. When she arrived there, she found that she had to transfer to the Wyoming & Missouri Valley Railroad to reach Aladdin. After she boarded the afternoon train, she was horrified that the seats were torn, the men were all in overalls, not uniforms, and the train was pretty rough looking for a girl from back East. This motorcar is said to have made quite a few trips to the dances in St. Onge, South Dakota. The young people would borrow the railroad handcar and pump down to the Rathburn barn for a night of dancing. Going down was fun, but going back up to get home was tough going. It is also said that Matt Whalen was known to borrow it on occasion. (Courtesy of the Crook County Museum.)

From left to right, Andres Pearson, Jalmar Nelson, Andrew Olson, and John Hanson sit in Belle Fourche, waiting to catch the train back to Aladdin. It looks like they found a good place to wait with cool drinks and where smoking a pipe was accepted. They could be at John Pearson's Lodging House, not far from the railroad station. When the coal was being shipped out on a regular basis, passengers could ride into Belle Fourche, do their shopping, and catch the train to return in one day. (Courtesy of Chuck Pearson.)

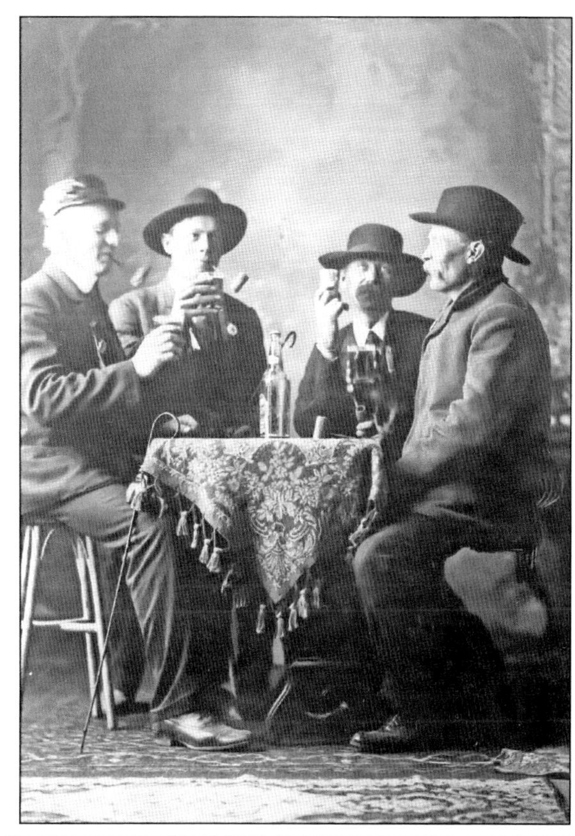

Old Rosie is about to pull out of the station in Belle Fourche for the return trip to Aladdin. The passengers are ready to board. On the left, Charlie Dayton, the conductor, is in his shirt sleeves and ready to take their tickets. Andres Pearson, Jalmar Nelson, Andrew Olson, and John Hanson will be home in just a few hours. The train made the trip every day except Sunday. It left Aladdin at 10:00 in the morning and returned by 2:30 each afternoon. (Courtesy of Chuck Pearson)

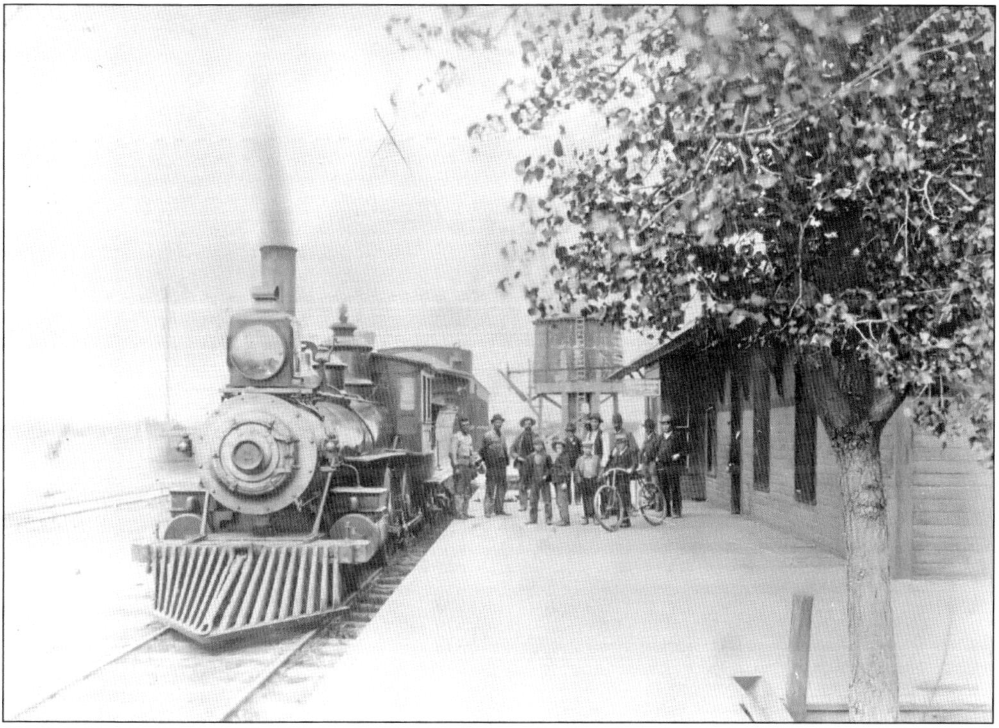

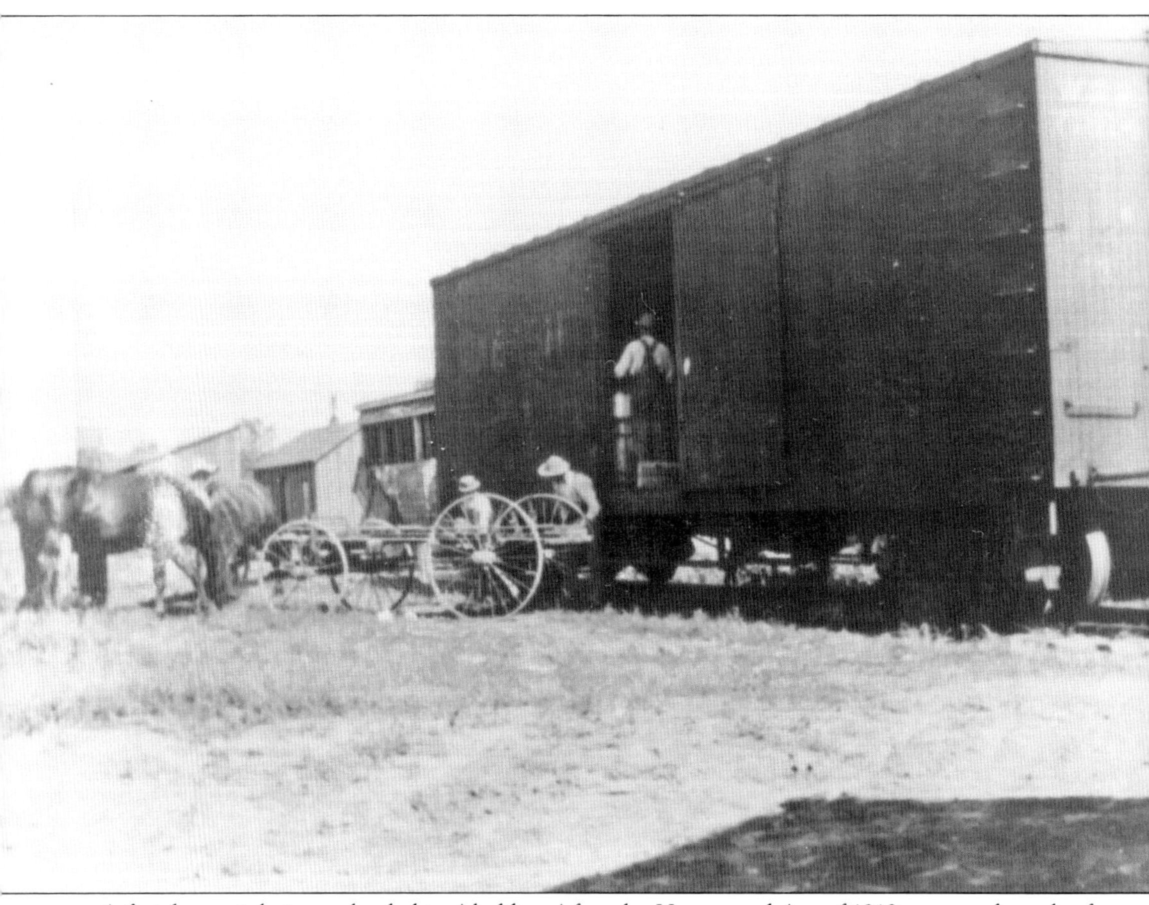

A freight car is being unloaded in Aladdin. After the Homestead Act of 1910 reopened much of the land in the West to homesteaders, people once again began to venture out into a new and different world. The railroads helped them to make this move. Aladdin was the end of the line for homesteaders who settled in the northeast part of Wyoming. They came with all their possessions. A family could load their livestock into a rented cattle car and one family member could ride in the car with them at no charge. Farm equipment and household goods could also be loaded into a rented boxcar. When the train reached Aladdin, some were met by friends or family members who would help them find their way home. It would take a team of four or six horses to haul a family's possessions and household goods. Others would unload into their own wagon and start off to find just the right place to begin a new life. (Courtesy of the Aladdin Store.)

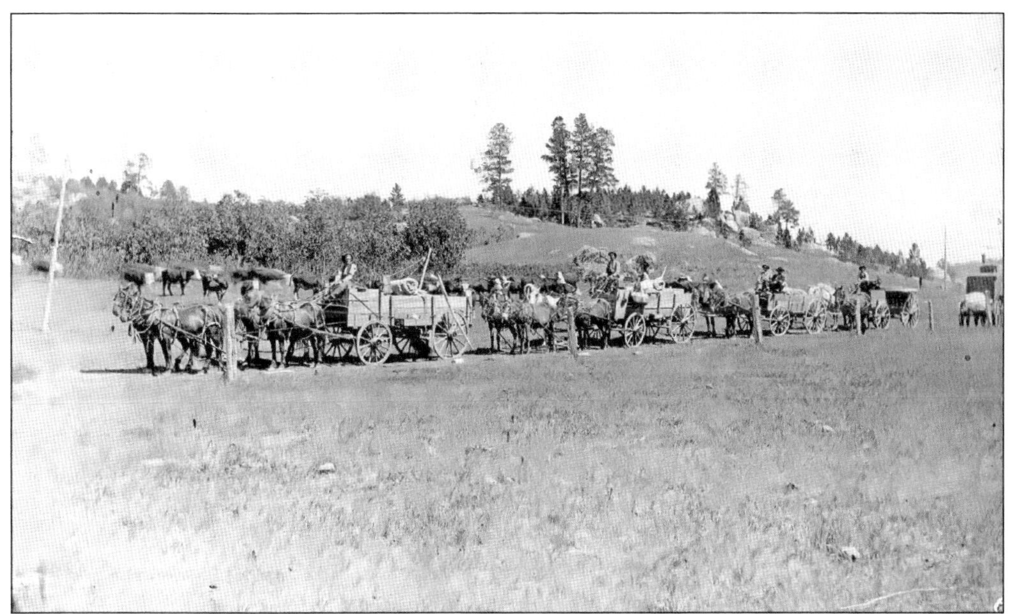

This 1911 photograph shows the freight train from Aladdin to Hulett. On the train are, from left to right, James Patton, Floyd Patten, Edgar Summers, and Burl Patton. They are delivering goods that came in on the train to families and merchants in and around Hulett. When freight came into Aladdin, it could be delivered by wagon to places as far away as Alazada, Montana, or even Sundance and places in between. Soon catalogs arrived, and then, "Katie bar the door," whatever people saw on those pages could come to their home. The trains carried tractor parts, wagon parts, seeds, glass windows, and fancy clothes. (Courtesy of Chuck Pearson.)

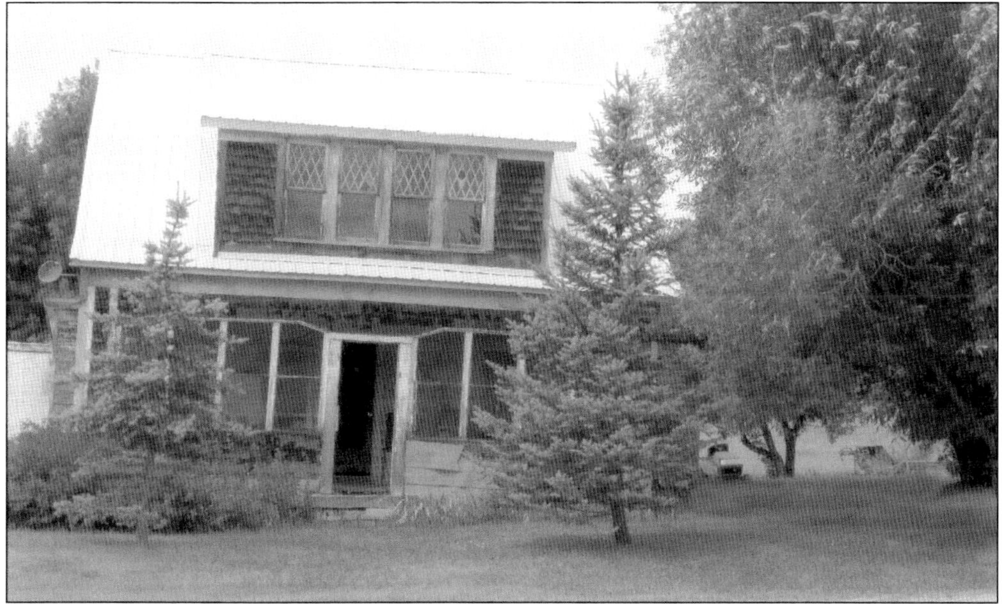

This fine old house still stands in Aladdin. The furnishings most likely came to Aladdin on the train. The Aladdin Mercantile would have been able to order most anything the family wanted. The fancy glass in the upstairs windows would have been wrapped very carefully for the trip; they not only made the train ride, but have lasted a very long time. (Author's collection.)

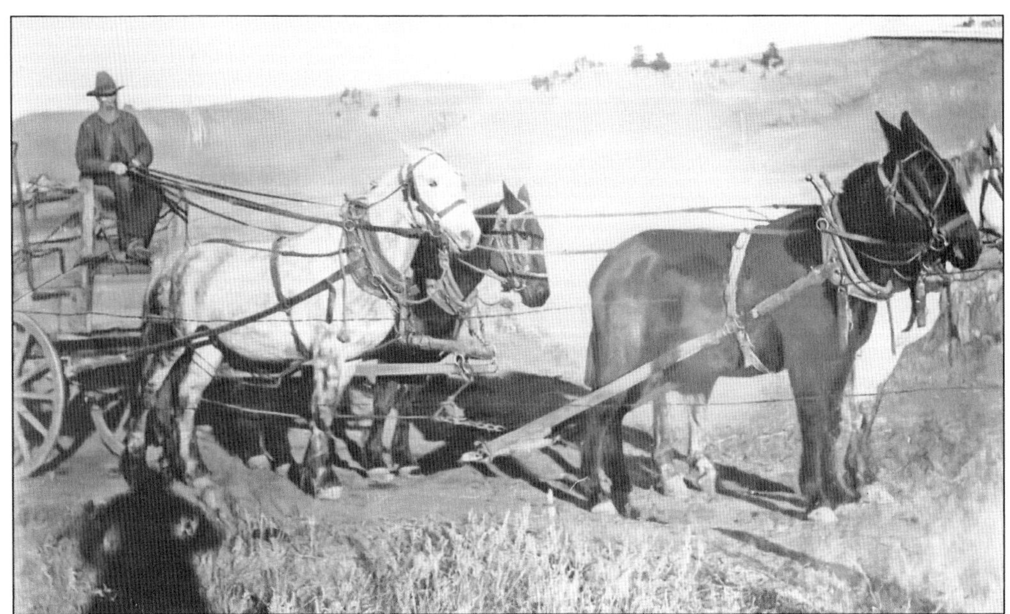

Here is a close-up of one of the teams used to haul freight from the railway station to the families and ranches who were waiting for their orders. The wagons also carried goods ordered by the merchants and other business establishments in towns all along the freight route. The horses that pulled these heavy wagons were very important to the freight operation. Because they were so important, they were well cared for—in fact, sometimes they were just plain spoiled. James Patton is driving the wagon, and the horses are named Pete, Boon, Stewart, and Guy. It is not known who the shadow at left belongs to. (Courtesy of Chuck Pearson.)

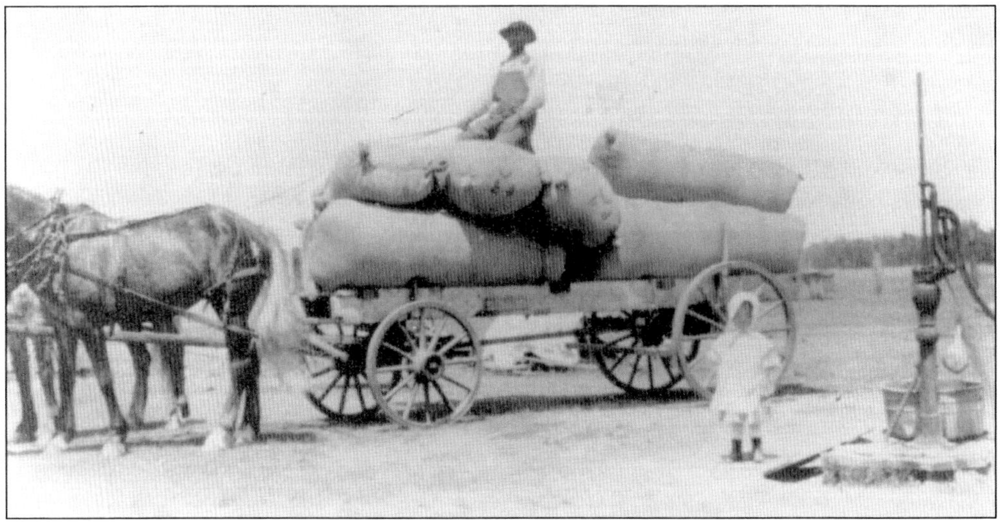

This load of bags of wool is being hauled to the freight office in Aladdin to be shipped back East to a clothing manufacturer, where it will be made into good warm clothing. The Marchant or DeFord shearing crews would take the wool from the sheep and stuff it into big bags for shipping. These bags were about eight feet long. When they were tromped down so they could be filled with as much wool as possible, each bag could weigh 300 pounds. The shearing was hard work, but stuffing and tromping the wool into those bags was worse. The father and daughter in this photograph are unidentified. (Courtesy of the Crook County Museum.)

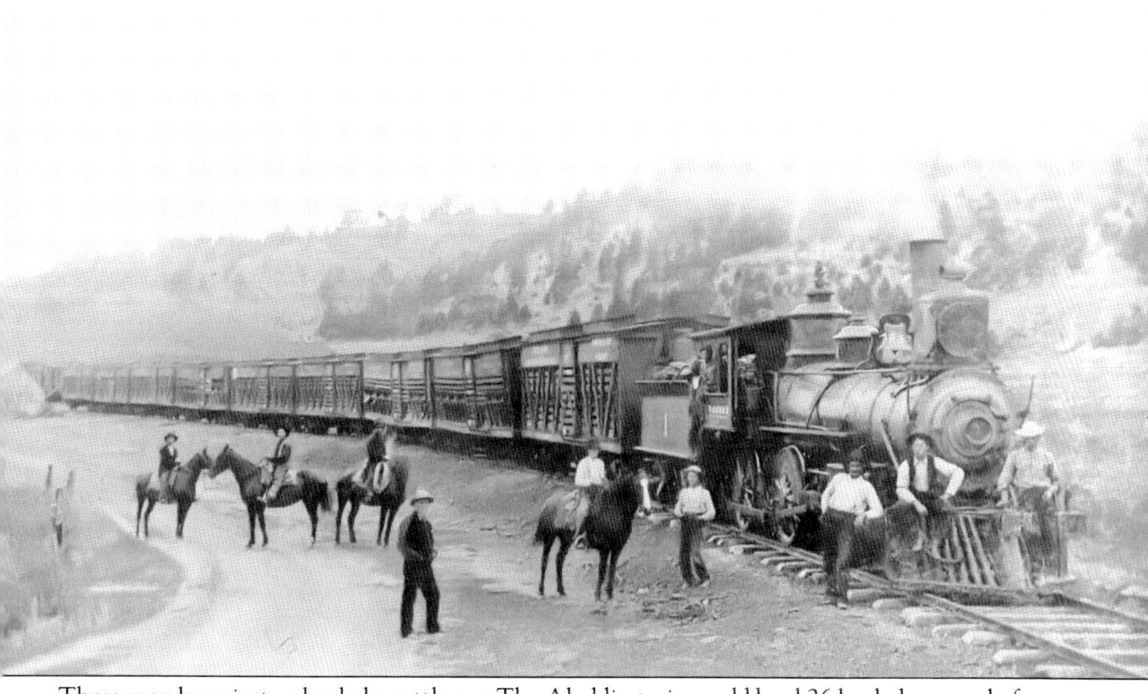

These men have just unloaded a cattle car. The Aladdin train could haul 26 loaded cars and often did, especially during the fall. There were two side tracks and loading pens east of Aladdin. One spur went to Chris Mortenson's ranch corrals. Another was near the Hoffman ranch. Pigs and hay were loaded at the Hoffman corrals. As the nearest railhead to many parts of Crook County, Montana, and the Dakotas, Aladdin soon became a loading point for cattle being shipped to market. In the fall, cattlemen from all around drove their cattle in to be loaded into cars and shipped to the market in Omaha, Nebraska. One could see herds of cattle in all directions waiting their turns at the loading pens. This continued even after the coal gave out and up to the time the railroad line ceased operation. Over 600,000 cattle are thought to have been shipped out of the Aladdin shipping pens. Frank Pearson and Richard Procter both drove their hogs to Aladdin, a distance of 10 miles or more, to be shipped to market. In 1925, three carloads of sheep were shipped off to Iowa. Fall shipping was an exciting time, and Aladdin teachers would bring their students to watch. (Courtesy of Chuck Pearson.)

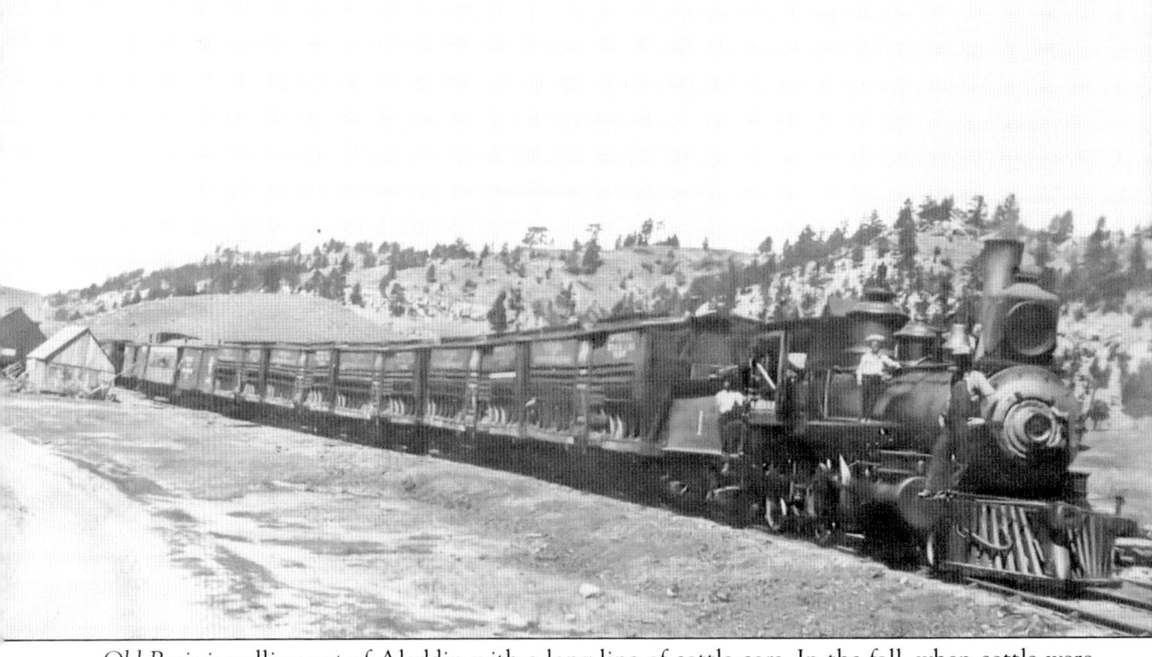

Old Rosie is pulling out of Aladdin with a long line of cattle cars. In the fall, when cattle were shipped to market, the ranchers would trail their cattle many miles to the loading pens, where the cattle would wait their turns to load into the cars to make the journey to market. Sheep and hogs were shipped to market in the same manner. Ranchers would usually travel on the train with their stock. Sometimes, they would take their families along for an adventure. Bill Morrison (standing in the cab) and Frank Houtz (standing on the cow catcher) are on the train and ready to go. The child is not named; he probably was not to be climbing on the engine. It looks like Morrison will get to be the engineer for at least the trip to Belle Fourche, and then on the trip home maybe it will be Houtz's turn. (Courtesy of Chuck Pearson.)

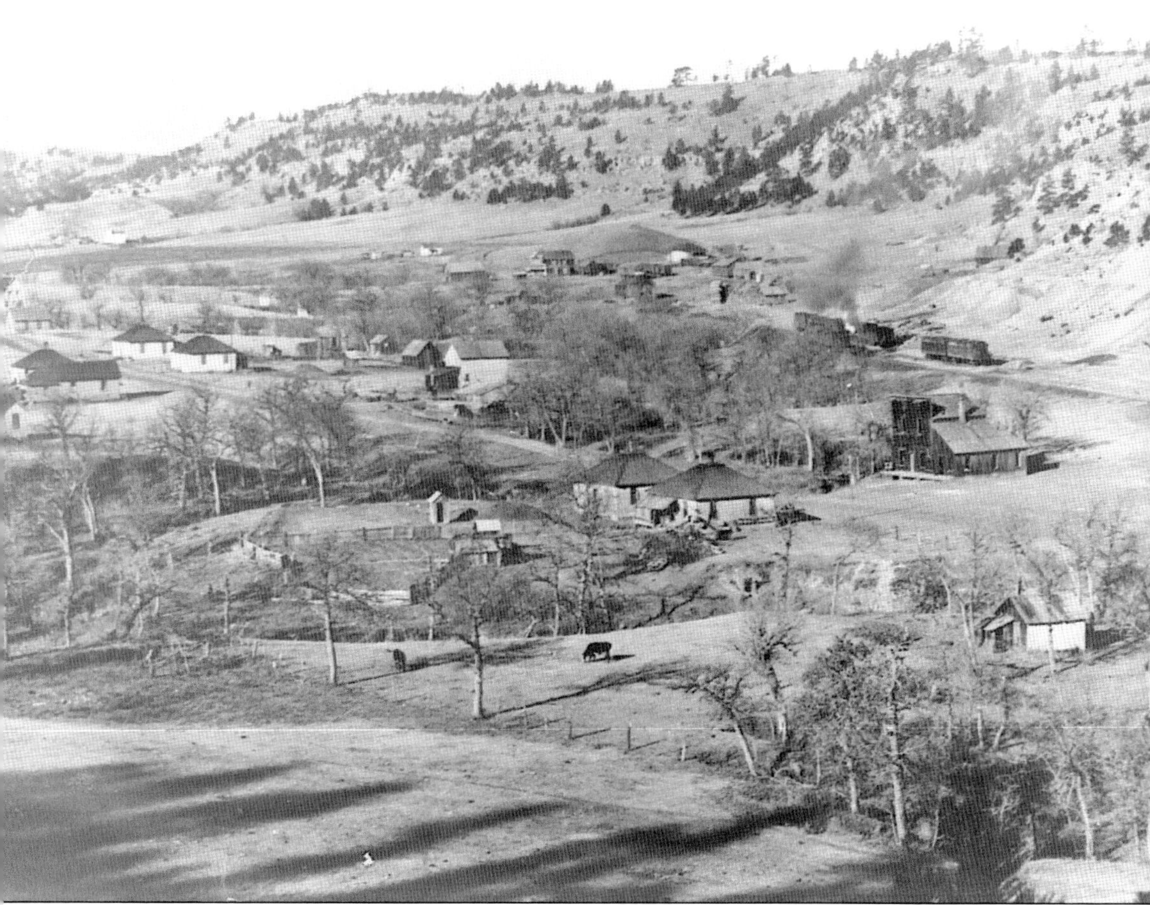

The little town of Aladdin was a lively place in the late 1890s and early 1900s after the railroad spur from Belle Fourche was built. It was known to almost everyone that the railroad bed was mostly a downhill grade. There is a story of a rancher who loaded a train car with hay to be shipped out of Aladdin to Omaha. For some reason, the railroad agency was a little slow that day starting the shipment on its way. As ranchers are wont to do, this man was getting impatient. So, he climbed aboard the car, released the brake, and coasted the load all the way to the station in Belle Fourche, 18 miles away. The engineer was just a little surprised to hear that the load of hay arrived without his help. (Courtesy of the Crook County Museum.)

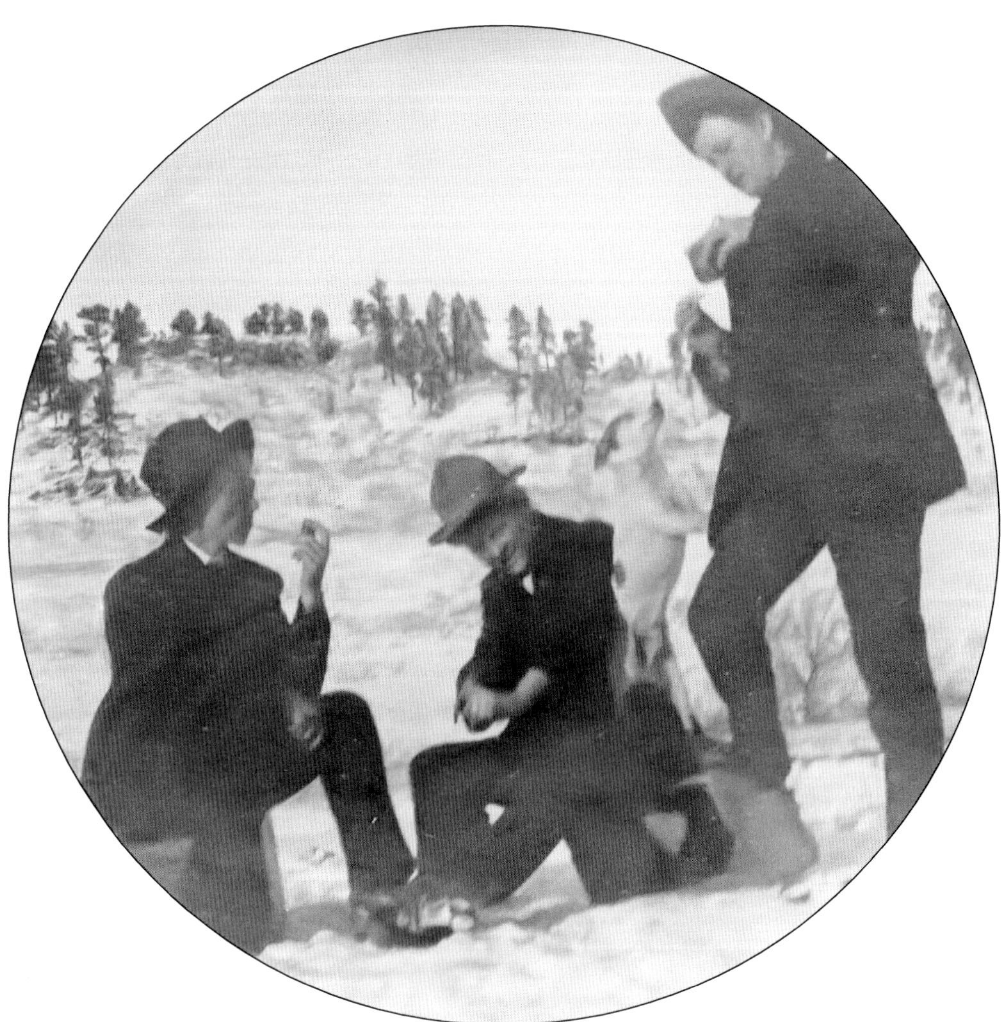

On one winter trip, there were four Crook County girls aboard the train on their way back to school at the Spearfish Normal School after Christmas vacation. It was a normal trip until, somewhere between Aladdin and Belle Fourche, the train broke down. The fireman on the train went to get help from the nearest farmhouse. The men returned with a team of four horses, and the train was at last pulled into Belle Fourche. These three girls are dressed in men's clothing for warmth and are having a fun time in the snow. They would have turned a broken-down train into an adventure. One of the girls stranded on the train was Rose Storm, the daughter of Lucy and James Storm. She did not make it home in time to join in the fun. Pictured here are Nancy Patton, Lizzie Patton, Edith Smeek, and Trix the dog. (Courtesy of Chuck Pearson.)

Four

ALADDIN

If coal was responsible for the development of the Wyoming & Missouri Valley Railroad, then the construction of the railroad was responsible for the establishment and growth of Aladdin.

The Wyoming Mercantile, now known as the Aladdin Store, was built in 1896 with hopes of a coal boom. At the turn of the century, the immediate valley boasted a population of an estimated 500 inhabitants. Aladdin is the only one of the coal-mine settlements to spring up in the area that is still in existence today. The Aladdin Store has always been the heart and soul of Aladdin and continues to hold the community together 120 years later. At one time there were about 27 houses in Aladdin, which, like the railroad, were all owned by the Wyoming Mercantile. Besides the store, post office, depot, and freight office, there was a school, a hotel, a boardinghouse, a saloon or two, a barbershop, and a pest house. There was a roundhouse for the train engine, and there were stock pens and loading chutes to load the cattle into the cars for shipping.

Aladdin's business continues to be ranching and timber. The Aladdin Store was built by Amos Robinson; when he died, the courts turned it over to the coal company. Dan Hickey became the second manager of the railroad and the store in 1899. In 1919, Fred Mann took over the store, replacing Carl Moeller. Irven Hejde worked in the store until he was inducted into the Army in 1918. Later, he would buy out his brother Jay in 1941 and the store became the Hejde Mercantile until 1953. In 1953, the store was sold to Verle Wagner, and when he left, Ralph Magelky bought it. Later, Astor Jordan bought it from Ralph. While Astor owned the store, he built a café and motel and a little house east of the store. Gayle Weaver bought the store in 1966 and kept it for 20 years before selling it to Judy and Rick Brengle. And now the Brengles are ready to retire and would like to find someone to love it and to care for it as much as they have.

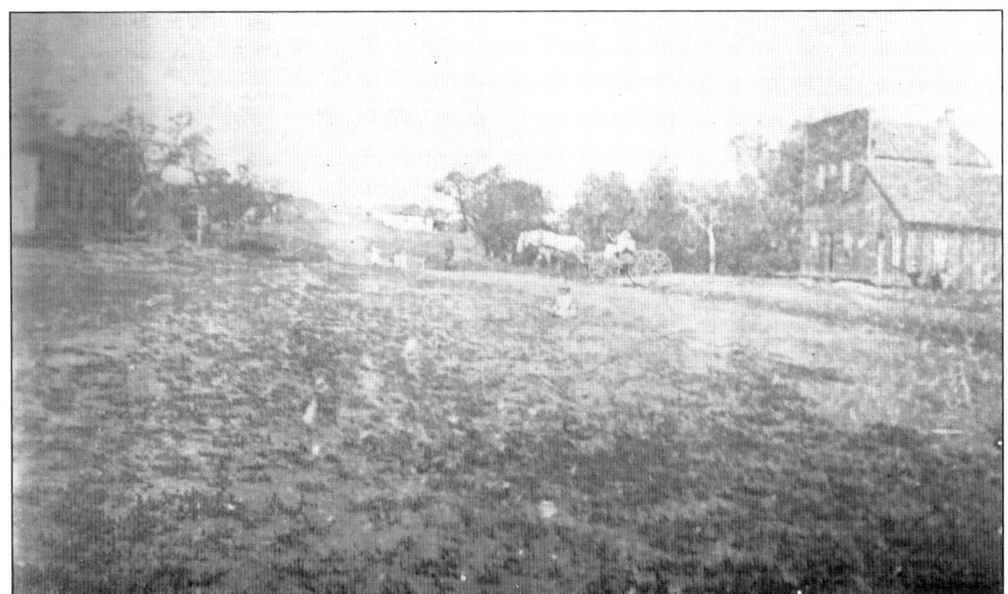

This is a very early photograph of Aladdin, the name given to the Hay Creek town that would become the terminal point for the Wyoming & Missouri Valley Railroad. Land records show that Amos Robinson was issued a patent for 40 acres in the Hay Creek valley on November 12, 1894. These 40 acres would become Aladdin. The coal mines were operating, but there was not much around. There was a barn south of the store. This barn could have belonged to one of the liveries that sold and rented horses and buggies to those who needed to travel. A newspaper advertisement for a livery in Hulett boasted that the stage would leave Aladdin every morning at 7:00 and arrive in Hulett by 4:00 in the afternoon the same day. (Courtesy of the Robinson family.)

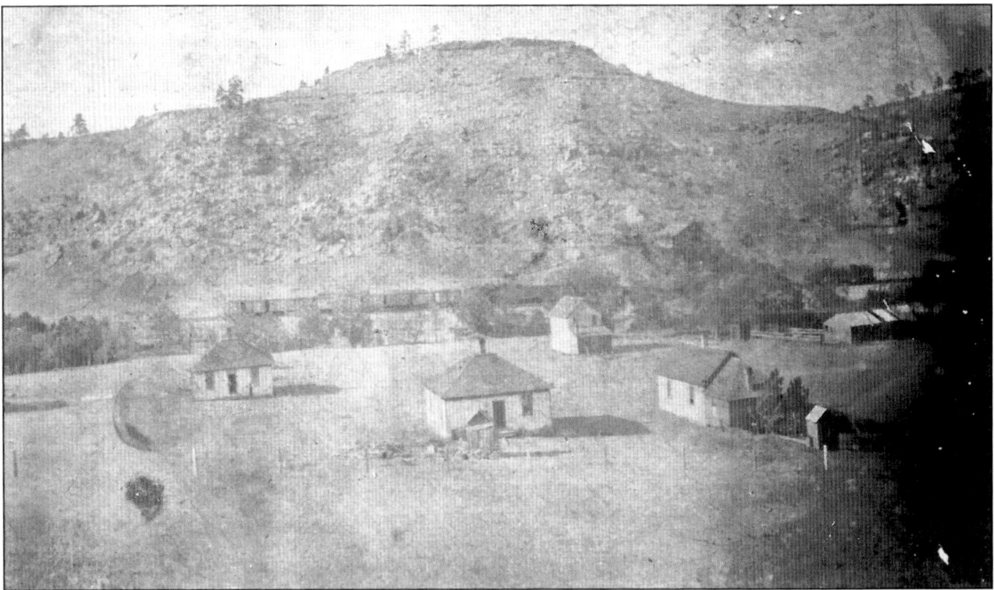

This is another very old picture of Aladdin, from June 1898, looking across the valley toward the train tracks to the south. There was really not much going on in Aladdin on this day. There are three or four square miners' houses spread out far apart, and a barn on the hillside across the way. It could be the same livery barn as in the previous image. (Courtesy of the Robinson family.)

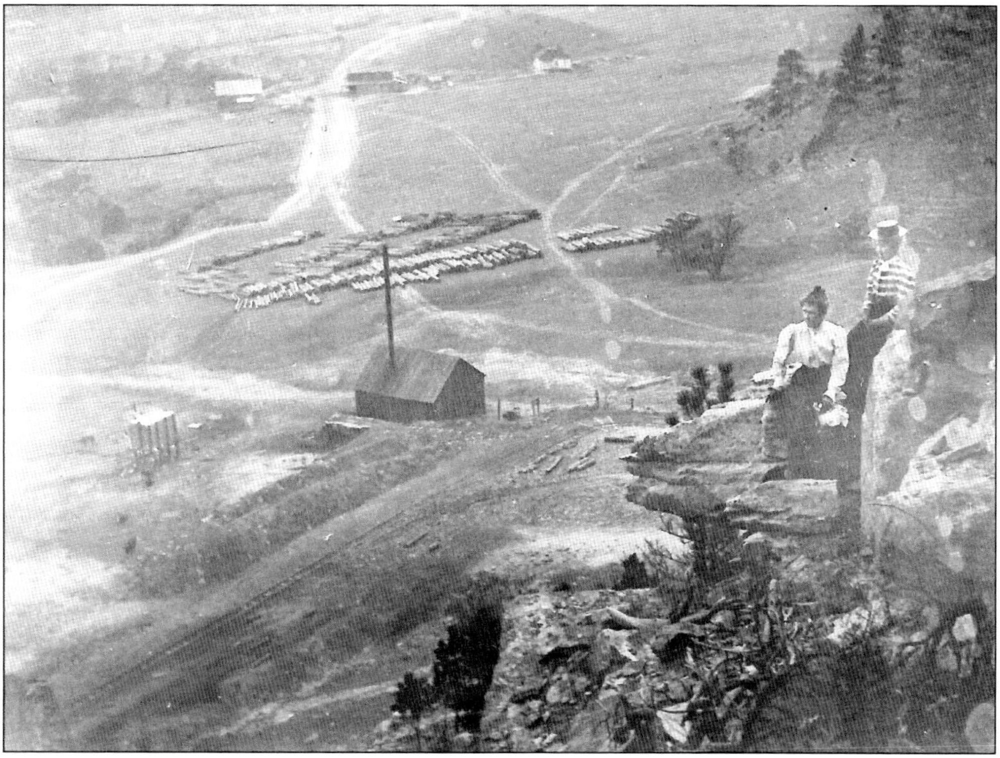

These two ladies are the Carlson twins, Hilda and Hilma. They have managed to climb up this rocky ledge of the Lakota Formation with the shale and sandstone outcropping in their long skirts and petticoats. Did they come to check out the buffalo skull in the rocks just below their feet? Below their perch, on the valley floor, the beginnings of Aladdin stretch out before them. The train has not yet made its way as far as the store, which is new. They can see the barn, the store, and Dan Hicky's home. There are stacks and piles of mine timbers delivered from the Pearson sawmill in Eothen. (Courtesy of the Robinson family.)

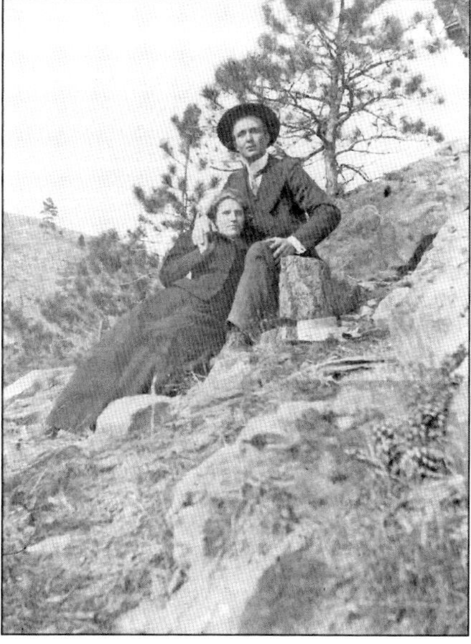

Thomas Robinson and Hilda Carlson are pictured in the rocks above Aladdin just before their engagement in 1899. The Robinson family lived next door or across the road from the family of Otto and Hannah Carlson. Thomas worked for the railroad in Aladdin for several years before he moved to Belle Fourche, where he owned and managed a pool hall. Thomas and Hilda would have two children. Their son, Thomas Jr., was born in Aladdin in 1900, and daughter Helen followed in 1902. Hilda died shortly after giving birth to Helen. Her children were raised by her parents, Otto and Hannah. Because they were raised by their grandparents, both children spoke fluent Swedish. Thomas and Hilda's granddaughter Helen Jane was raised by the Ernest Bunny family. (Courtesy of the Robinson family.)

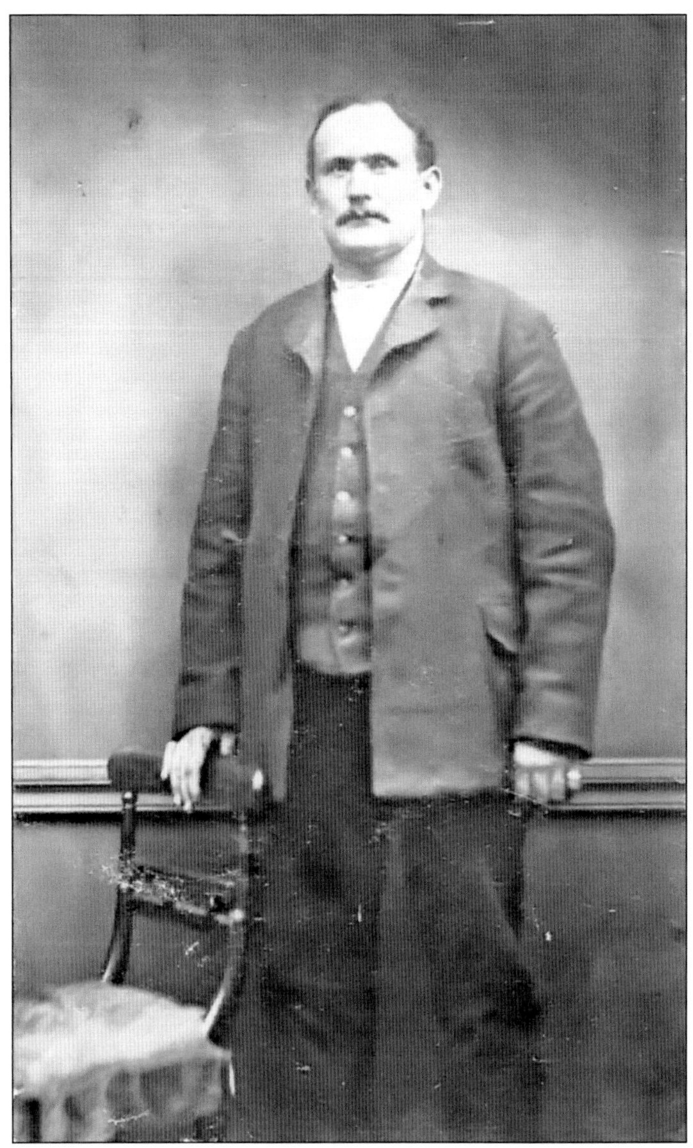

Amos Robinson built the Wyoming Mercantile as a saloon and commissary for the miners in 1892, some reports say. The building was constructed with lumber from the Pearson sawmill in Eothen. The mercantile held a general store, post office, and saloon. Business was going well, and Amos decided to build another saloon in Beulah. Ed Ross already ran a saloon in Beulah, and did not appreciate the new competition. On June 24, 1896, as Amos was playing high five, Ed Ross came in and sat next to him. Amos asked that he not interfere. Ed gave Amos a good slap alongside his head. The game continued, but after last call, Amos closed up and stepped outside, where Ed was waiting, and the confrontation started again. Shots were fired. Amos stumbled to the hotel next door and called, "I'm done for." Ed Ross yelled for someone to call the sheriff because "I just shot the belly off old fatty Robinson." Newspapers did suggest that Amos Robinson was the most obese man in Wyoming. Ross was tried and convicted of second-degree murder and sentenced to 99 years. He appealed and lost. The Wyoming Supreme Court ruled that one cannot goad someone into pulling a weapon and then claim self-defense. Ed Ross served eight years and three months. (Courtesy of Tom Robinson.)

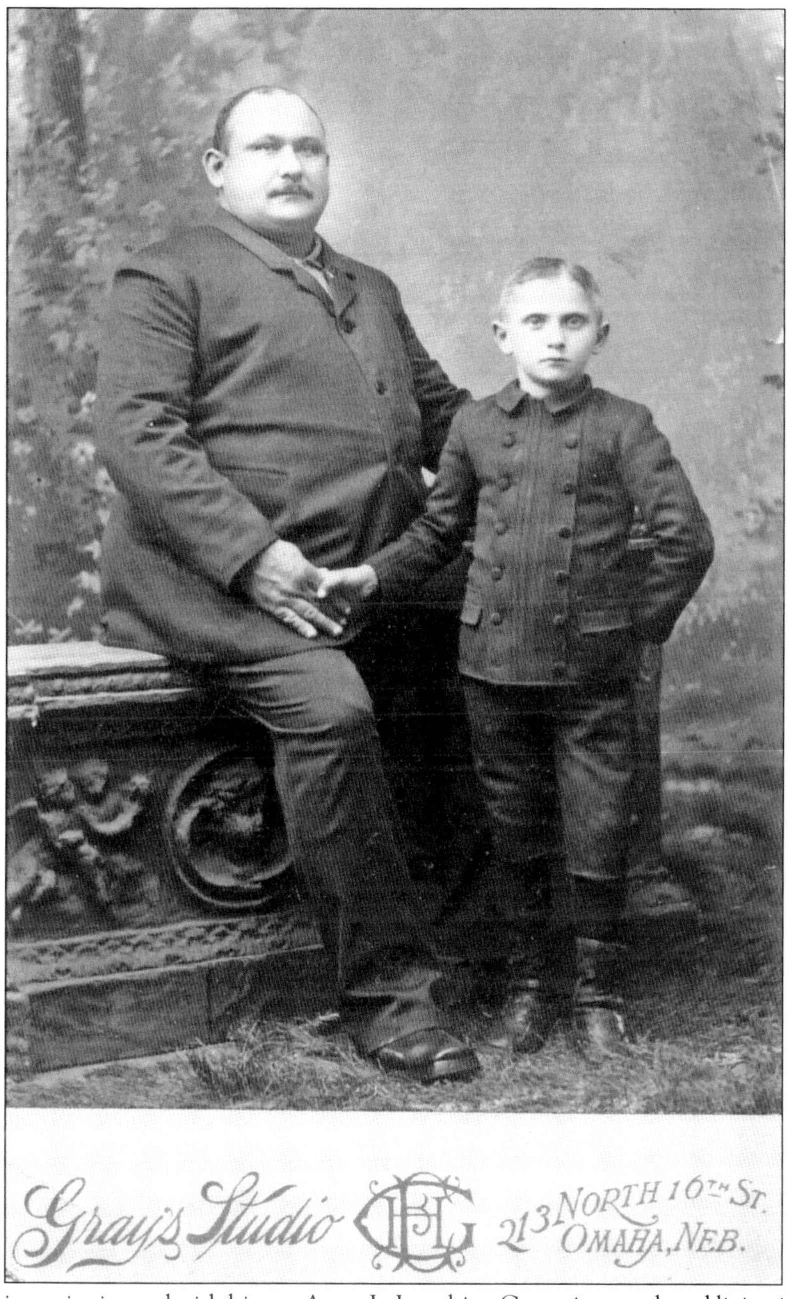

Amos Robinson is pictured with his son Amos Jr. Josephine Gervasi remembered living in Aladdin next door to the Robinson family. She remembered that Hannah Robinson was always in a wheelchair. The Robinsons had one daughter, Emily. Emily was a nurse in Chicago and did not come home to Wyoming often. There were also two sons in this family, Amos Jr. and Thomas. They did most of the house work for their mother. Thomas also worked as a fireman and as an engineer on the railroad. Across the street lived Otto Carlson and his family. Otto worked in the coal mine, while his wife boarded miners. They had twin daughters, Hilma and Hilda. Thomas married Hilda. Hilma moved to Belle Fourche and married Almon H. Dean. Hilda and Thomas lived with her parents in Aladdin. (Courtesy of Tom Robinson.)

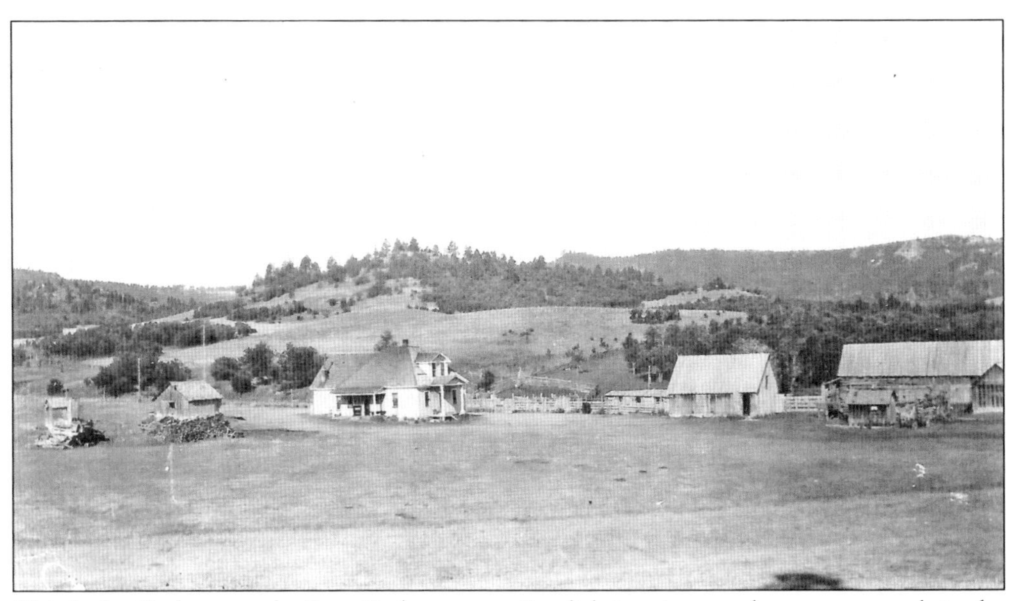

This is the Carlson ranch. Otto Carlson was a Swedish immigrant who came to work in the coal mines. In an accident at the mine, Carlson's hand was smashed by falling rocks. Shortly after arriving in Crook County, he had begun acquiring land. By the time he died in 1927, he had three ranches in the Bear Lodge Mountains of the Black Hills National Forest. After his namesake, great-grandson Otto, moved to Idaho, the Carlson ranch was sold several times. It is once again in the hands of the Carlson family. Under the care of Bruce Carlson, the ranch Otto started continues to thrive. (Courtesy of Chuck Pearson.)

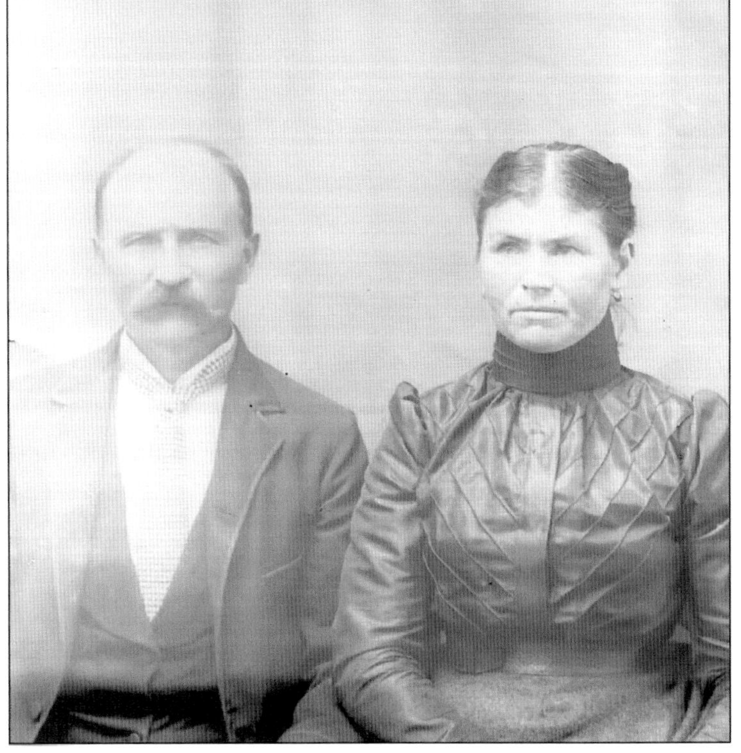

Pictured are Otto and Hannah Carlson. After the death of his first wife, Otto found Hannah and asked her to become his second wife and to travel with him and his twin daughters to northeast Wyoming. It took a very brave soul to take a chance on the man and venture into the great unknown. An injury to his hand caused Otto to give up mining, and he became an accomplished rancher. Otto continued to farm and raise cattle until the time of his death in 1949. (Courtesy of Tom Robinson.)

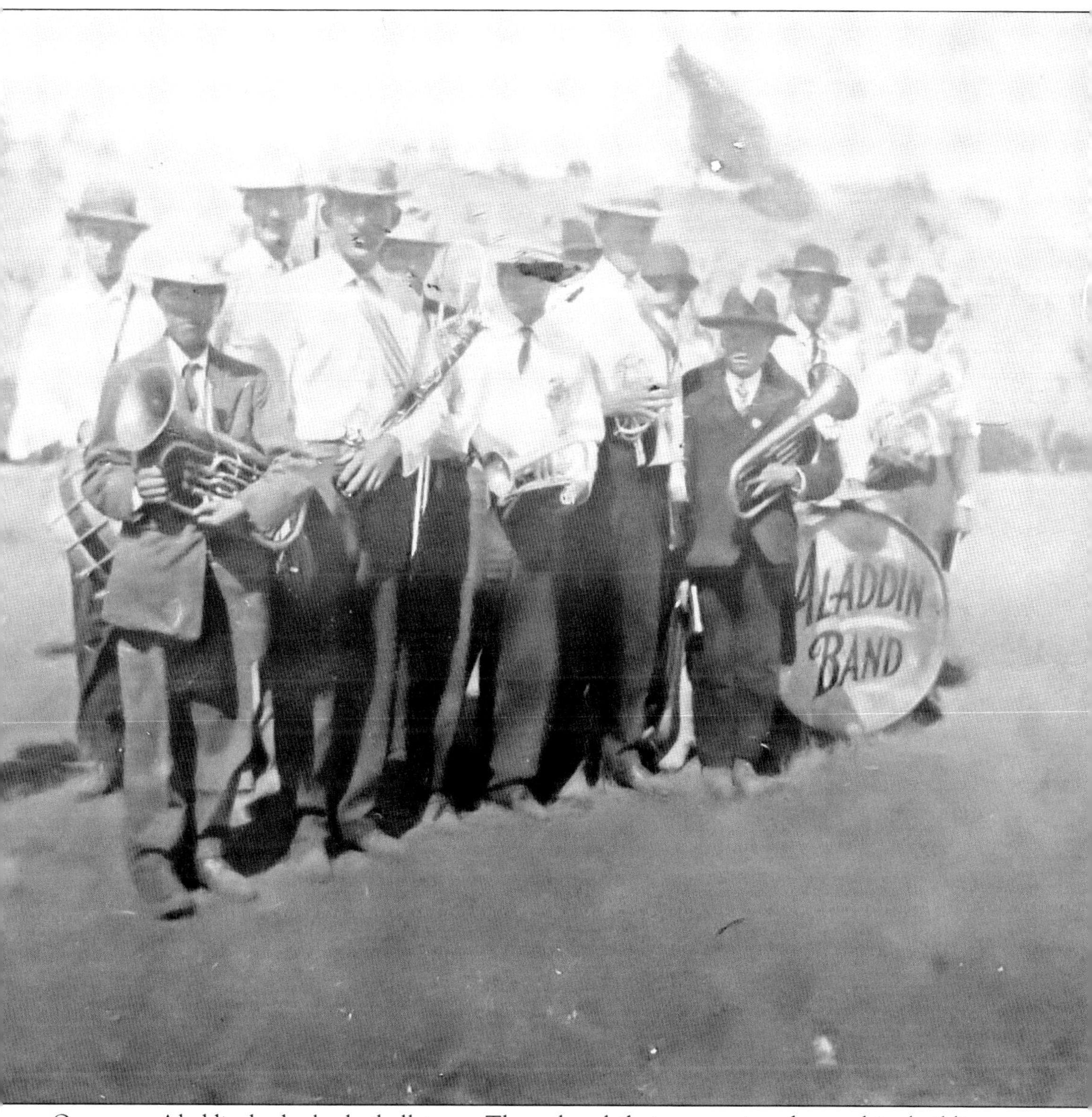

One year, Aladdin had a basketball team. They played their games in a large white building that was also used for dances and community meetings. Irven Hejde was the basketball coach. Members of the team were Walter Tracy, Buster Whalen, and Frank, Joe, and Leo Gervasi. The players could never tell how many games they won or if they ever did win. Many of those playing basketball were also in the band. Vern Willard, the band leader, lived west of Jim Marchant out along Oak Creek. Band members pictured here in unknown order are (first row) Fred Aikman, Elmer Heetland, Irven Hejde, and Johnny Pearson; (second row) Richard Knoff, Fred Mann, and Frank O. Pearson. To the west of the dance hall was a smaller building where basketball players and dancers could grab a sandwich before starting home at the end of the night. (Courtesy of Chuck Pearson.)

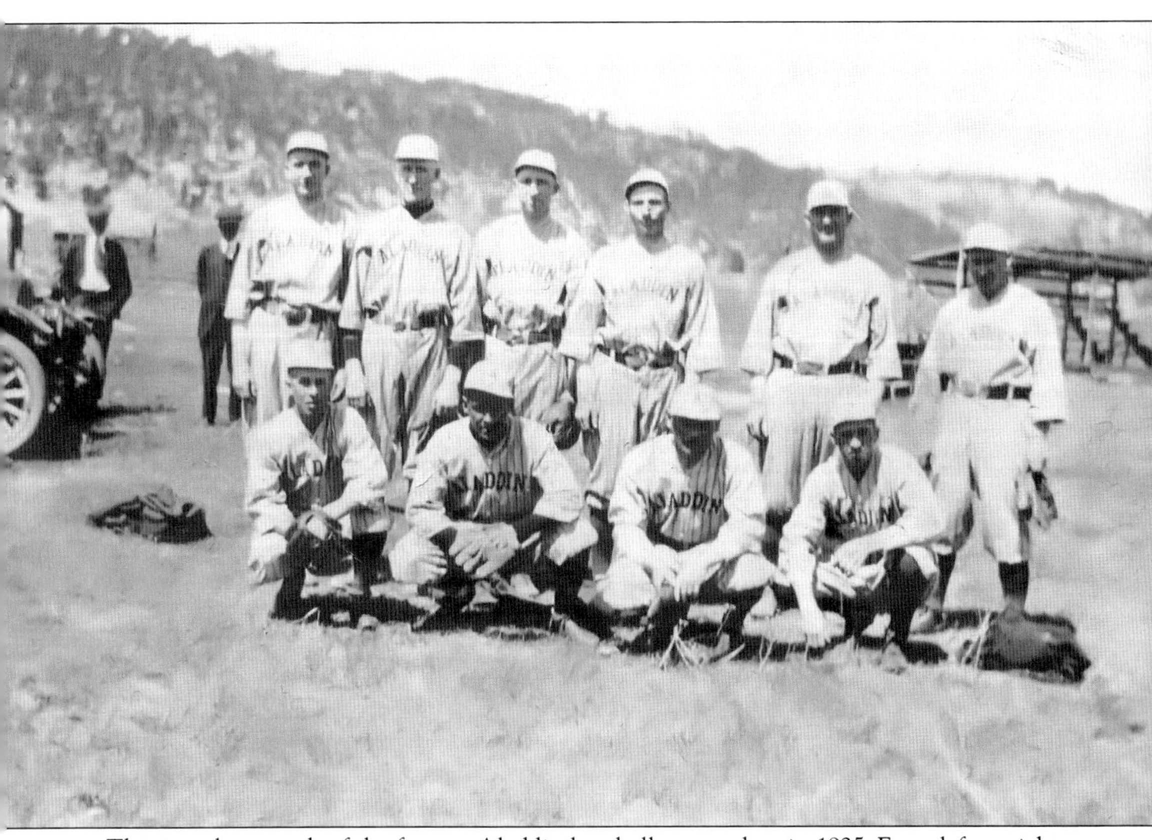

This is a photograph of the famous Aladdin baseball team taken in 1925. From left to right are (first row) Elmer Heetland, Frank Gordon, Fred M. Tracy, and Paul Heetland; (second row) Francis Hejde, Irven Hejde, Jay Hejde, Cess Glaudo, Ralph Nickelson, and Harry Tracy. Irven was the pitcher, and his brother Jay played first base and sometimes shortstop. Francis played the outfield. Frank Gordon was the shortstop and Ralph was the catcher. Another member of the team was Dillon Ruland, who played center field and also played with the Hulett and Alva teams. John Whalen, who still lives on his ranch just west of Aladdin, remembers being the batboy. This was the team to beat. The team from Gillette even brought in two or three ringers, unknown players from the big city, in an effort to beat Aladdin. It didn't work. Irven had the honor of being one of the Black Hills players chosen to play in an exhibition game in Deadwood, South Dakota, where he pitched to Babe Ruth. With the count at two balls and two strikes, Hejde threw a fastball high and inside, and the mighty Babe struck out. (Courtesy of the Crook County Museum.)

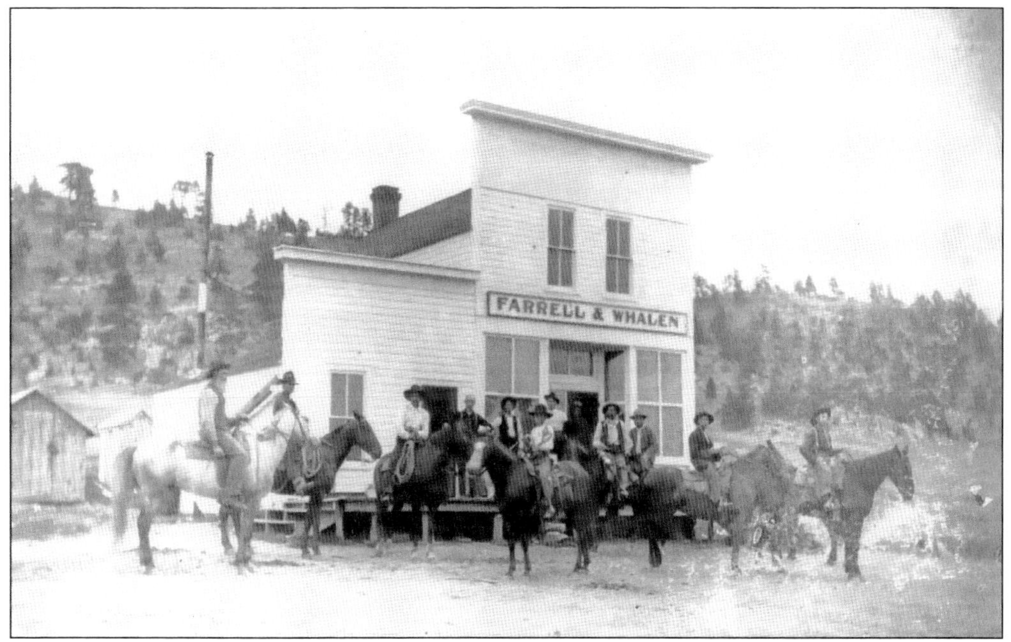

Matt Whalen and Joe Farrell first opened their saloon in Barrett. The establishment was one of the first to open for business there. When the post office moved to Aladdin, most everything moved with it, and the men decided to move their saloon as well. The Farrell and Whalen Saloon sat west of the Aladdin Store. Today, an old orange combine is near the spot where the building stood. Judging by this crowd on horseback in front of the building, it looks like they had a thriving business. (Courtesy of Chuck Pearson.)

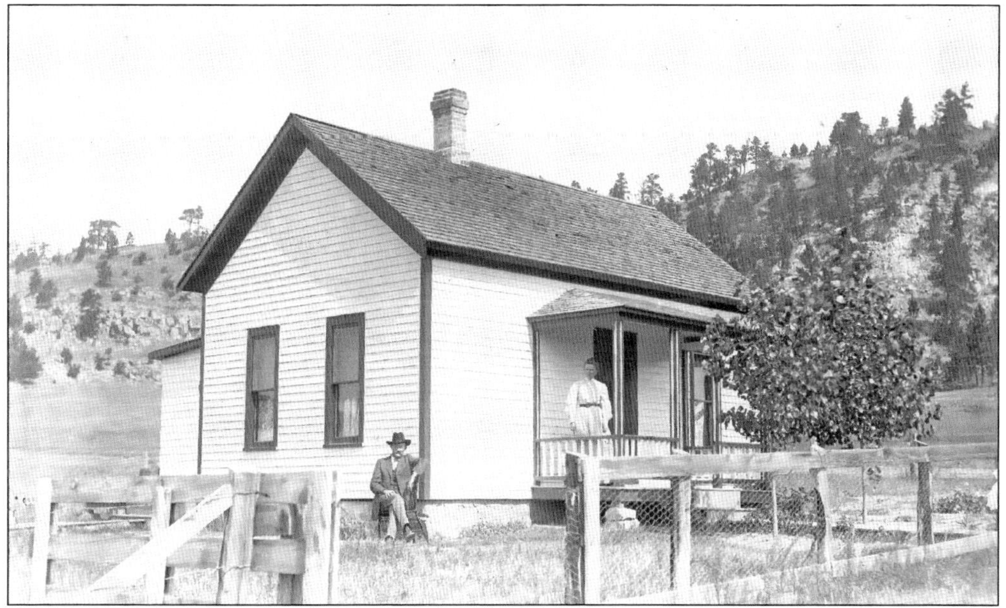

Joe and Julie Farrell are pictured at their home in Aladdin. Julie is on her front porch watching Joe while he takes a well-deserved rest in the shade. Their home was just west of the Aladdin Store and east of the Farrell and Whalen drinking establishment. The first schoolhouse was north of the Farrell house. (Courtesy of Chuck Pearson.)

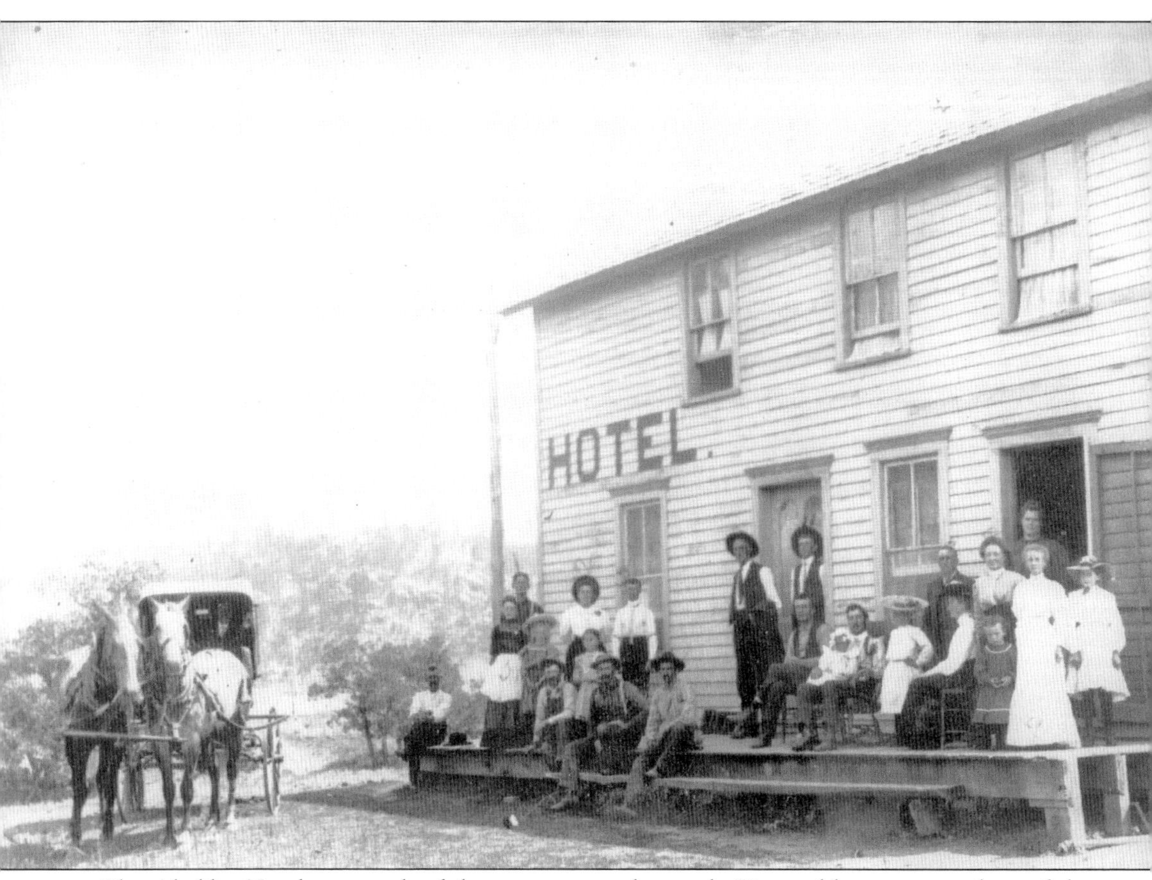

The Aladdin Hotel was south of the store across the creek. Pictured here are members of the Taylor family from the Bear Lodge Mountains. Mark Megotti is sitting on the porch, wearing a striped shirt. There was a hotel at one time or another in each of the towns along Hay Creek. Calamity Jane stayed in this hotel on her way to Sundance, a trip related in a Deadwood newspaper. She had surprised two cowboys along the way by shouting "High low jacks and the game. Got a beer?" They told her they had no beer, as they were working. When she asked for a smoke, she was offered a chew of tobacco. The freight wagon driver told the newspaper reporter that she had taken a "chew that would have made a Kentuckian ashamed of himself." (Courtesy of the Crook County Museum.)

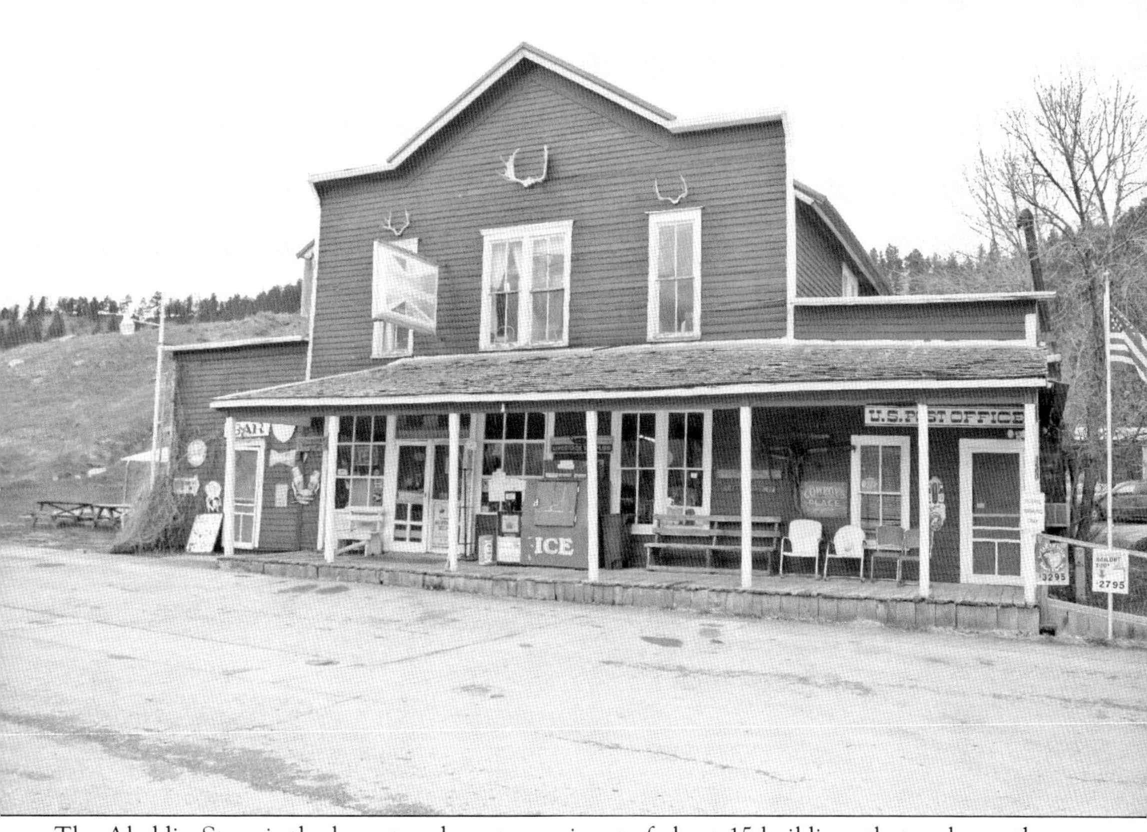

The Aladdin Store is the largest and most prominent of about 15 buildings that make up the present town along both sides of the highway. The store itself is comprised of a tall, two-story, gable-roofed central portion with flanking one-story, shed-roofed wings on the east and west and a shed-roofed addition on the north. The main gable roof is covered with brown wood shingles. A set of elk antlers can be seen high up on the gable end. Below this, a wooden sign with black letters proclaims this to be "Aladdin, Wyo." The building itself is of wood frame construction with red clapboard cladding; the addition is of board-and-batten siding. The building measures approximately 42 feet north to south by 57 feet east to west. A notable feature of the building is its classic false-front facade on the south elevation. A wooden porch covers six of seven windows on the facade. The porch flooring is built of unpainted two-by-six lumber and is covered by a low-pitched shed roof that projects from between the first and second stories. Two signs hang from this porch; one points out that "Package Likker" can be had inside. The other offers "Package Beer." The porch roof is covered in weathered wooden shingles and supported by seven painted wood posts. (Courtesy of the Crook County Museum.)

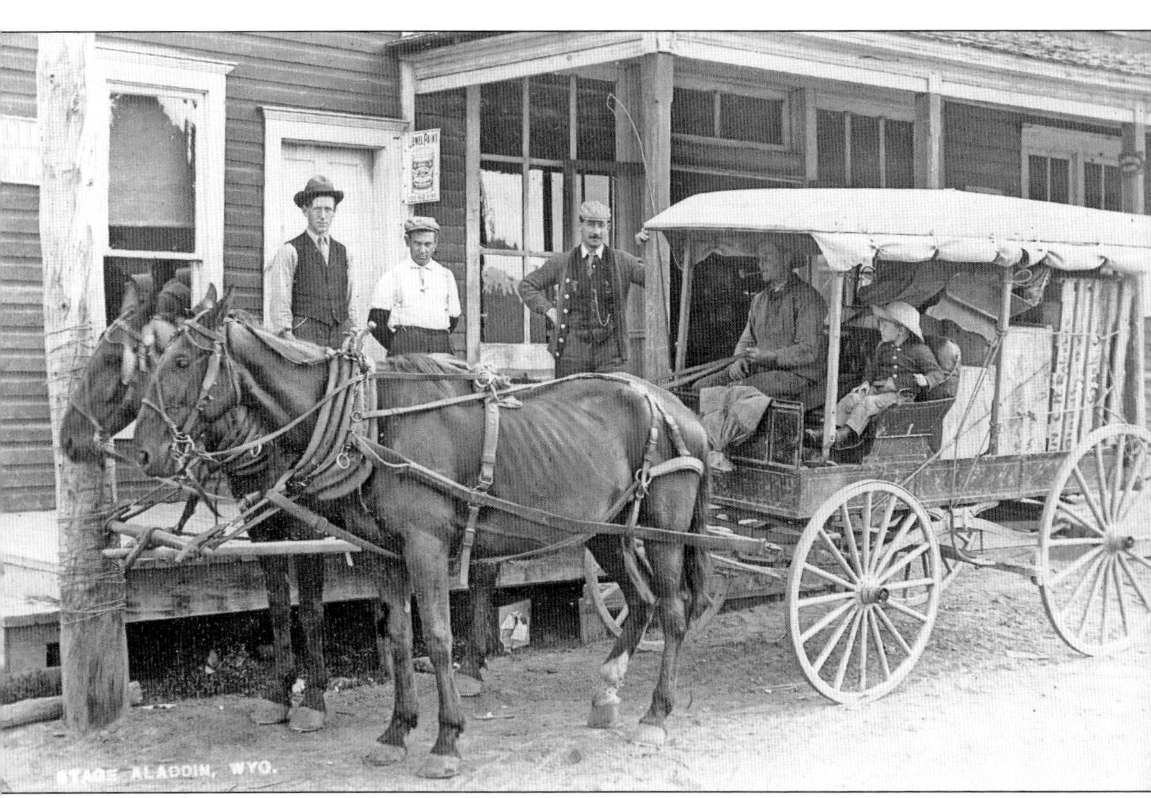

The back of this postcard reads "I was down at Aladdin tonight and got a few cards. This is the Hulett stage. I go to school on it sometimes. The first fellow is Mr. Irven Hejde, you have heard of him before. This picture was taken a long time ago. The next fellow is Post Master Henry Tracy; next to him is the Honorable Fred H Mann. He is the express agent. In the stage is the driver. I don't know who he is, but it is not Jack. And young Walter Tracy is sitting next to the driver. Of course they are all in uniform. I will have a better picture of Aladdin when I can get it. I am having a very pleasant summer but am anxious to be in Illinois. Please, write. EMP." This stage ran between Aladdin and Hulett. It would carry passengers and light freight. (Courtesy of the Aladdin Store.)

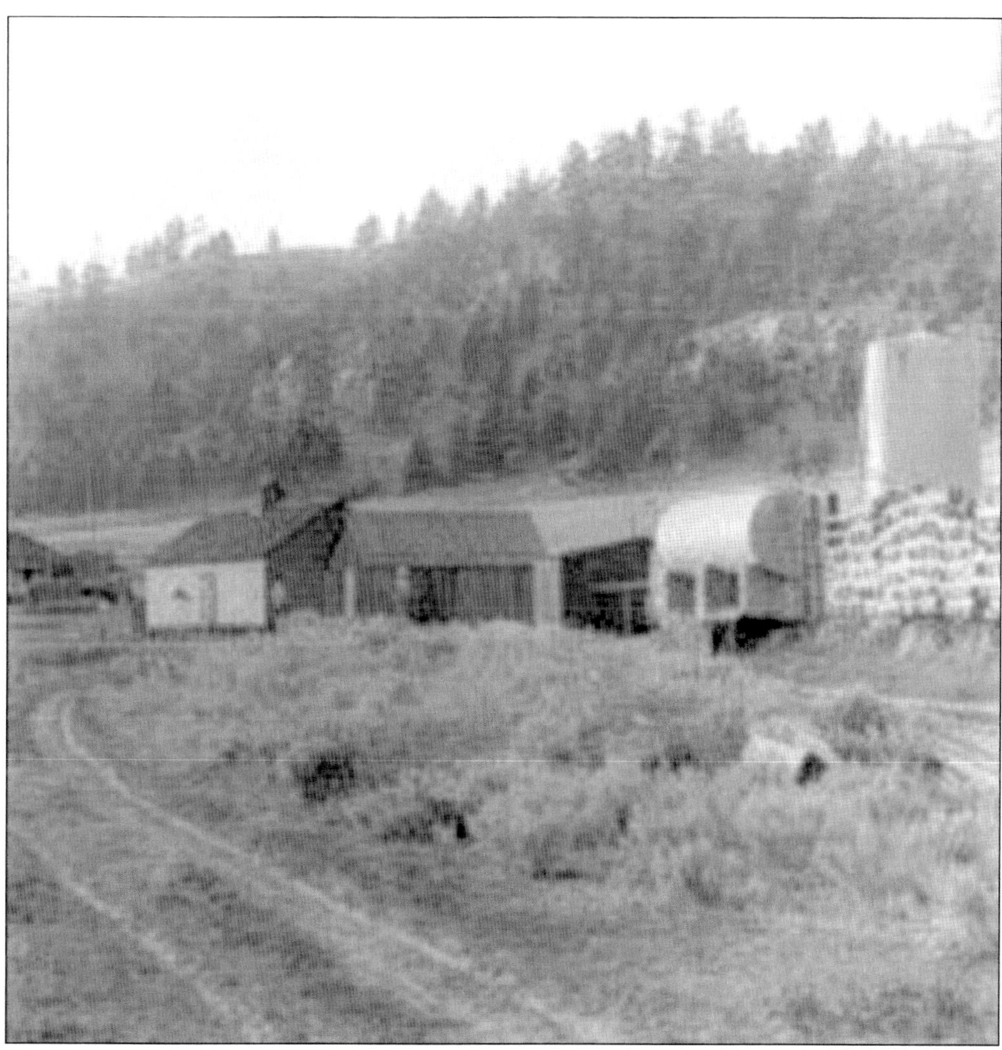

Aladdin is a small community in the far northeast corner of the state. It is situated in Crook County, nestled within the scenic Black Hills region. Belle Fourche is 17 miles to the east, while the nearest Wyoming town, Alva, is 15 miles to the west. Sundance, Wyoming, the county seat, is 30 miles to the southeast. These days, when one enters from either the west or the east, a sign boasts a population of 15. Most residents will state that at any given time there could be anywhere from 13 or 20 to 750, depending on the month. Names of families within a five-mile radius of Aladdin from 1910 to 1922 included Whalen, Pearson, Hejde, Tracy, Mann, Hantz, Hoffman, Nelson, Berry, Finn, Scott, Brimmer, Chittim, Stevens, Patterson, Richard, Summach, Ripley, Mollers, Mortenson, Schnitger, Miller, Glaudos, and Gervasi. Most of these families are still in residence in the valley today. (Courtesy of Chuck Pearson.)

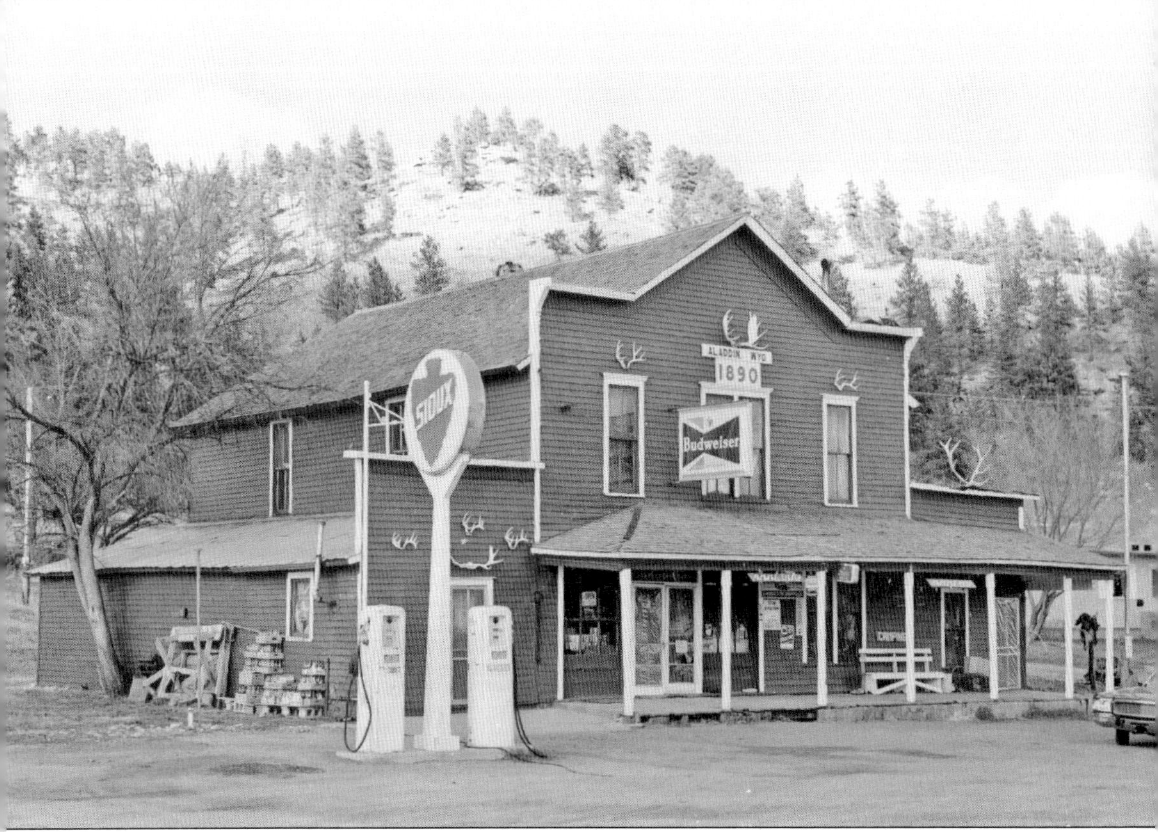

The Aladdin Store has not been the Wyoming Mercantile for many years now. Elk antlers are still hanging from the gable, and more have been added. Soda pop boxes are stacked along the outside of the liquor department of the store. The door to the beer and spirits has sprouted its own crop of antlers. A fancy Budweiser sign has been added and reminds travelers of the passing years. The sign on the gas tanks tells passersby that Sioux is what is on tap for the modern automobiles of the day. On the porch, a liar's bench has been added that is occupied more often than one might think. The door on the right leads into the post office, which probably has not changed much since it opened in 1898. Mail is delivered to that door once a day. It is taken inside and sorted before the carrier picks up the departing mail and goes on his way. (Courtesy of the Crook County Museum.)

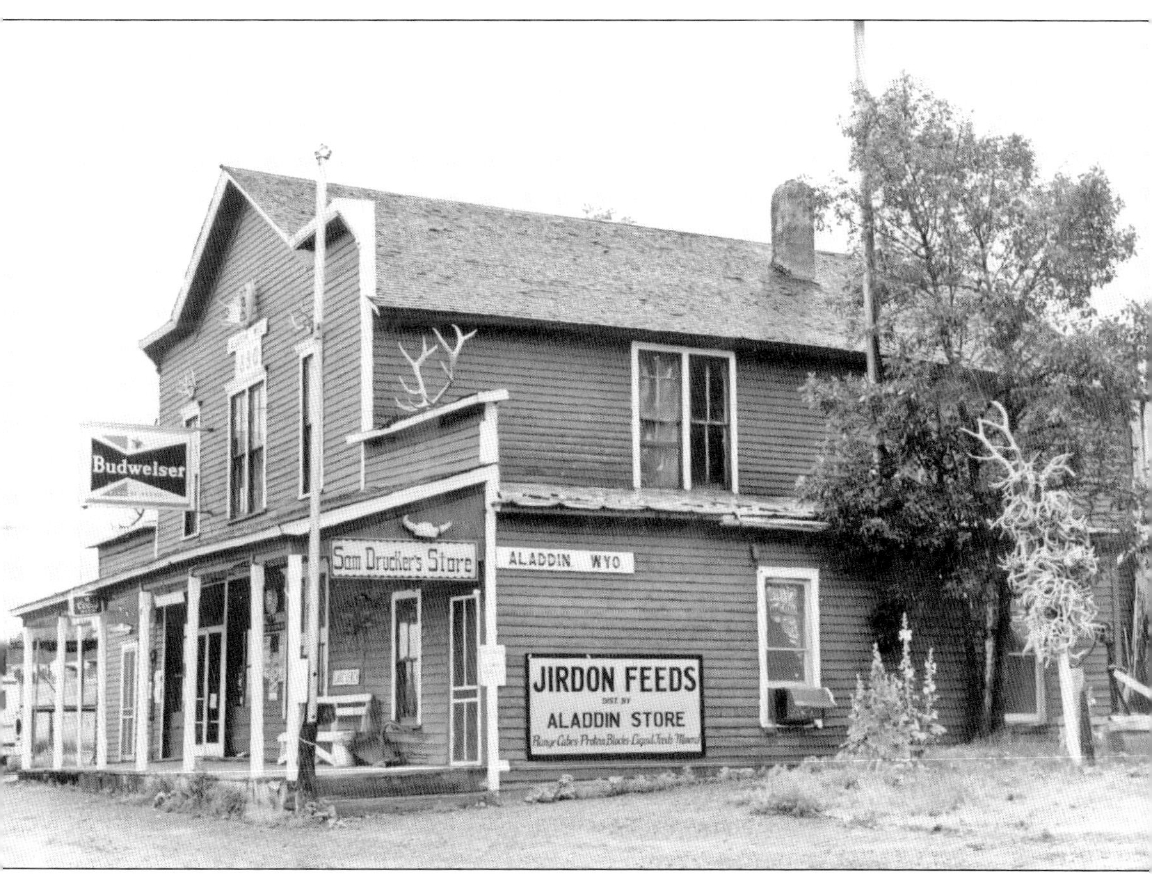

This is the east side of the Aladdin Store. The sign that declares it to be Sam Drucker's store was put up one dark night by someone who missed the *Petticoat Junction* and *Green Acres* television shows. The store has always been the heart of the community and its center of activity; it continues as such today. Through the years, the Aladdin Store and post office have been many things to many people. The building has housed a general store, a bar, a post office, a barbershop, and a telephone office, and served as a depot, freight station, and gasoline station. The gas pumps now replace the hitching post where customers tethered their horses, but the same hospitably can be found in Aladdin today as in days gone by. The store still has much of what one might need. Groceries, supplies, snacks, caps, gloves, forgotten anniversary gifts, and garden supplies are still to be had. Travelers often stop, attracted by the obviously authentic old country store. The store has been listed in the National Register of Historic Places since 1990. (Courtesy of Black Hills State University, Case Library, Watson Parker Collection.)

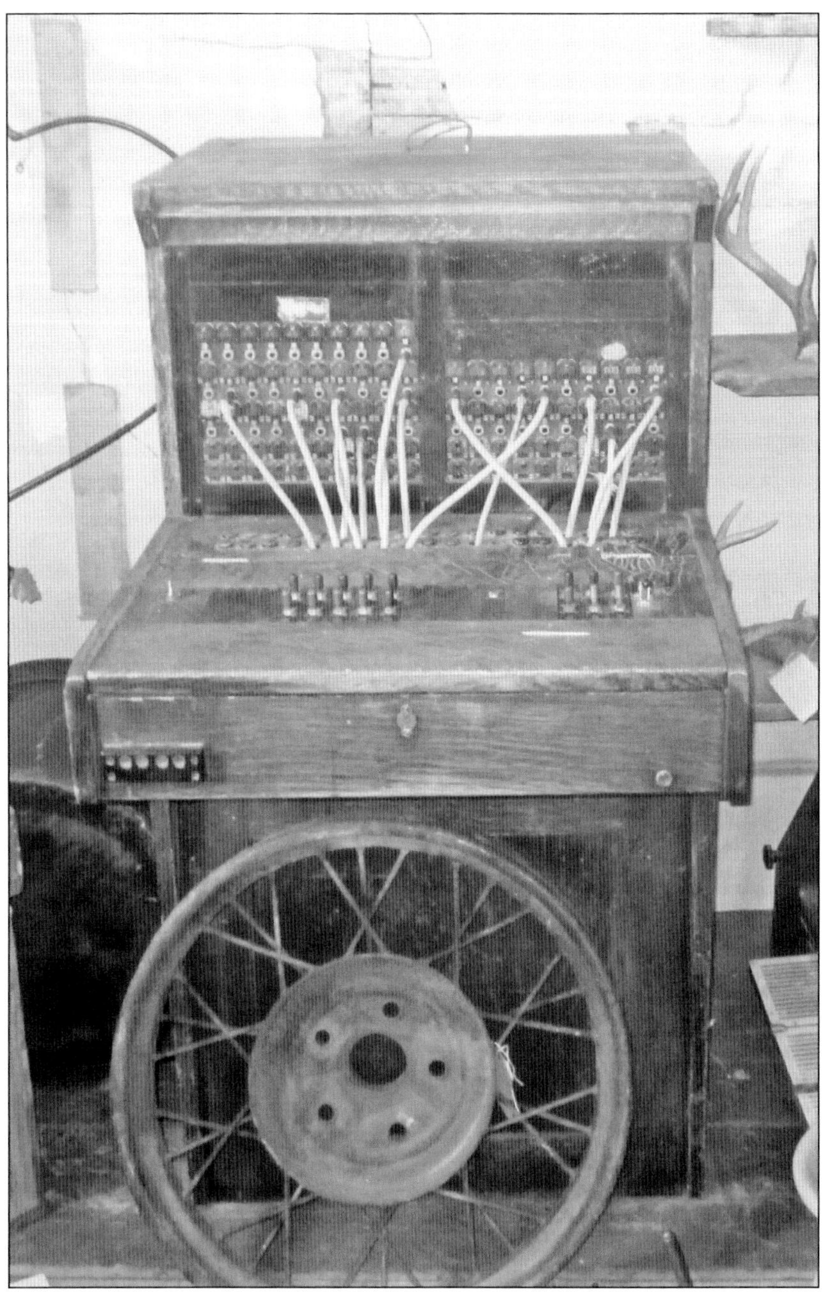

This is the Mona Short Line switchboard. It sits upstairs in the Aladdin Store in the same place it has been since the day it was carried up the stairs. Jack Kunerth was instrumental in organizing the telephone line into Aladdin. For many years, the phone line was owned by the neighboring ranchers. These progressive-thinking men also maintained it. Many different men and women acted as the switchboard operator. Some of them lived upstairs over the store while they worked for the Mona Short Line. Besides being the local telephone office, the upstairs was also used as a family home, a boardinghouse, and a hotel. It remains the home for two departed young ladies who joyfully haunt the rooms, play with the merchandise, and startle the unsuspecting. (Author's collection.)

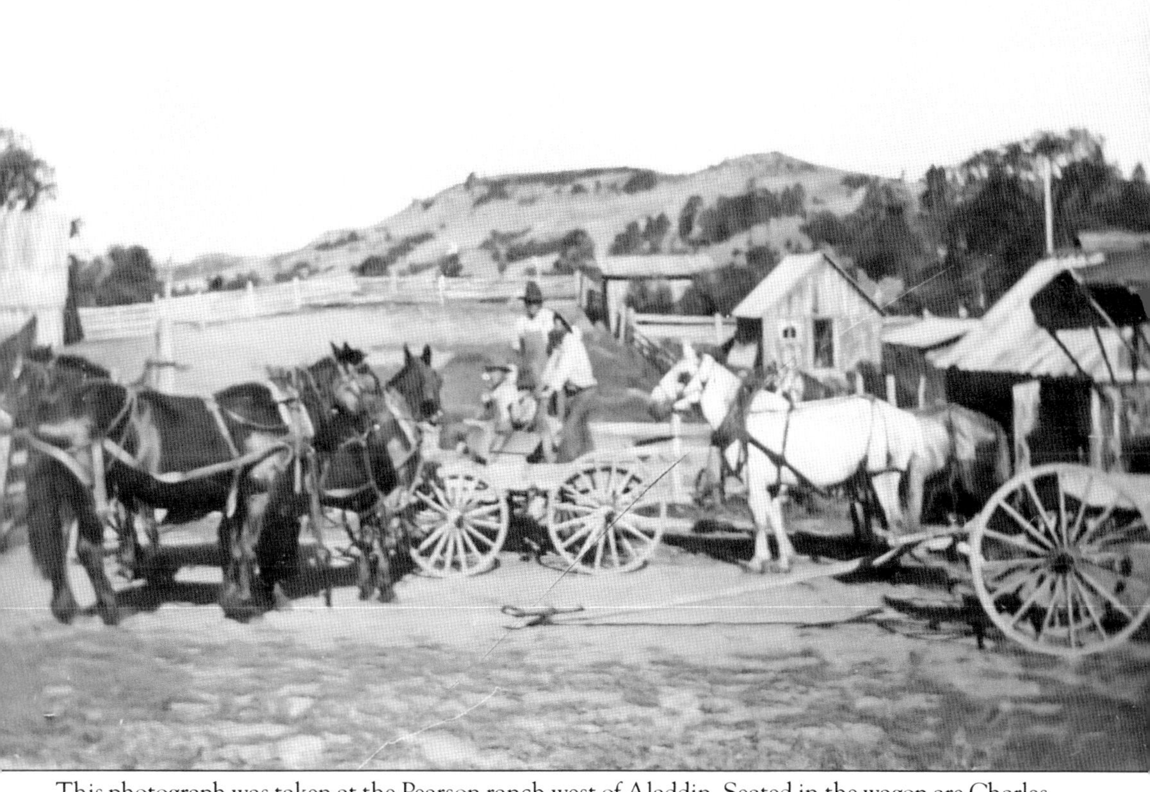

This photograph was taken at the Pearson ranch west of Aladdin. Seated in the wagon are Charles Pearson and his son Frank A. Pearson. Standing behind them are Sam Leitner (left) and Archie Zink. There are two or three teams of horses in the picture. There is one team ready to be hitched to the buggy and four horses in front of the wagon. That many horses would be used with a wagon if there was a heavy load to be pulled and if there was a big hill to climb. The horses could have just finished a long day's work in the fields and are waiting for their harnesses to be taken off, have a nice brushing down and a good meal of grain and fresh hay, and find a quiet place to nap and dream of wild runs in clover fields. (Courtesy of Chuck Pearson.)

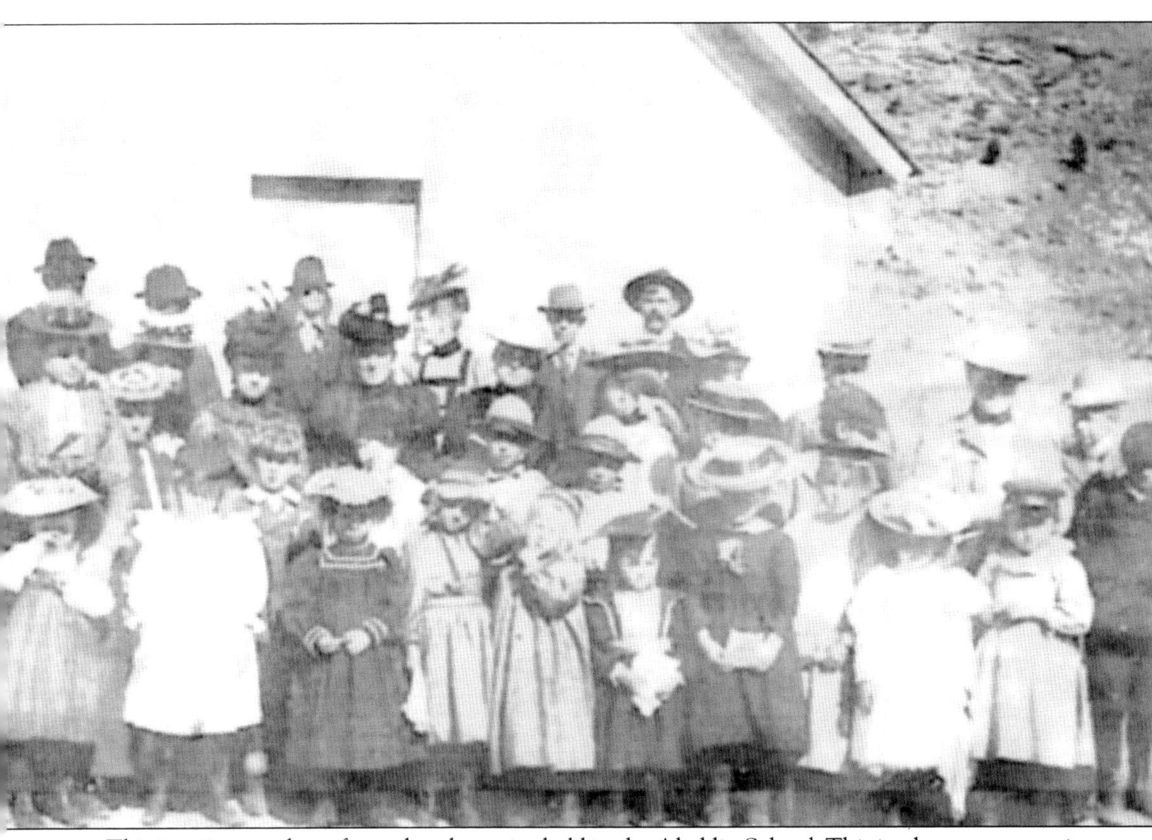

This is a picture taken after a church service held in the Aladdin School. This is a large congregation for a town the size of Aladdin. People must have come in from a few miles away. Chances are that Rev. Wes Tracy did the preaching this morning. Church services were often held in schoolhouses or in people's homes. Records do show that there was a Methodist-Episcopal church in Aladdin for a few years. There was a Catholic church about 10 miles north of Aladdin on the Ryan ranch. Preacher Tracy traveled around the county to marry people. Sometimes he just could not make it to the ceremony on time. That did happen in Riverdale one evening. Justice of the peace John Pearson in Eothen was sent for, and John saddled up and rode through a cold, 40-below night to get Mary Belle Baxter and Edward Wilson married. (Courtesy of Tom Robinson.)

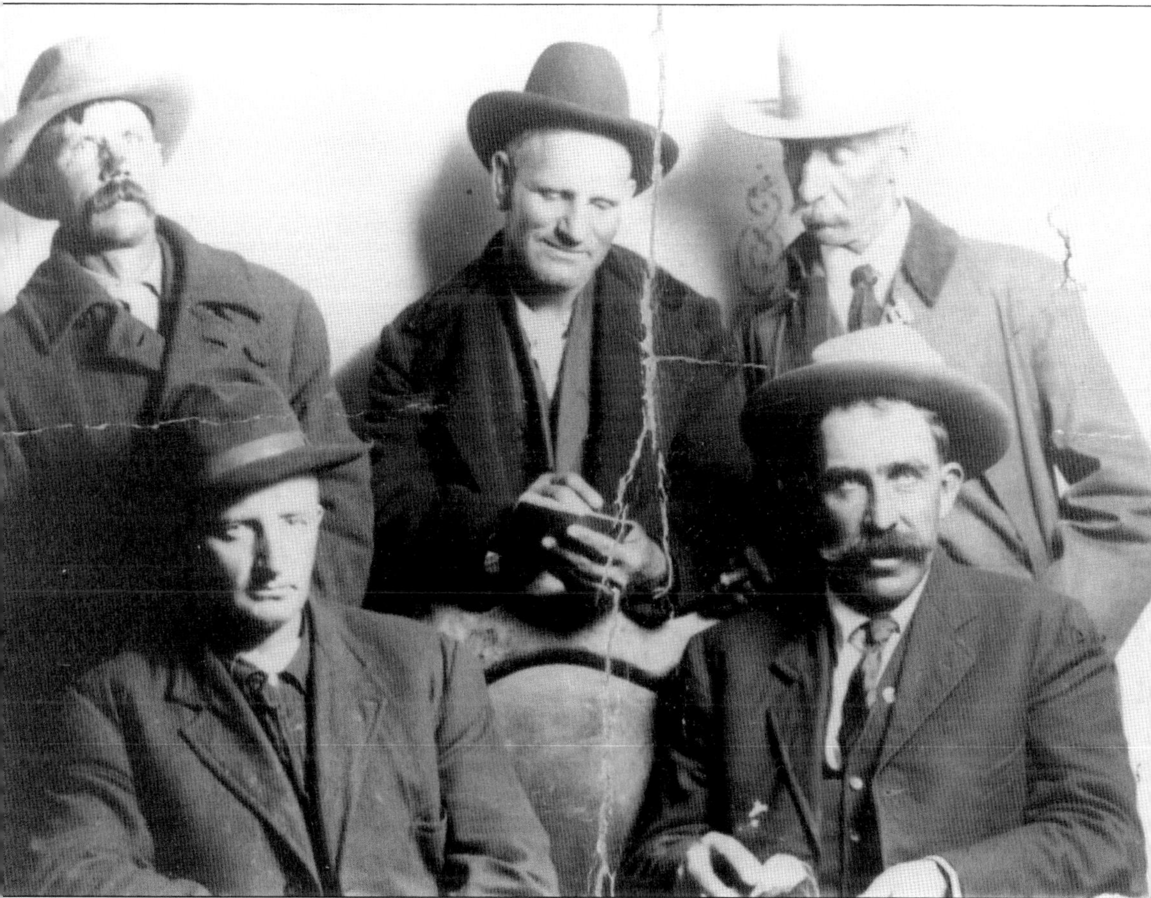

Here are a few of the men who would gather in the store around the stove to discuss crops, market prices, weather, and maybe politics. There was always a fire in the wood stove and cards, checker boards, and sometimes even a cribbage board waiting for them at the codgers' table. From left to right are (first row) Charles Pearson and George Brownfield; (second row) Nils Nilson, Herb Sims, and Fred Aikman. Nils Nilson was a surveyor and a civil engineer. He was elected county surveyor for several years. During his last year, he made a complete map of Crook County, locating all dams and roads. When George Brownfield was 65 years old, he was arrested for the murder of Theodore Thomas and for assaulting his 22-year-old wife. On March 10, 1930, after bidding the prison chaplain goodbye, Brownfield calmly walked to his hanging. Word of his hanging was received with approval around the community. (Courtesy of Chuck Pearson.)

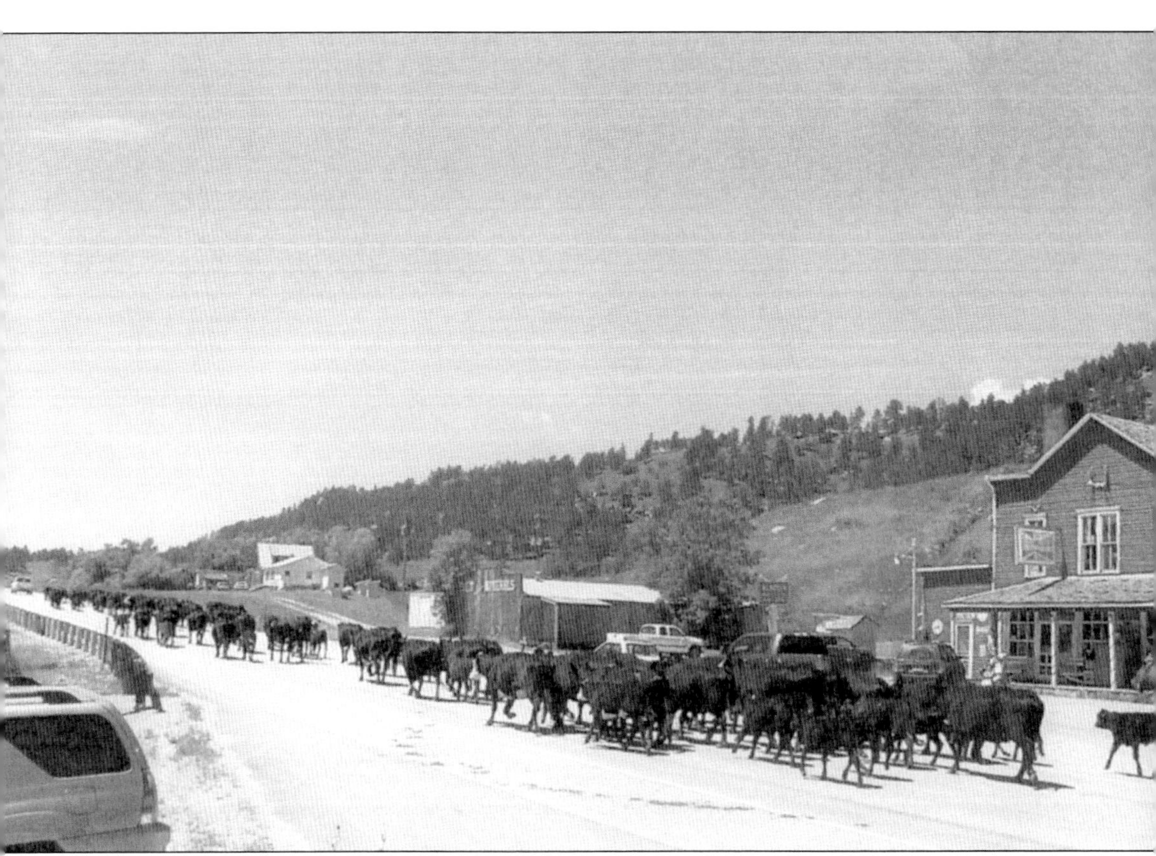

Even in these modern days of the 21st century, the old ways are often the best and most efficient. On a sunny day in June, the Ray Marchant family is moving their cattle through Aladdin. The cattle spent the winter on the home ranch about eight miles north of the store along Oak Creek. When the two-day drive is over they will be spending the summer in the Black Hills National Forest. When the weather starts to change and the leaves begin to fall, it will be time for the return trip. The cattle will travel along the highway for a few more miles before they turn west and enjoy moving slower, away from busy traveled highways. There are a few differences from the olden days. Today's riders will take turns coming back to Cindy B.'s Aladdin Café for lunch and maybe a big piece of pie. And at night they will have a hot shower and sleep in their own beds. (Author's collection.)

Five

The Schools

In 1887, there were 28 schools in Crook County, Wyoming. In 1914, there were 110. The school superintendent, Priscilla Clark Pattee, reported that in June 1885 she had traveled 256 miles in eight days to visit the seven schools in the Aladdin area.

Schoolhouses were usually log with dirt floors. Often a spare room, a ranch harness shop, or even an empty granary would be put into service as a school. Many times the classroom would be in someone's home. Schools moved about as the number of children changed as parents moved in and about the school district. School would be near where the greatest number of children attending lived, and sometimes, the school was as close as possible to the youngest child attending classes. Five students were needed to open a school. Some school terms were short summer sessions, and some were long winter terms.

Some schools had a place for the teacher to live near the school. Often the teacher would board with families of the students. In rural schools, a teacher was nurse, mother, janitor, and the law. Teachers were assigned a school each new term. In 1890, a teacher's salary was $42 per month.

All schools had a door in the front and a large blackboard across the back wall. The desks for pupils were double or single. Under the top of the desk was a place to keep their books, tablets, and anything else that would be needed. There was an inkwell and pens for penmanship. Most days were filled with reading, writing, arithmetic, language, geography, physiology, Wyoming civics, and spelling.

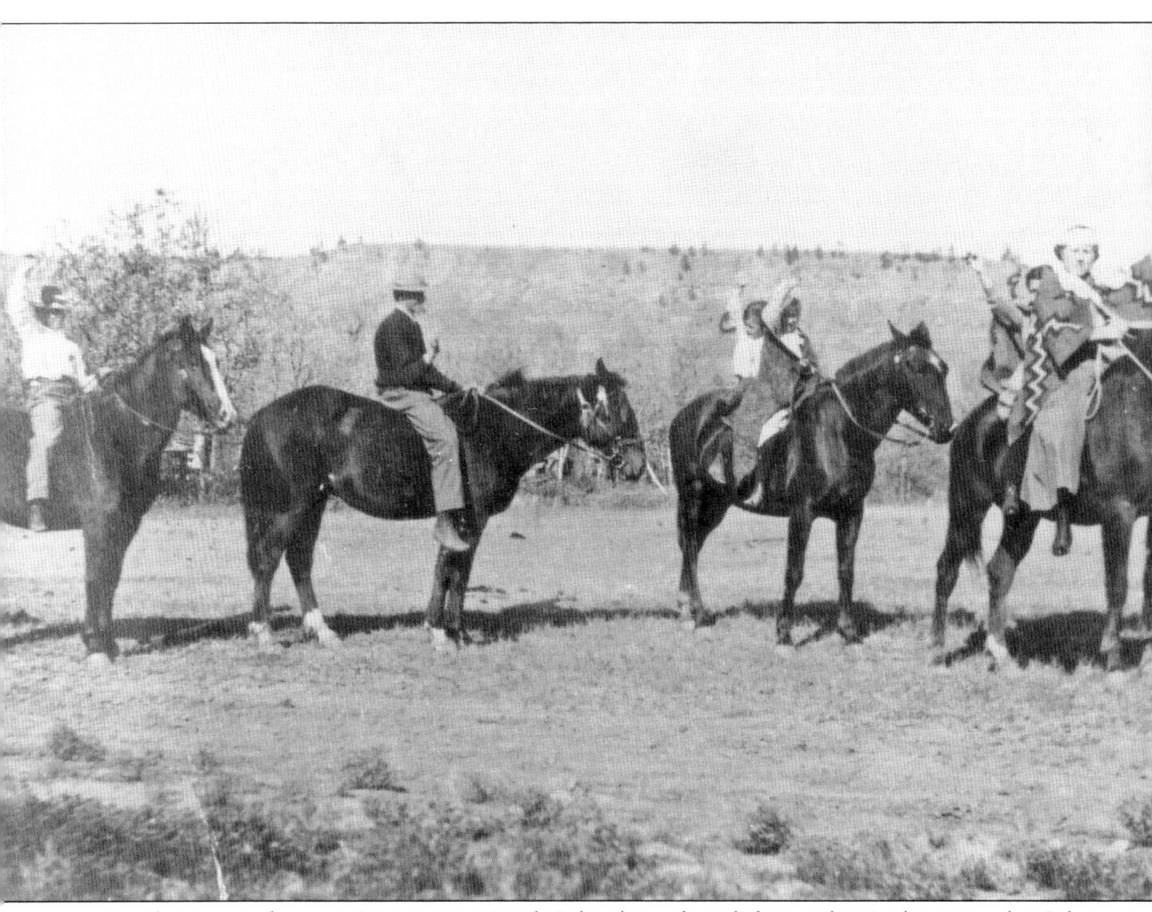

On the way to classes in Upper Pine Creek School are, from left to right, Arthur Knowles, John Reddington, Ida Waddington, Chester Smith, Eva Smith, and Edna Waddington. Upper Oak Creek was also called Basin School or Mitchell School. Arthur Knowles rode horseback to school from the first grade. He came down off Stoney Point past Major Miller's ranch. William Crago and his sister sometimes rode a cow the one and a half miles to school. (Courtesy of Chuck Pearson.)

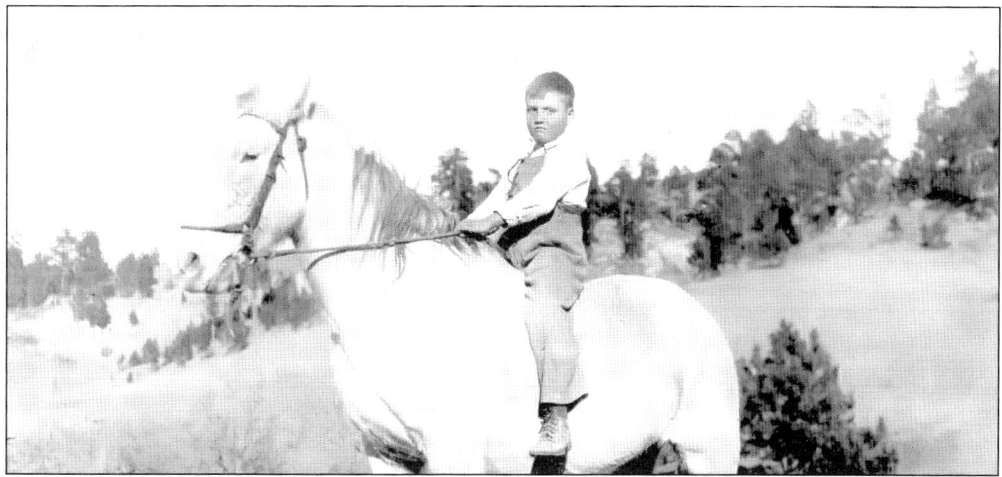

One more small boy is on his way to school, and he appears to be none too happy about it. In 1897, this school was housed in a newly constructed log cabin. A man whose name seems to have been long forgotten was helping raise the building, and as he reached to lift the next log into place, a rattlesnake bit him on the end of a finger. Without a moment's hesitation, he picked up an ax, laid the doomed finger on a log, and cut it off. In 1918, the log building was replaced by a frame structure set on a sandstone foundation. The builders were Charlie Parsons, Charlie Pearson, and Zea Russell. At an earlier date, a barn had been built for the horses that were ridden to school. (Courtesy of the Thompson family.)

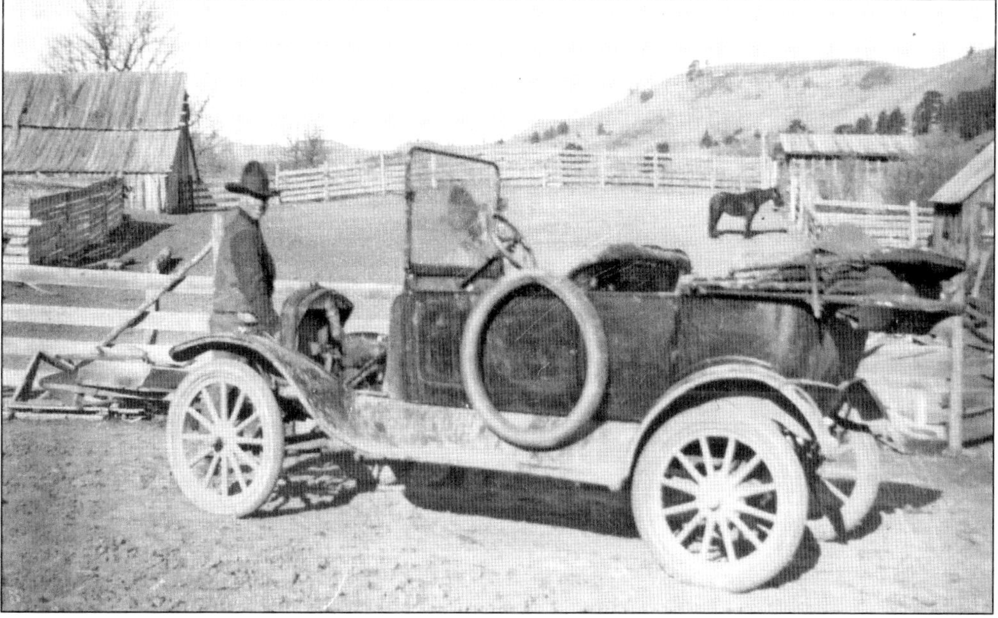

Here is Arthur Knowles with different means of transportation. This is Arthur's first automobile, and a fine one it is. It was one of the first such contraptions in this end of the county. Some thought it was the way of the future, and others thought it was just a passing fancy. His horses were not too happy about the whole idea. There were many new inventions appearing all the time to catch a child's interest. When airplanes flew over, classes came to a halt so that the children could all run outside to watch and wave. If the pilot saw them, he would waggle his wings to wave back, and they would cheer. (Courtesy of Chuck Pearson.)

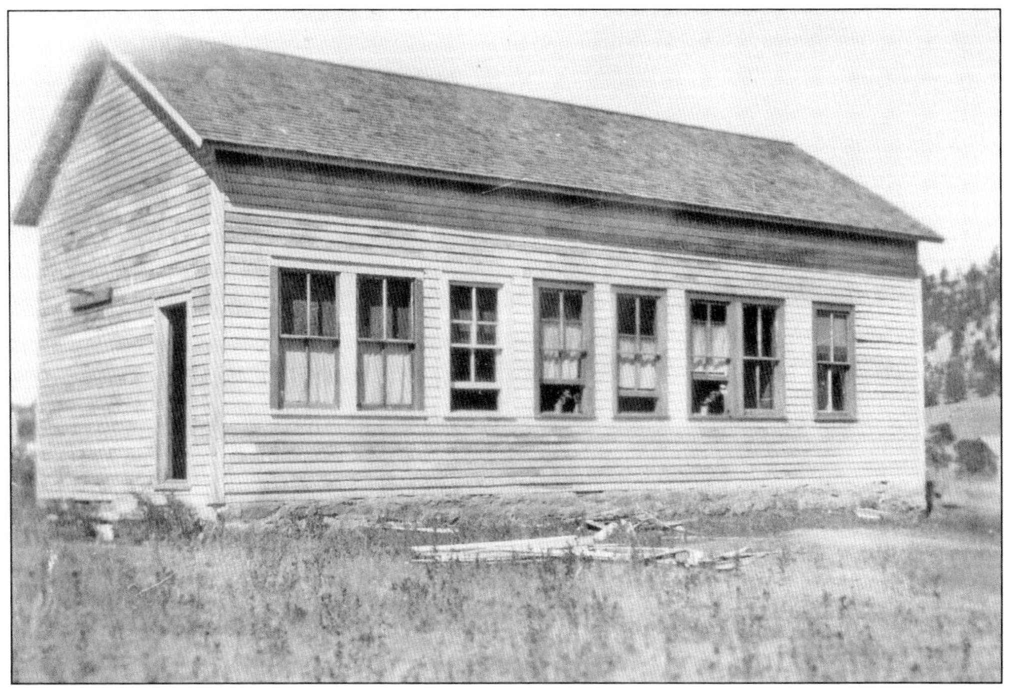

At one time, the county superintendent of schools reported that Florence Culver was the teacher of the Aladdin School, which was two miles from the town itself. It appeared that even at that distance the children attended regularly. The school contained English, French, German, Italian, Swedish, Norwegian, and Danish children, all of whom seemed to be learning fast, and the teacher managed to keep the peace among all these nationalities. About 1901, the Aladdin School sat across the road from the store and some distance up the hill at the edge of a wooded area. It was a solid building and larger than most country schools. It had a large heater and many windows, and at one time a porch was added. This school was moved over the Bear Lodge Mountains to Hulett and continues to this day in its new occupation as a church. (Courtesy of Chuck Pearson.)

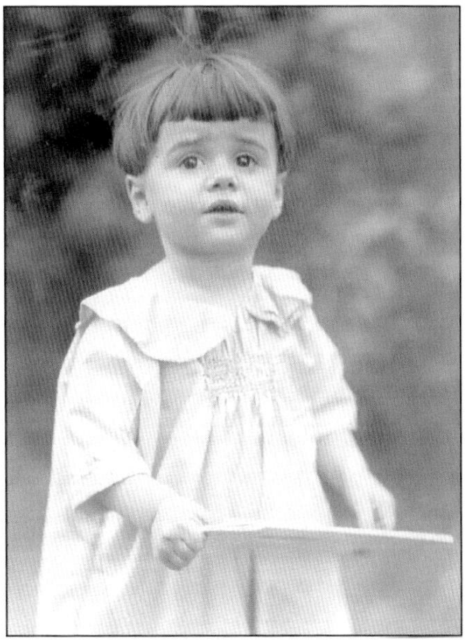

No one remembers her name, but they do remember that this little girl wanted to go to school with the older children. She carried books and paper around to show she was big enough to go to school. Teacher Florence Culver would have to tell her not yet, she had to be at least six years old. She would answer the teacher saying "Please, school." This school never had a shortage of students. Her family must have moved from Aladdin before she reached school age. (Courtesy of the Thompson family.)

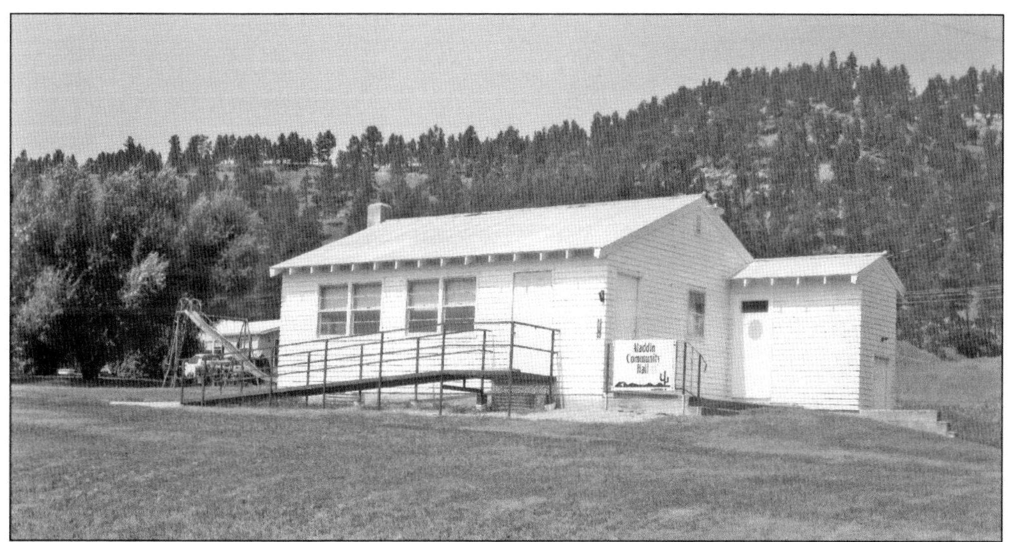

This school that sits on the western edge of Aladdin was built where it stands. There never was a need to move it to other locations. The stage, the teacher's desk, and the blackboards remain inside ready for any time they might be needed. It is one of the few schools with a basement. This Aladdin schoolhouse no longer serves as a school, but it continues to serve the community. In 2004, men fighting a 7,000-acre wild fire were fed in the basement. The residents of the Aladdin voting district cast their votes inside at every election. The Aladdin School continues to be used for meetings, dinners, parties, and pie socials. (Author's collection.)

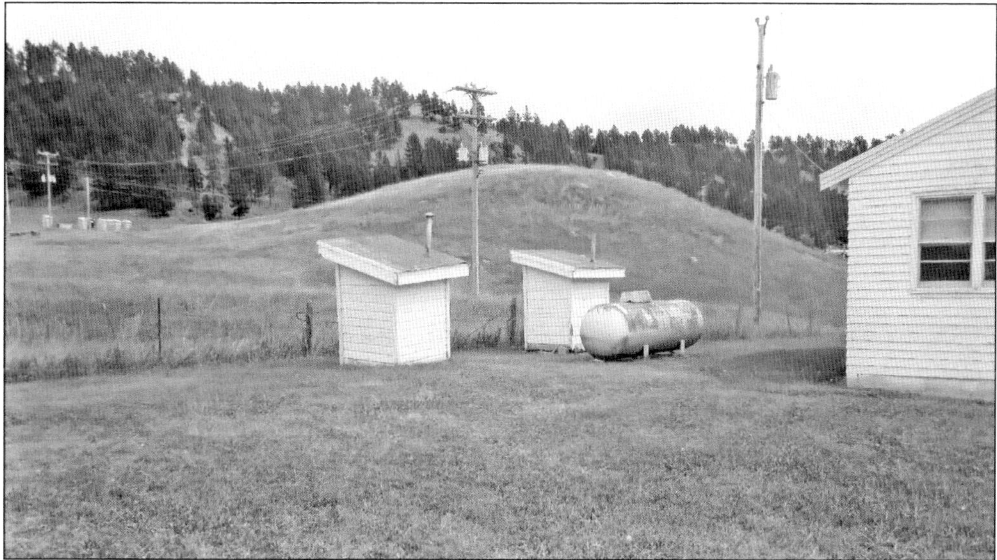

In all rural schools, the bathroom was located a varying distance from the schoolhouse along a path that could be dry or not depending on the season. The Work Projects Administration (WPA) employed millions in the 1930s and 1940s to carry out public works projects, including construction of public buildings and roads. Keeping these buildings in good shape was not always easy, as porcupines could wander in and chew on the seats. Like the roads and bridges that were built during that time and are still in use today, many schools, parks, and ranches have outhouses built by the WPA that are still standing and functioning as well today as they did the day they were built. (Author's collection.)

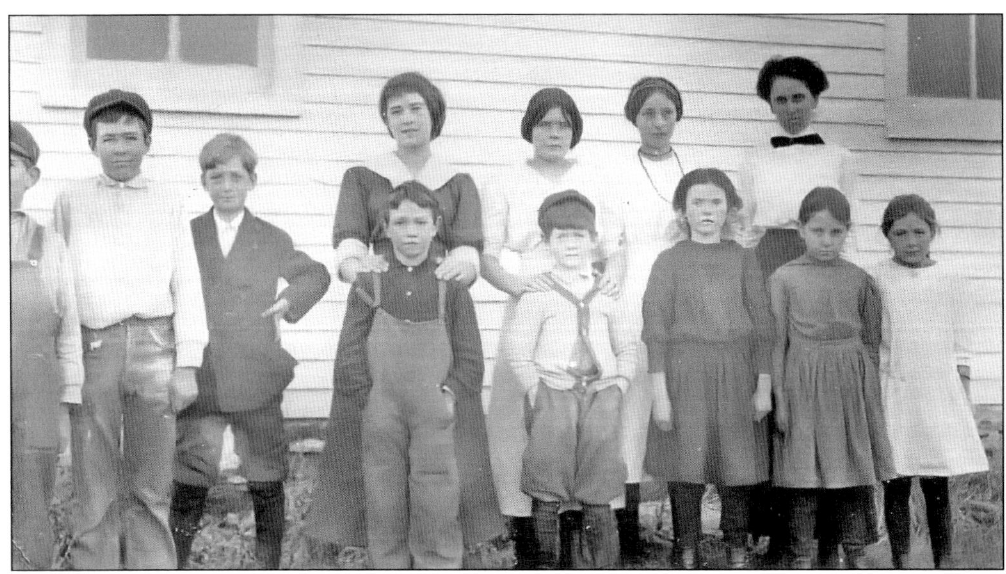

This postcard was sent by Hazel Linscott Kendall and addressed to her parents Frank and Cloe Kendall of New Haven, Crook County. Hazel traveled from Ewing, Nebraska, at the age of 18 to homestead in Crook County and to teach school. She was quite a catch for some young man. She had a paying job and homestead land. The postcard is postmarked from Aladdin, Wyoming, and reads, "Dearest Folks, Will treat you to a postcard. I will write a real letter for the next mail. I am getting along just fine. How are all of you? We are sure having fine weather. Yesterday was cold. Will all of you write to me? This is a picture of my school at Mona. We are all here, but for one boy, who is only half seen on the left side of the picture. From left to right are; Ernest Cremeens, Arthur Knowles, Daniel Phillips, Carrie Burnett, Robert Waddington, Frances Ginnegan, Hazel Phillips, Josie Ginnegan, Yours Truly-me-Hazel Kendal, Eva Phillips and Lottie Phillips. With dear love, as ever, Hazel." (Courtesy of the Thompson family.)

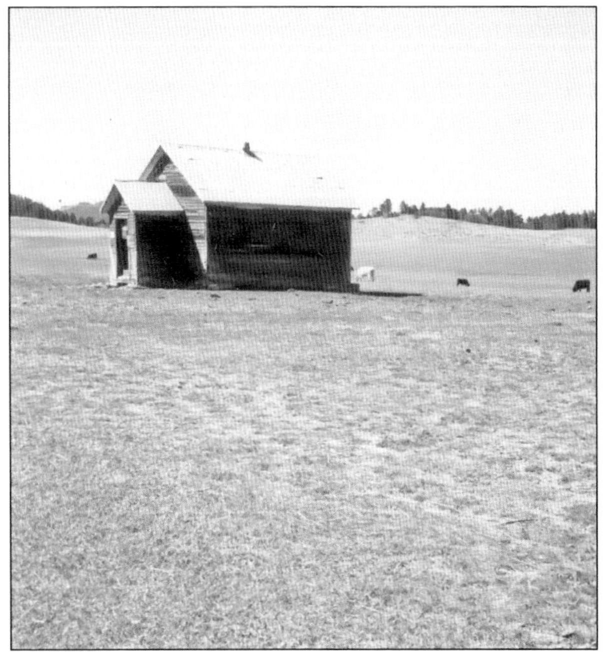

The schools were named for the nearest landmark, like a creek or a hill, for the ranch where the school sat, or for the people who had built them or moved them. That was how the KMP School got its name. Tony Koyek, Marshall Miller, and Harry Parsons moved the school into place and made it a sturdy, safe school for their children. Pictured is the Mona School. This school was moved around many times, much like the Mona Post Office. After one such move, the children and their teacher planted flowers so that there would always be a reminder that there once was a school on that spot. Those flowers do continue to remind people that students went to school there. It is a struggle, but they keep blooming. (Courtesy of the Crook County Museum.)

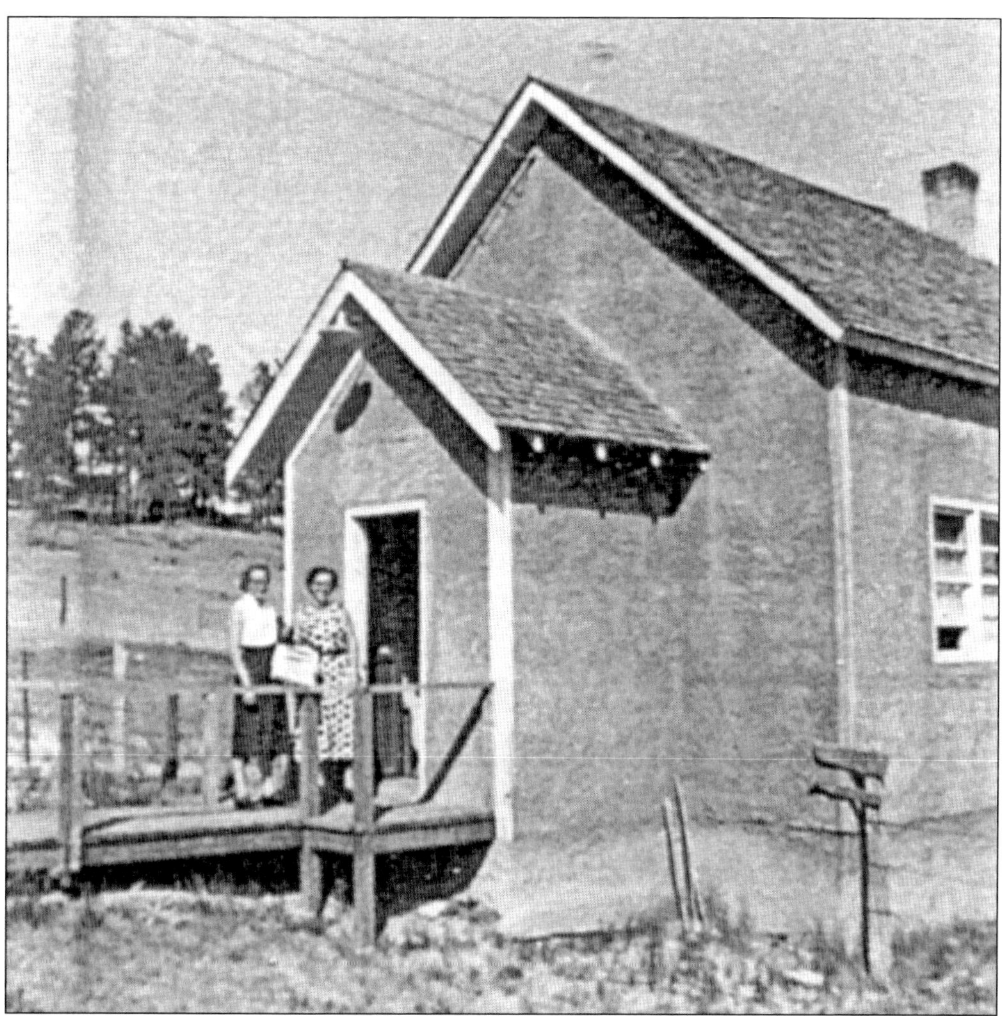

Annual meetings for School District No. 2 were held at the Eothen schoolhouse. For some parents, it was a four-day trip. Many families would bring a picnic lunch along. Some even brought bedrolls and cooking supplies. They were prepared for the long haul. Everyone had a chance to talk, and talk they did. There were always one or two curmudgeons on hand to vote down the need for more teachers or better salaries because "teachers have an easy time." All of those present wanted to voice their opinion on school business and the kind of teacher they wanted for their children. The no-fighting rule inside the schoolhouse caused many men to take their discussions outside into the schoolyard and beyond. It was probably a good thing there was no drinking of adult beverages on school property. There were no rules about yelling, shouting, foot stomping, or hair pulling, and a lot of that sort of thing was reported to have happened during these meetings. (Courtesy of the Crook County Museum.)

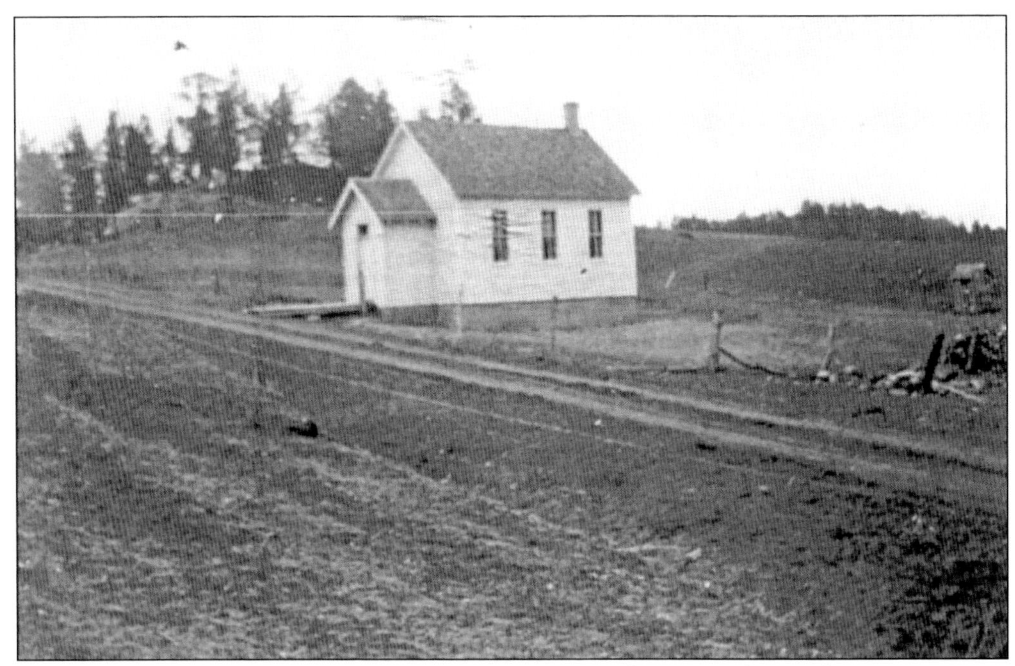

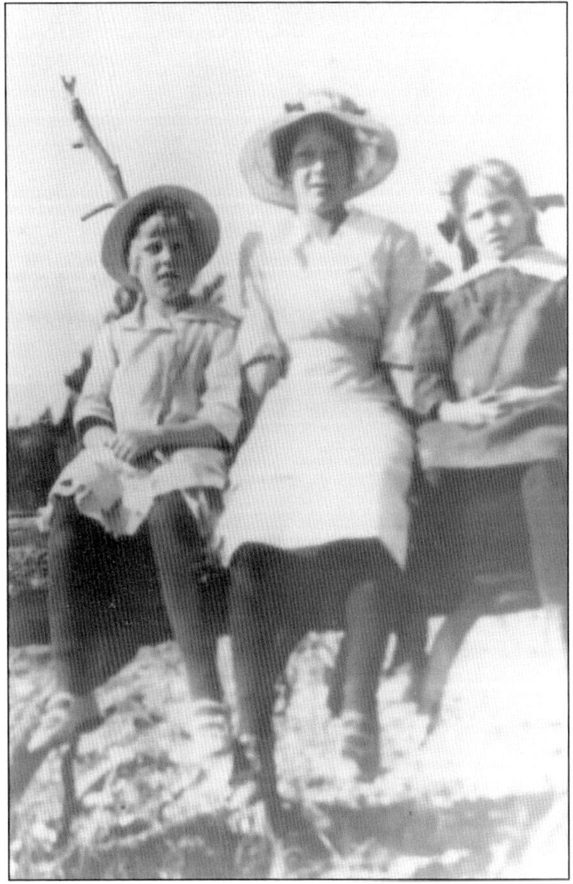

Chester Hjede says there was not any playground equipment when he went to school at the Eothen School. Robert Wyman went to the first grade early because of the need to have five students to start a school. He went to school for his first of two years in the first grade so that his older sister would not have to walk four and a half miles to the Aladdin School. (Courtesy of the Crook County Museum.)

These three are taking a break from classes to enjoy a spring-like day. Their teacher somehow talked the other two into climbing a tree to sit among the branches. Many of the teachers would use the outdoor environment as a classroom and as a way to introduce new ideas and experience new activities. Many times, the students would use the outdoors to give the teacher a new experience. Many a teacher learned about snakes, raccoons, spiders, and bugs from her students. (Courtesy of the Crook County Museum.)

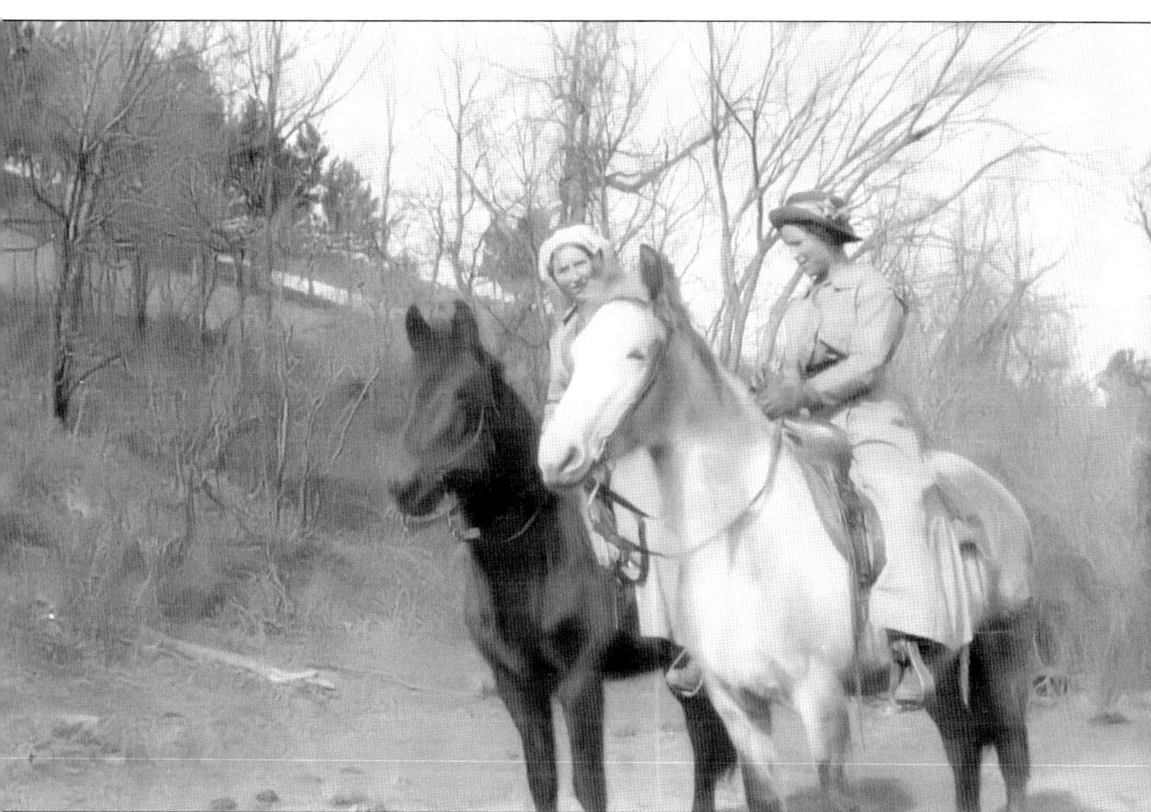

Here are two new teachers riding off to their schools for the first time. Someone thought to take a picture to record the day in the lives of new teachers, but they forgot to record their names on the back of the picture. Many women did travel from different parts of the country to come to Crook County to teach. Some lasted only a year, some not that long. Others stayed for the rest of their lives. (Courtesy of the Thompson family.)

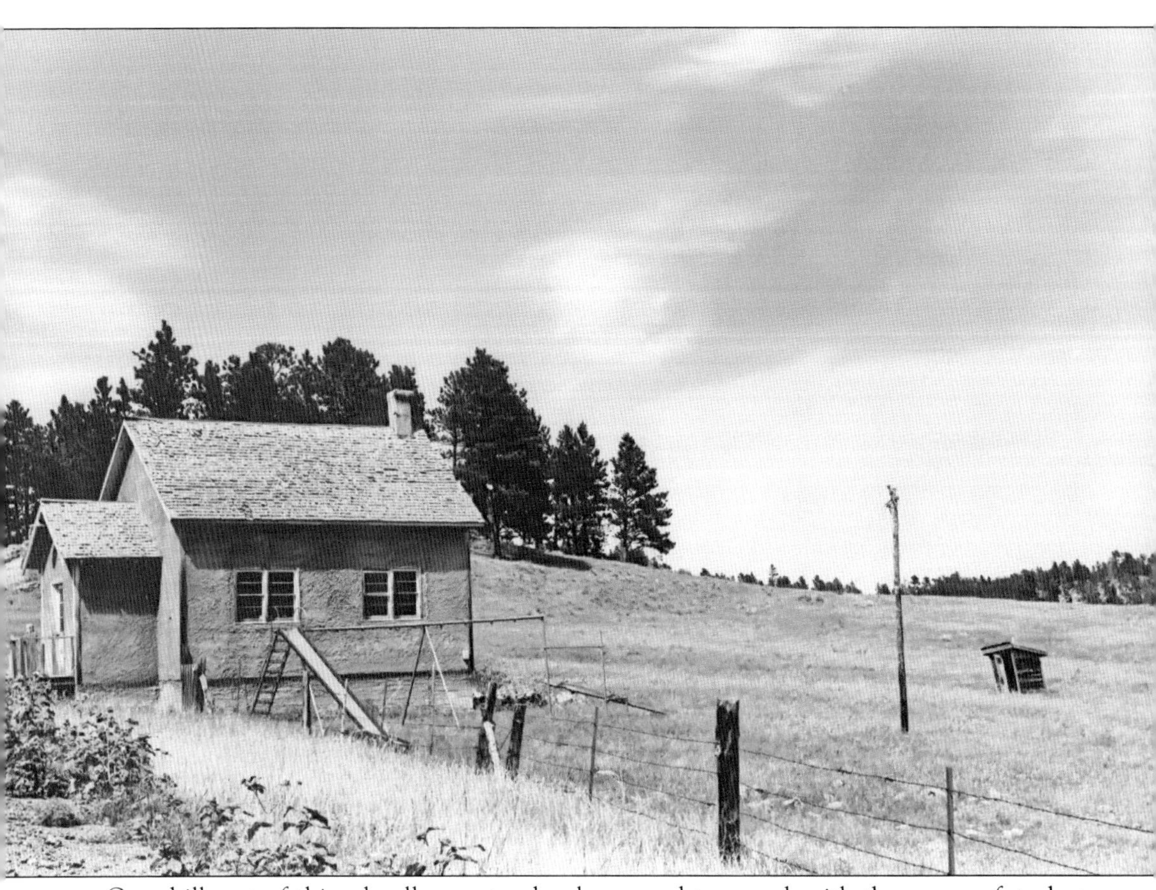

On a hill west of this schoolhouse stands a large sandstone rock with the names of students who attended the school carved into it. Names and dates come from 1894, 1902, and the 1940s. Some of the names that appear on the rock are Julius Hattfield, Charley and Frank Pearson, and a Dungey. Maybe it was Kay Dungey who carved his name into the rock. This school sat in the same location until it was moved or torn down in the 1970s. Now only the rock holds all of the school-day memories. (Courtesy of Chuck Pearson.)

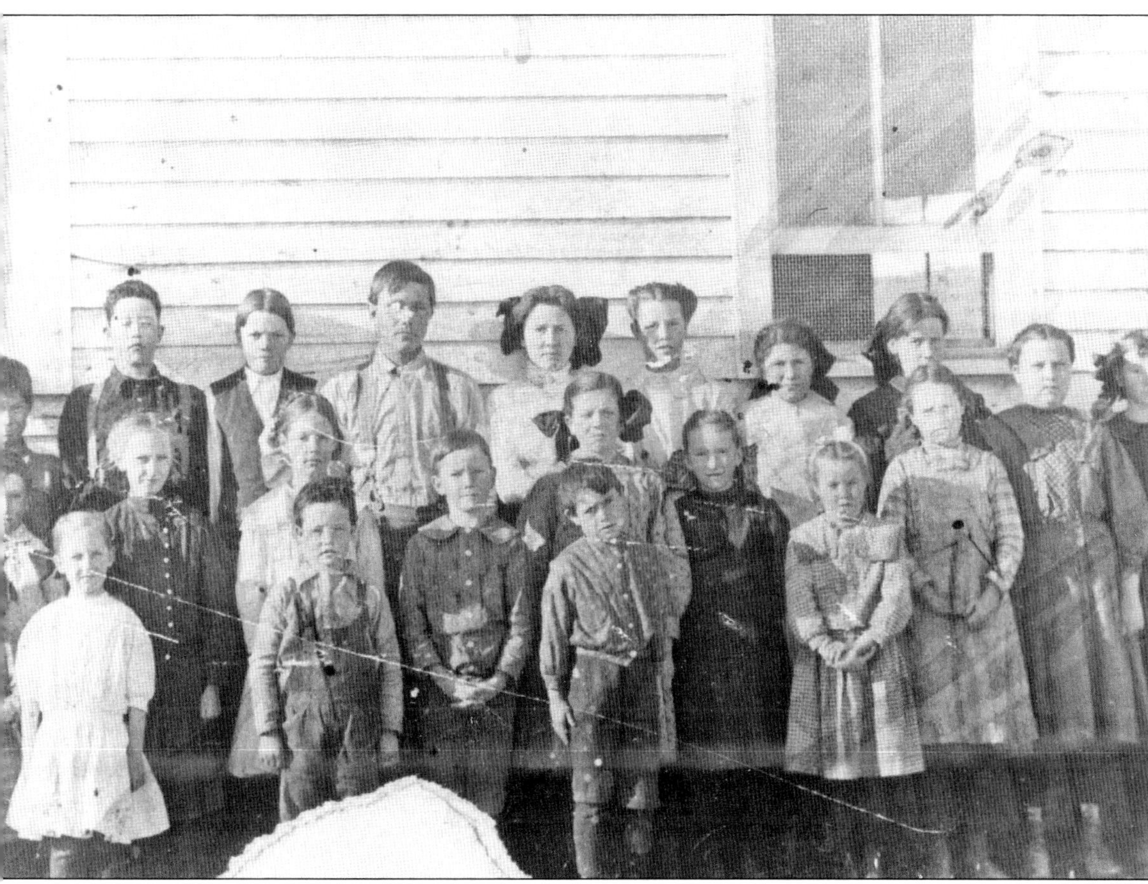

In 1896, the Hay Creek School had a baseball club, and even teacher Minnie Butterfield took her turn at bat. Patrons of the school were said to be "pleased as punch" with her work in the schoolroom, just as the youngsters were with her assistance on the baseball diamond. The school superintendent noted that on her visit the teacher and the students did seem affected by spring fever. This school group does not look too happy. Maybe they were the visiting team that just lost a game to the Hay Creek School students. (Courtesy of Chuck Pearson.)

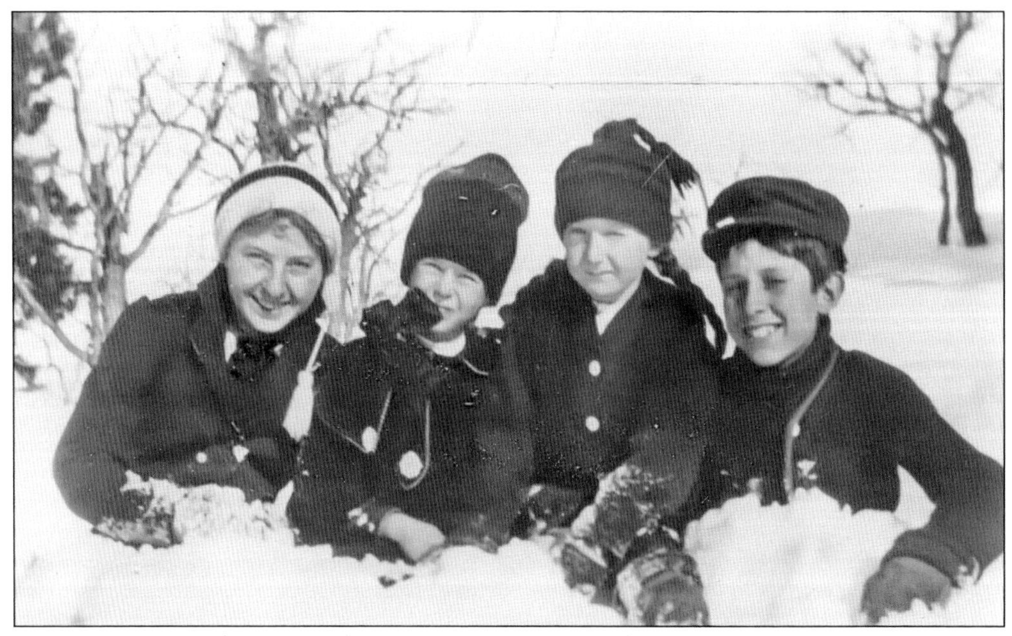

In 1910, these snow bunnies took time out from classes at the Oak Creek School to enjoy being buried in the first snowfall of the year. From left to right are teacher Sophia Landers, Frances Nilson, Marion Kimball, and Sam Aikman. (Courtesy of Chuck Pearson.)

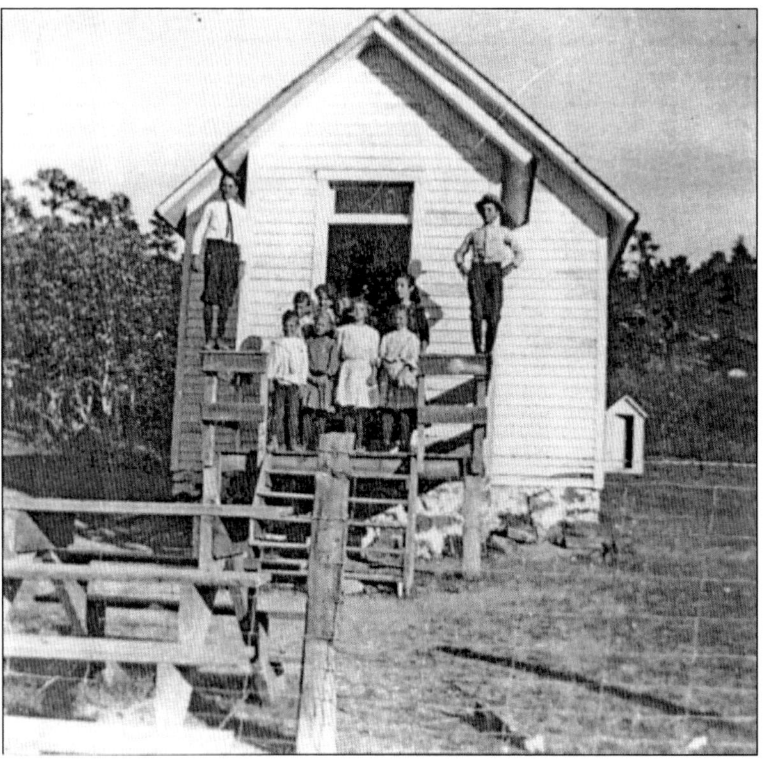

When the weather was warmer, more students gathered outside the school and took time for a picture before returning inside for schoolwork. From left to right are (first row) Oscar Nilson, Frances Nilson, Helen Robinson, and Elaine Kimball; (second row) Tom Robinson, Delia Derrickson, Theo Derrickson, and Esther Aikman; (on the porch railings) Winthrop Kimball and Sam Aikman. (Courtesy of Chuck Pearson.)

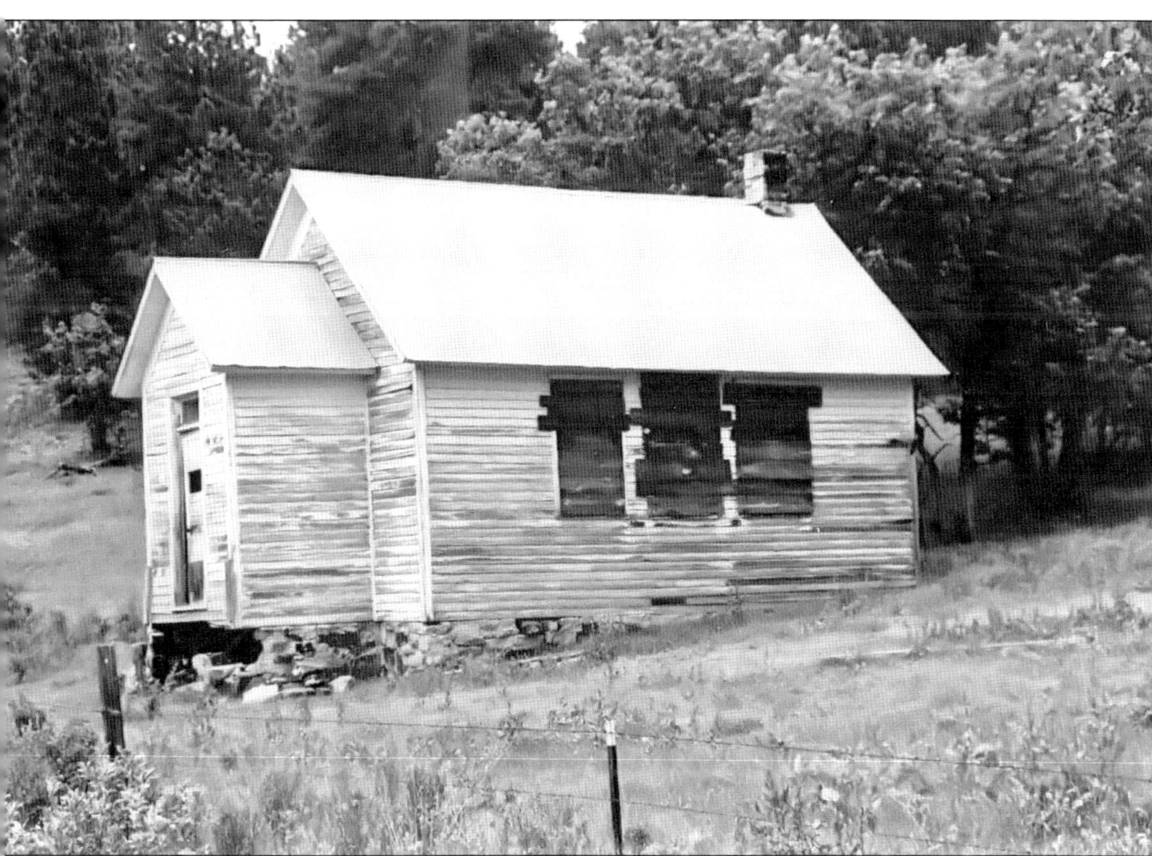

Historian Watson Parker wrote in his notes as he traveled throughout Crook County that the Forest Service map showed the Aikman School and the Pearson ranch so continuous as to be almost a community of sorts on a creek that runs northwest into Oak Creek. The area is in the northeast quarter of Section 3, Township 54 North, and appears not to be near anything. The school was about eight miles east and one mile north of Alva, Wyoming. Except for the Viergutz ranch a mile northeast, the Aikman area looks deserted. On closer inspection, Parker concluded that the considerable ranch across the road must not be the only basis for this school's population, and he was right about that. The whole area is not as empty of people as its isolation might have led a person to believe. The Aikman School stands today in the same spot across from the Pearson ranch. (Courtesy of Black Hills State University, Case Library, Watson Parker Collection.)

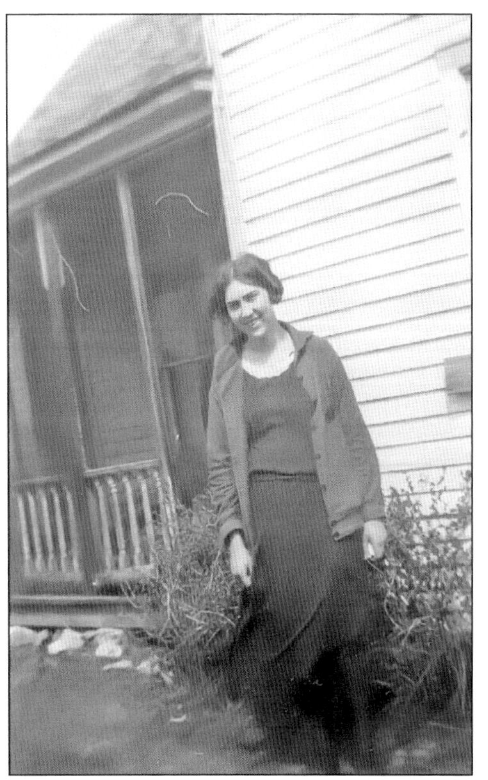

There were many rules a teacher must follow, and it was not always easy to remember them, let alone follow them. Included were: teachers could not marry during the term of their contract; they were not to keep company with men; they were not to loiter in ice cream stores; they were not to ride in a carriage or automobile with any man unless he was the teacher's father or brother; they could not under any circumstances dye their hair; they must not dress in bright colors and must always wear at least two petticoats; and they must be home between the hours of 8:00 p.m. and 6:00 a.m. And they must be quiet during these hours, as Marion Thompson found when she received a letter from the school superintendent telling her that Mr. Walter had sent word about the noise coming from her living quarters during late hours. The walls were thin, and the Walter family, passing by, could hear everything Marion said and did unless she was very quiet. The superintendent asked her to avoid all noise after 9:30 in the evening. Marion does not look in this picture like the type of person who would raise the roof. (Courtesy of the Thompson family.)

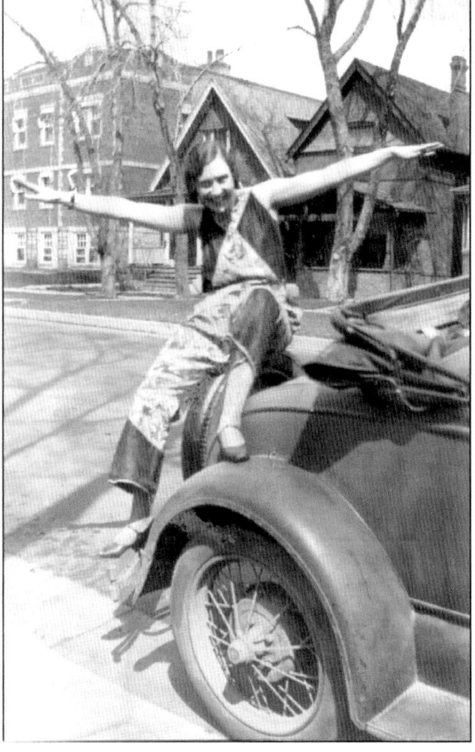

Here, perhaps Marion Thompson does look like she could raise a ruckus. She took classes from the normal school in Spearfish, South Dakota, while still in high school and received her certificate to teach elementary school. She soon decided that maybe teaching was not for her and went to business school in Denver. She retired as vice president of the Sundance State Bank in Sundance. (Courtesy of the Thompson family.)

Six

The Post Offices

When homesteaders arrived in the West, the mail was the only link to the folks back home and to the outside world. Until a mail delivery system was established for the Wyoming Territory, there was no mail service for these people, so they improvised and made do. Residents of these communities took turns traveling to Minesela, South Dakota, on the east bank of the Belle Fourche River to gather the mail for themselves and their neighbors. Later, they could pick the mail up at Forks, just inside the Wyoming state line.

For many years, there were no permanent buildings for post offices. If the postmaster was a merchant, a corner of the store was used as the post office. Often the post office was in the postmaster's home. If the postmaster was a rancher, the post office could be in a barn, tool shop, or in the living room. Ranch wives often became the postmaster simply because they were available more often. Contracts for these early mail routes were issued to the lowest bidder. Troed A. Pearson had the fourth contract issued. He carried the mail in a two-wheeled cart. He traveled to Forks on one day, picked up the mail, and delivered mail to communities as far as Hulett the next day. He made this trip three times a week.

As modes of transportation changed, the routes and methods of moving the mail changed. The Wyoming & Missouri Valley Railroad reached Aladdin in 1899, bringing the mail from Belle Fourche, and made getting and delivering the mail quicker and more reliable. Mail was received from and delivered by carrier three times a week, a lot like today.

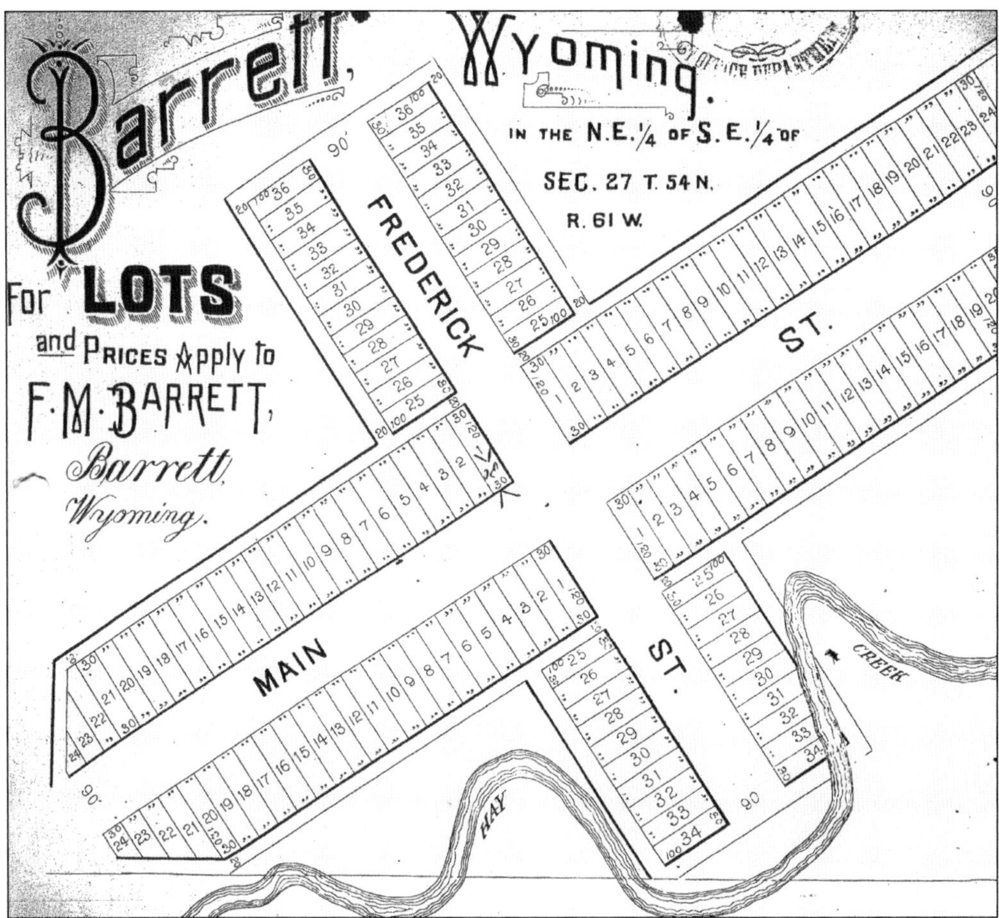

US Post Office records show that on October 17, 1890, the Barrett Post Office was established. This post office was in Township 54 in Crook County. The most prominent river nearby was the Belle Fourche. The nearest creek was Hay Creek, and the post office sat on the north side of the creek. The nearest established post office to the east was Forks, just four miles away. The nearest post office in the other direction was Eothen, just six miles to the west. The nearest town listed and not on this mail route was Beulah, nine miles to the east. This new post office was 18 miles from the station of the Wyoming & Missouri Valley Railroad. Barrett was the farthest mining town to the east of Aladdin. For a while, Barrett boasted a large general store that housed a drugstore as well as several large frame buildings. The entire town was owned by Fredrick "Dogie" Barrett. This is a plat map of the Barrett townsite showing plans for growth that would never happen. (Courtesy of the Crook County Museum.)

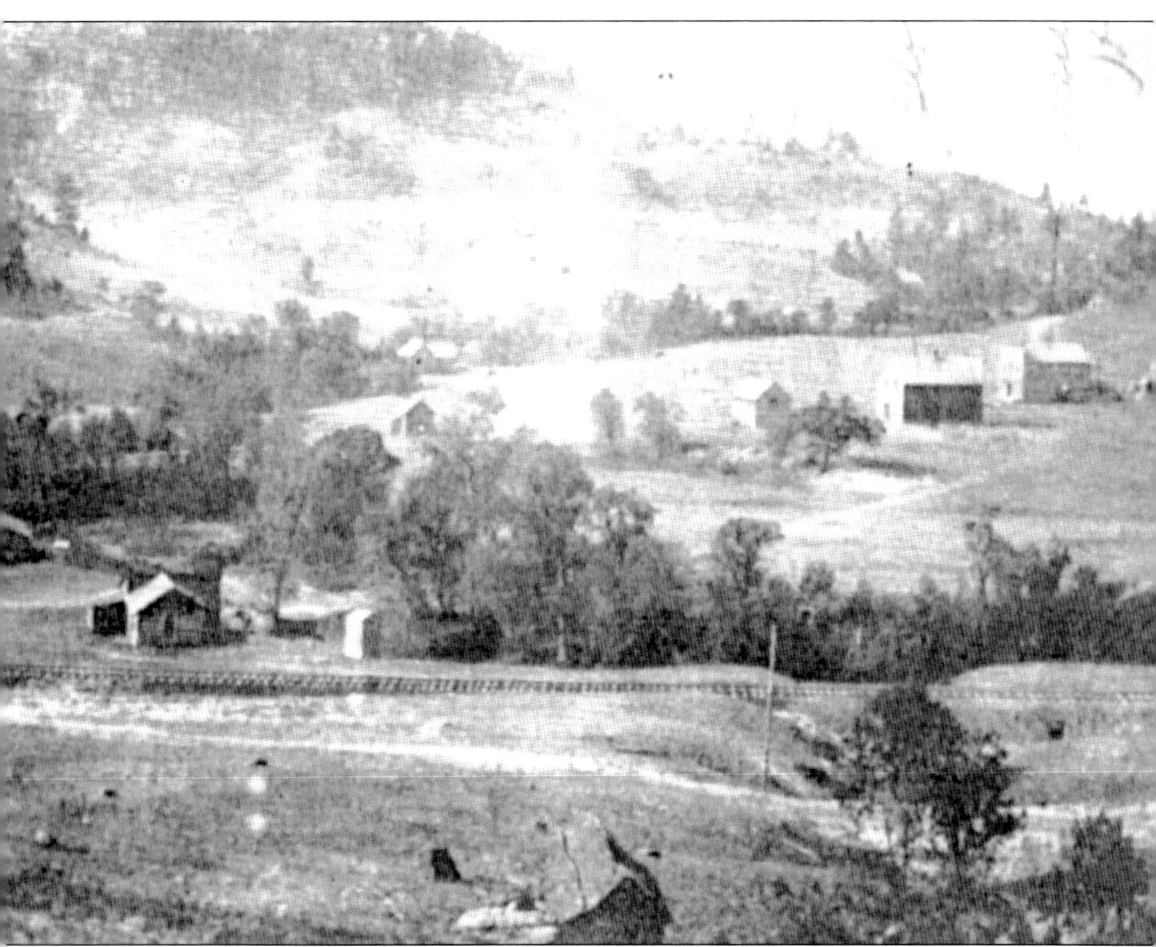

On November 9, 1898, the assistant postmaster general received a request to change the name and location of this post office. The request asked to change the name from Barrett to Aladdin and to move the office one and a half miles down the road. The request shows that the mail was delivered six times a week from Belle Fourche as far as Hulett, Wyoming. The report states that Aladdin sits on both sides of Hay Creek. The farthest post office not on this mail route is now Farrell. The Aladdin Post Office would be at the terminus of the Wyoming & Missouri Valley Railroad. Effie Estelle Hauer had a store with a hall upstairs where dances were held. The picture shows Barrett, the saloon, a hotel, a general store, and a pest house. The log house in the foreground is where the miners stayed, but in later years, it was used to house the mules that worked in the mine. (Courtesy of the Crook County Museum.)

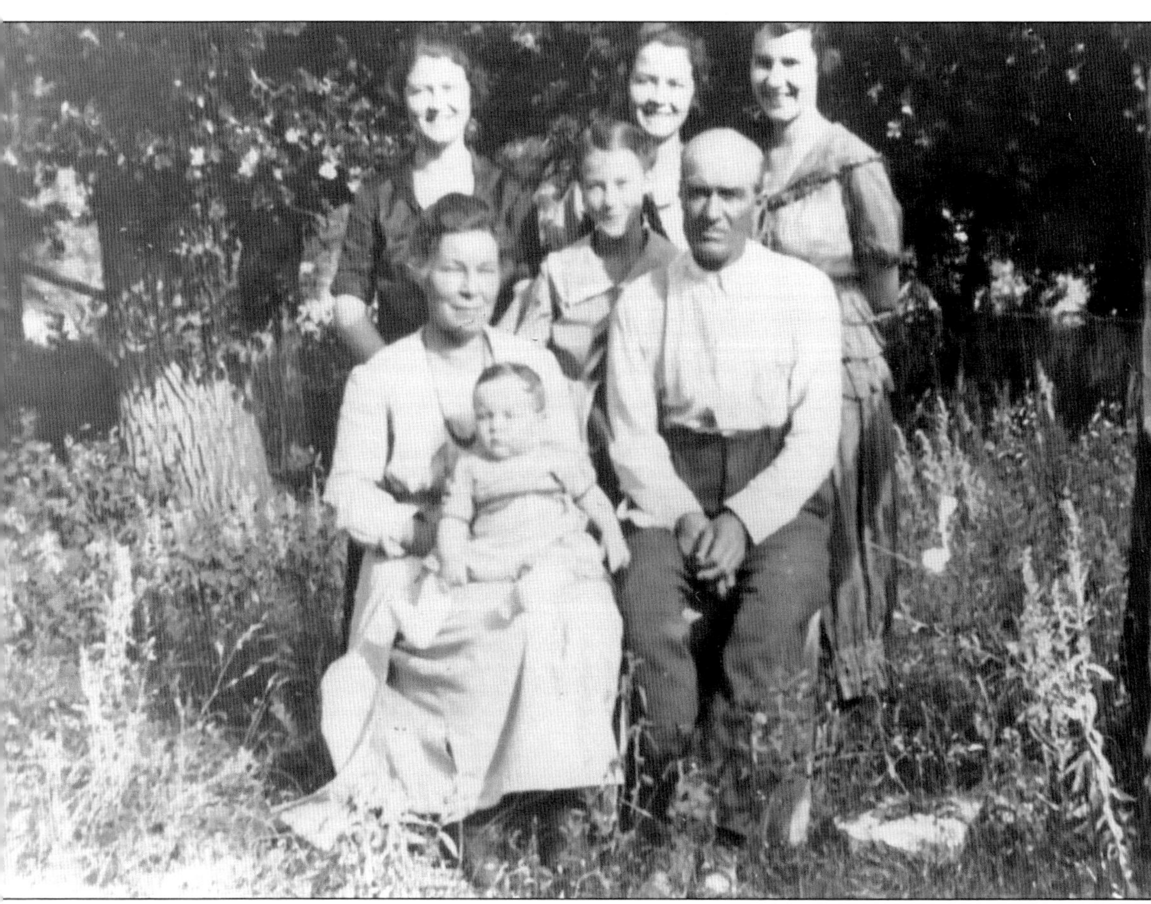

On October 9, 1886, page eight of the *Sundance Gazette* reported that the new post office on the Belle Fourche River had received no mail as of yet. The reporter noted that "the contractor has switched his buckboard and now runs about an office. He probably thinks the route was established for his benefit. He surely believes that he is not that far out of the way." Other names suggested for this post office were Clyde, Glendalle, and Lochwood. Riverdale was established on May 2, 1881, with William T. Hazelton as postmaster. The post office established at Riverdale also served as a stop for the Spearfish to Miles City, Montana, stage route. All roads led to Deadwood, and the road from Miles City was no different. Pictured here is the Baxter family, who lived and ranched in Riverdale and ran the post office for many years. From left to right are (first row) Lizzie with Pauline's baby boy, Clark Baxter Nowak, and Fred Baxter; (second row) Rose, Edith, and Pauline; in the center is Mary Belle. (Courtesy of the Thompson family.)

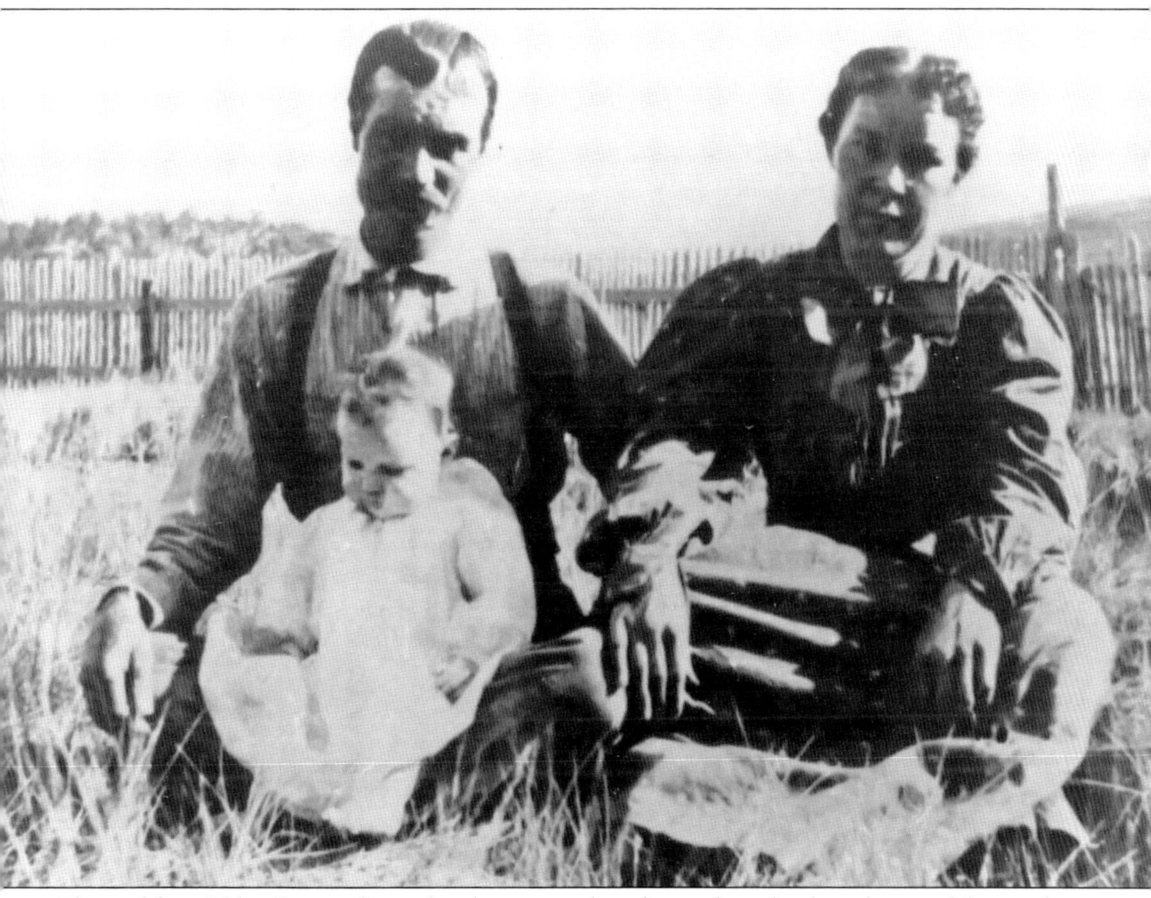

The trail from Miles City was littered with cacti, rattlesnakes, wolves, desolate plains, gulches, and wide rivers. These much-traveled trails have long since disappeared as nature reclaims and hides what little remains. Those who traveled these byways have left only stories and faint memories. Along the way, the traveler would cross the Sourdough Flats before coming to Baxter Crossing and the community of Riverdale. The 1890 census show that there were two Civil War veterans living in Riverdale. Charles Dorset, from the 1st Missouri Cavalry, was not in good general health. David D. Ross, from the 2nd Nebraska Cavalry, still suffered from a gunshot wound in his left hip. Joseph Baxter's ranch was located in the northeast corner of Wyoming at Riverdale. The Baxter family operated the post office after William Hazelton and raised roan saddle horses. Their brand was the Circle 8, so of course their ranch was called the Circle 8 Pony Ranch. The three in this picture are Fred and Lizzie Baxter and their daughter, Pauline. (Courtesy of the Thompson family.)

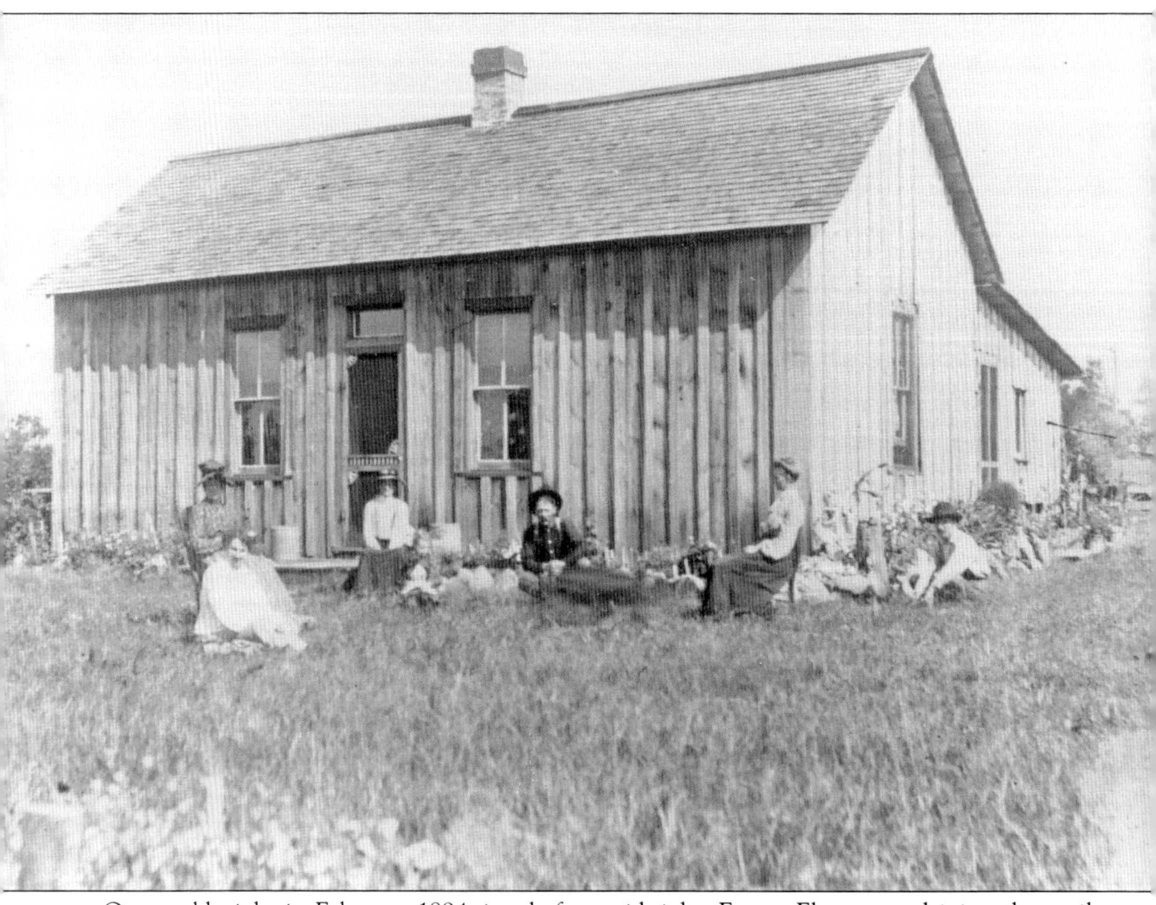

On a cold night in February 1894, just before midnight, Ernest Flynn was driving the mail buckboard when two men pulled the wagon over and helped themselves to the mailbags and Ernest's tobacco. But before leaving with their ill-gotten gains, they returned the tobacco to Ernest's pocket. These daring men were never caught, nor were the stolen items recovered, but a letter mailed at Riverdale and believed to be in the stolen mailbags was delivered to Dr. James B. Massie in Houston, Texas. Dr. Massie was the brother of Susan Baxter, the wife of the Riverdale postmaster, Joseph Baxter. Did these thoughtful robbers send this letter on its way at the next post office they passed through on their way out of Wyoming? Here is the Baxter family sitting outside of the post office and their home in Riverdale. Are they waiting for a letter from Texas? (Courtesy of the Thompson family.)

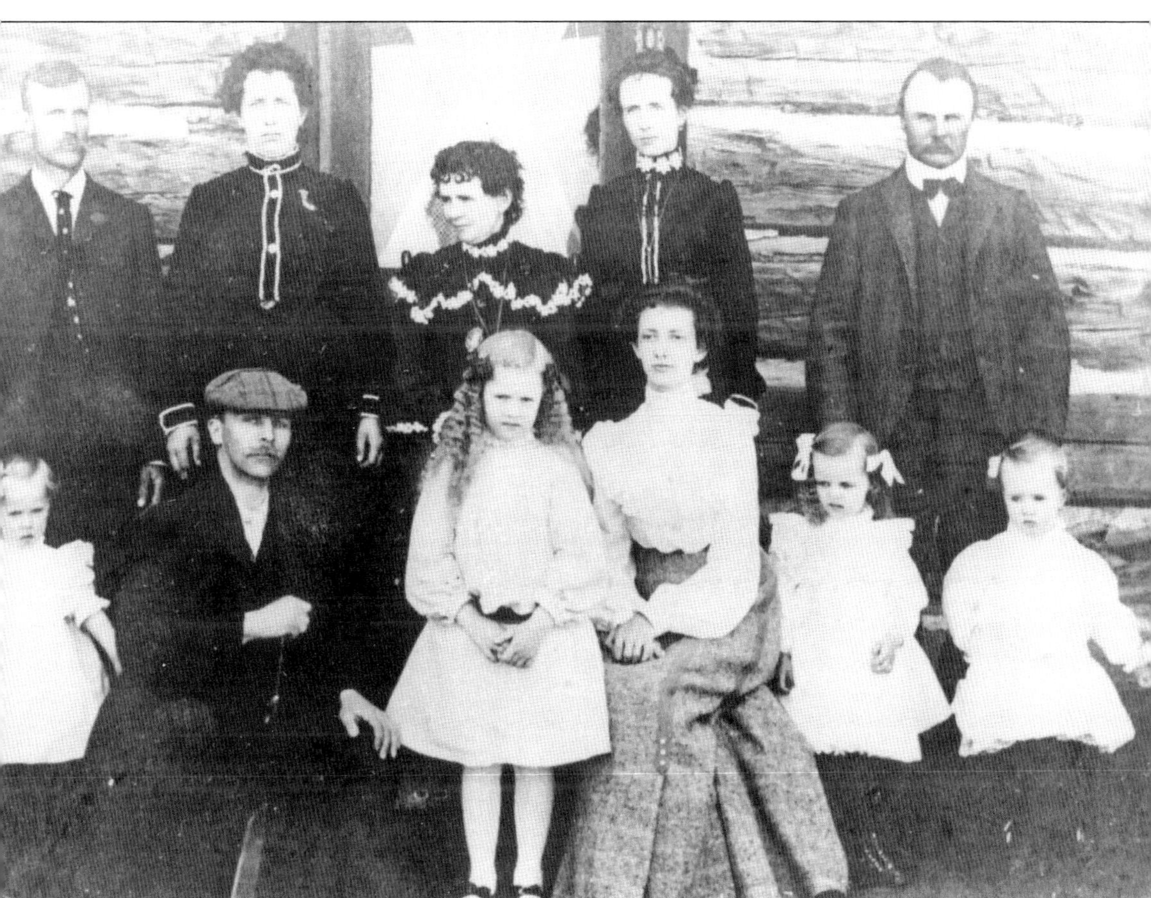

The Donald Post Office was established on March 28, 1906, with James O. McDonald as its postmaster. The post office was on the McDonald ranch. The original proposed name for this station was Boneta. The post office was in the McDonald home and was run by Lulu McDonald. Lulu became upset with Mr. Halley when he spanked the "little darlings" Gerda Oberg and Jennie Morse for racing their horses to school. The post office was discontinued on July 30, 1921. At that time, its mail was handled by the Aladdin Post Office. Stock raising was and still is the principal industry around Donald. This picture shows Bate Baxter, Nellie Baxter, Helen Cady, Lulu McDonald, and J.O. McDonald. In the front row are Lilian Baxter, Harold Baxter, Helen Baxter, Clara Cady, Lela McDonald, and Francis J. McDonald. (Courtesy of the Thompson family.)

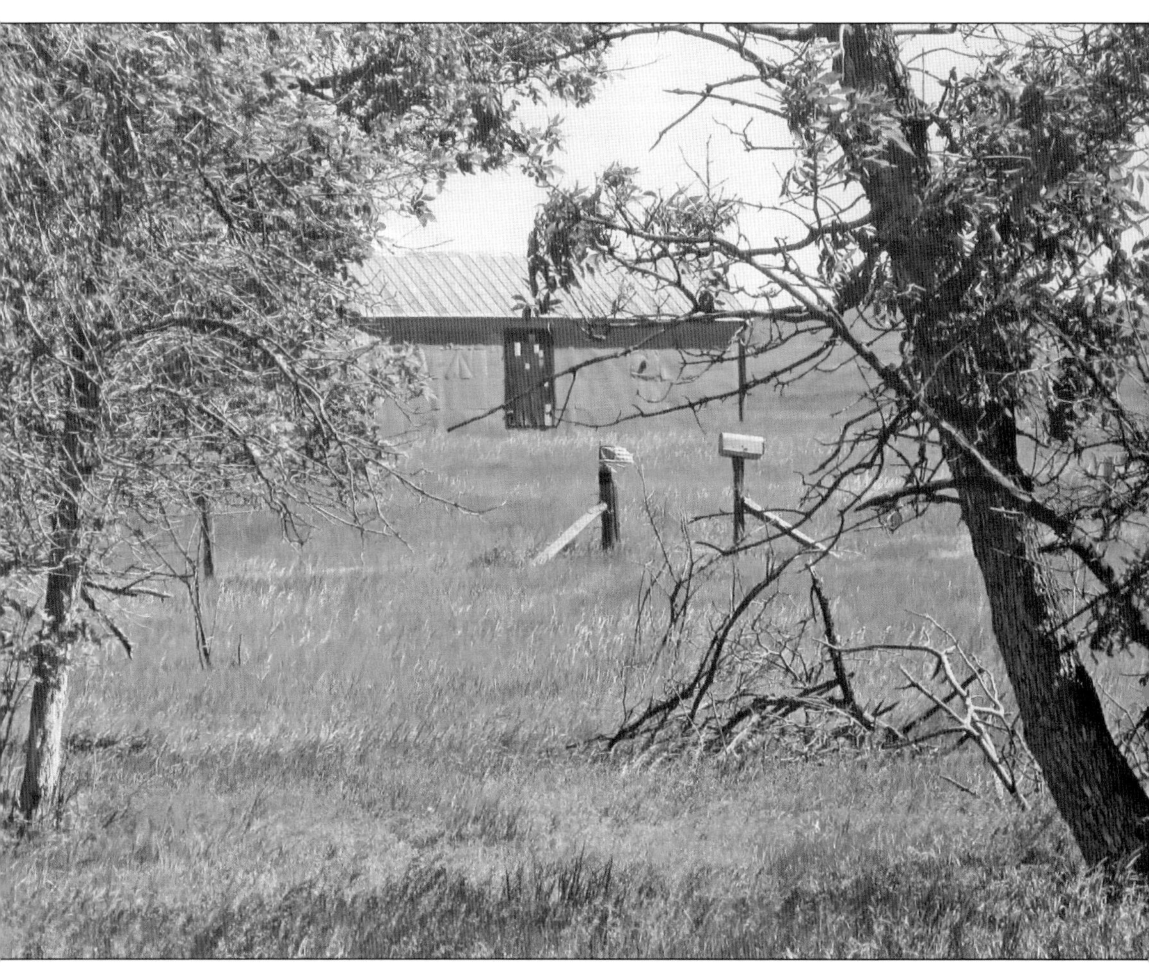

Forks is the name of a post office at the junction of several branches of Hay Creek. Located at the intersection of roads to Sundance; Beulah, Wyoming; Minesela, South Dakota; Spearfish, South Dakota; and Miles City, Montana, Forks was an ideal place for a stop for the Miles City to Deadwood stage route. The Forks Post Office was established on June 15, 1883. At this time, it was believed Inyan Kara was the only other post office in the county, but new mail routes were continually being petitioned for, and several new post offices were created every month. Higby Wisner as postmaster kept the office as well as a general store, a hotel, and a ranch business. Phoebe Wisner cared for Thomas C. Brown, who had been a sergeant with the 15th Illinois Cavalry during the War Between the States. Other Civil War veterans living in Forks at this time were George Drane and Lafayette Snow. Lafayette had been shot through the knee. Postal service to Forks was discontinued on December 20, 1899, and its mail was handled by the Aladdin office. This picture shows a small post office through the trees. (Courtesy of the Thompson family.)

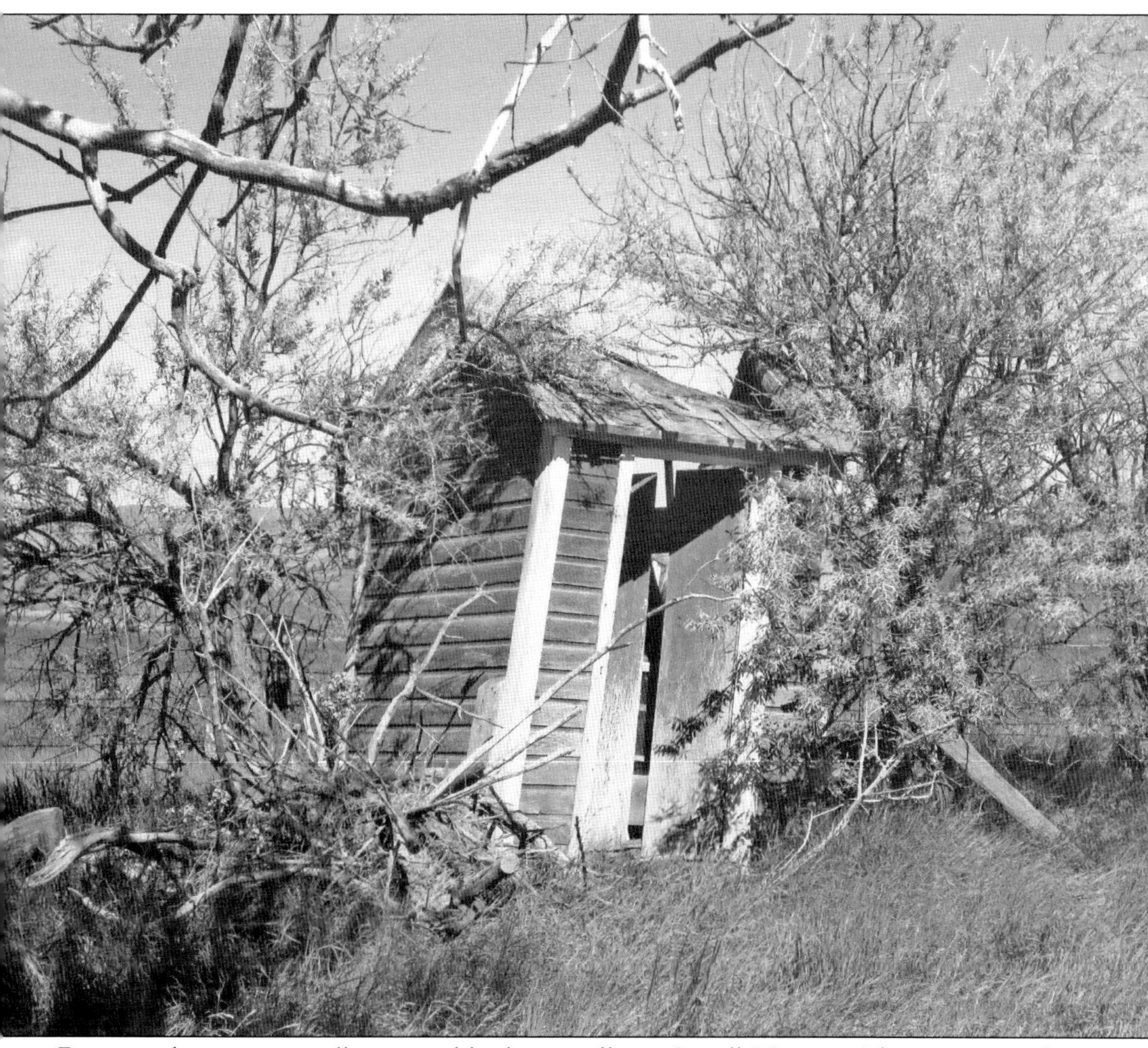

Faries was the name originally suggested for the post office at Carroll, Wyoming. This was suggested in honor of the postmaster, Frank P. Faries. The Carroll office was established on September 23, 1896, with Frank as the first postmaster. The elevation for Carroll is listed as 3,999 feet. The Carroll Post Office was established on what became the Viergets ranch. This post office was discontinued on June 30, 1902, after which its mail was handled by the post office in Aladdin, seven miles away, which was also the nearest railroad. Stock raising was and continues to be the leading industry around Carroll. According to the Wyoming State Business Directory, in 1901, the population in Carroll was eight adults. This post office has seen better days, but imagine the stories it could tell. (Courtesy of the Thompson family.)

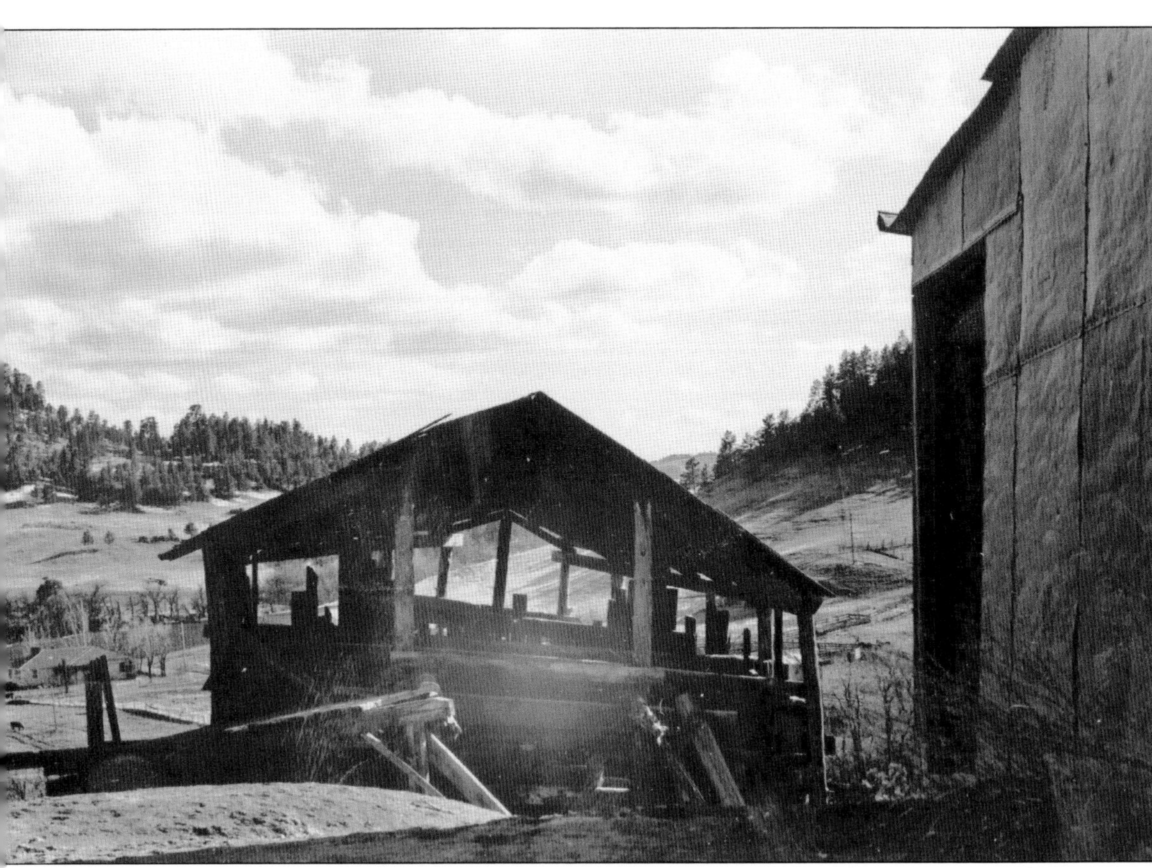

Bear Lodge was a gold-rush town that took its name from the Bear Lodge Mountains. There is also a story that the name was suggested for the town because of the fact that Henry Mason, an early homesteader, was killed by a bear at the very spot where the new community had its beginnings. Someone somewhere thought Eothen would be a better name, and so the little community became Eothen. Watson Parker tells in his notes, kept in the Francis Case Library at the Black Hills University, that an 1879 book by Lady Brassey was entitled *Eothen*. Alexander William Kinglake notes in his 1844 narrative of his travels in the Near East that Eothen was a popular place, so there are at least two places with the name. This picture shows the post office as it stands looking out over the valley. (Courtesy of Chuck Pearson.)

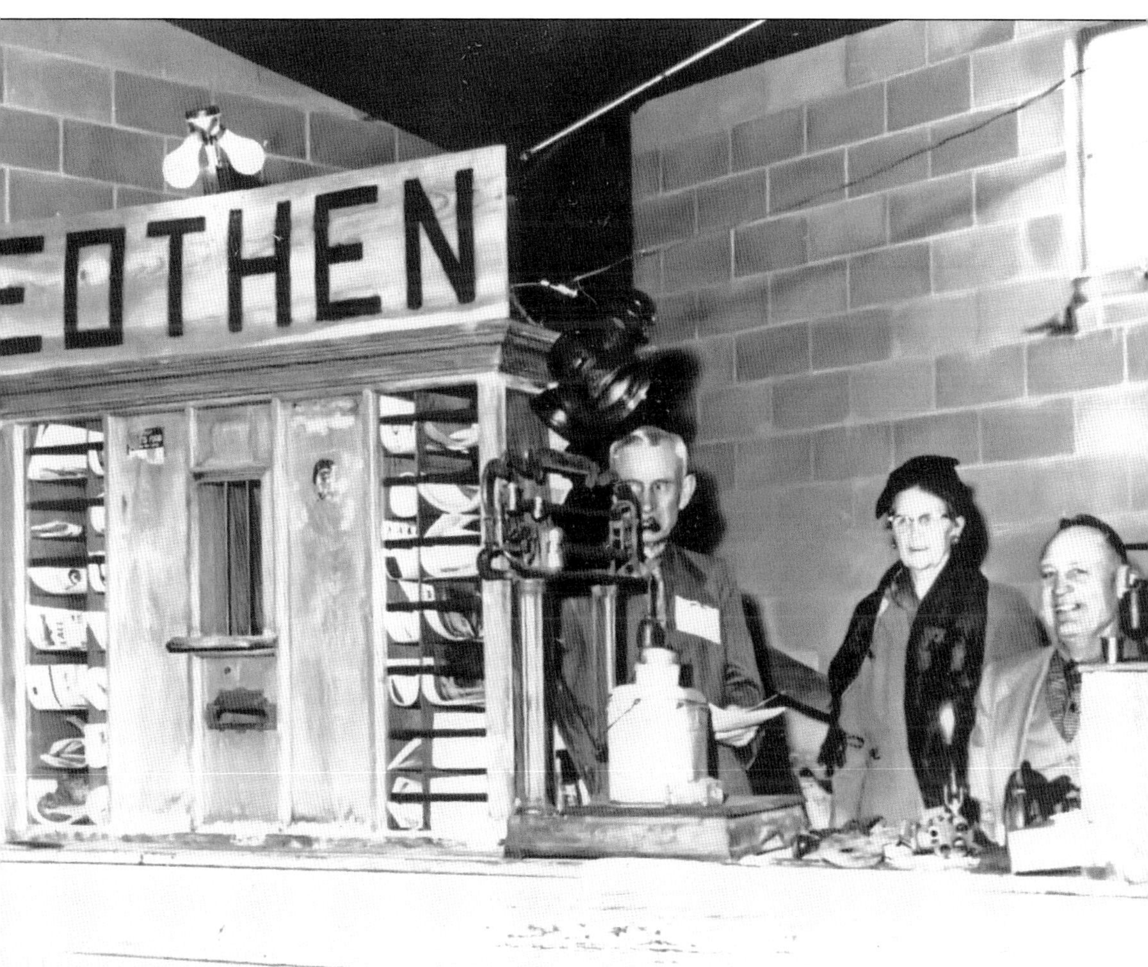

Wyoming's Eothen sits in the northeast corner of the state in Crook County. The elevation at the foot of the Bear Lodge Mountains is 4,199 feet. The town of Eothen was founded in 1882 by John Pearson, a Swedish immigrant. The Eothen Post Office was established on January 11, 1887, at Pearson's ranch. This post office was discontinued in February 1913. The mail service was moved to Aladdin, seven and a half miles to the south. Eothen was a small stock raising and sawmill community on the Hulett-Aladdin stage line and mail route. The Eothen Post Office shown here is now part of the Crook County Museum. (Courtesy of the Crook County Museum.)

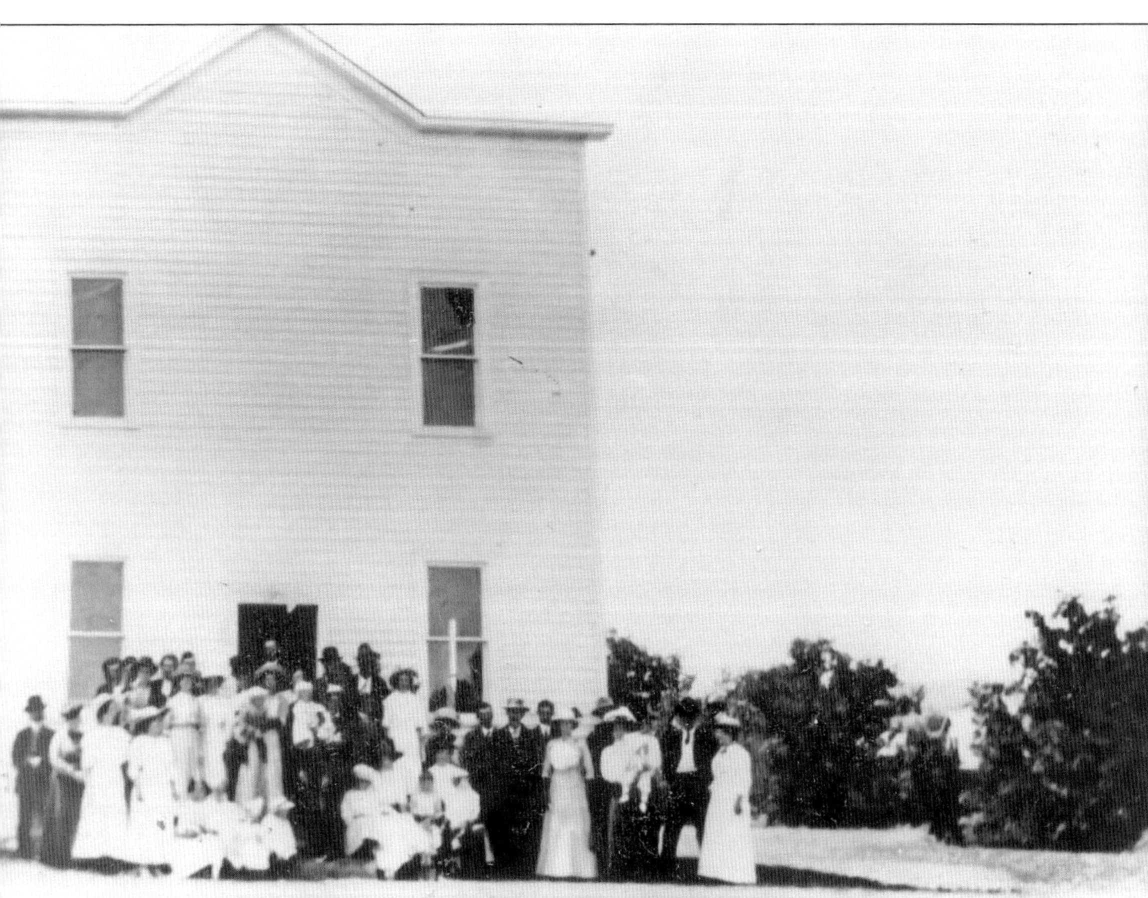

William Farrell Smith named the post office in Farrell, Wyoming, after his mother's maiden name. William was the postmaster for four and a half years. The post office was established on November 10, 1894. After the post office was discontinued, the mail was handled by the Aladdin Post Office. Aladdin was the nearest railroad and shipping center to Farrell. Stock raising was and is the leading industry around Farrell. William Farrell is one of the Wyoming men mentioned in the book *Progressive Men of Wyoming*, published in 1903. It is written that he was a candid, outspoken man of positive convictions and fearless courage in voicing them. He was said to be one of the inspiring forces of mental, moral, and commercial advancement for his community. He was a total abstainer from intoxicants, never gambled in any way, and never was arrested or had a lawsuit brought against him. Among the people pictured here at Farrell Hall are (standing in the doorway) Mr. and Mrs. Gilbert Goodson, Emma and Elmer Smith, and Charles Smith. (Courtesy of the Crook County Museum.)

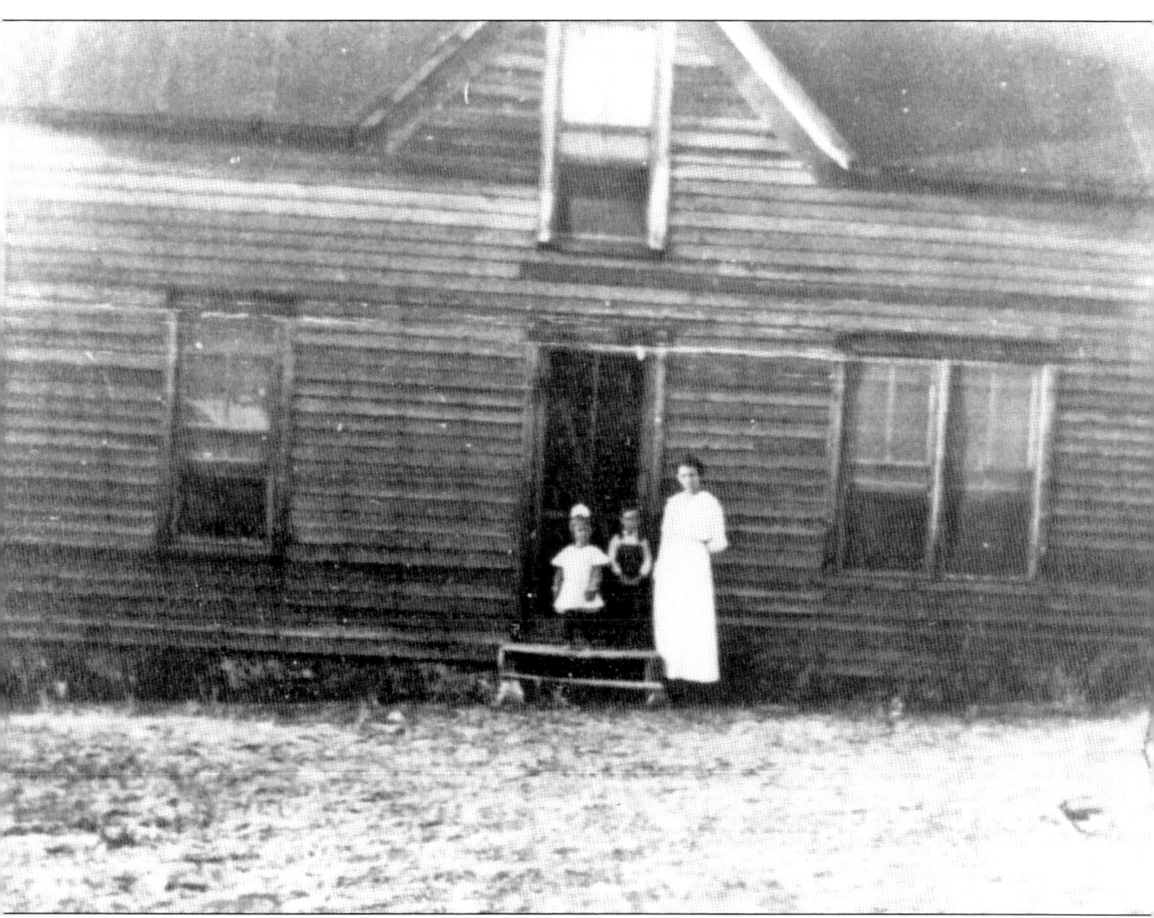

The office at Mona was established on May 29, 1897, with Eliza Mortimer as postmistress. The post office was in her house, and she found that people came at meal time to collect their mail and stayed to partake. She put a stop to that by serving her family an early breakfast and a late dinner. The old-timers in Crook County tell that at one time, the Mona Post Office was at the top of the Bear Lodge at the Knowles-Sims sawmill, deep in the Black Hills National Forest. Kate Sims was the first postmistress and Albert Knowles was the first mail carrier. By the time the post office was discontinued on December 5, 1942, it was owned and operated by Wick and Margaret Carr. The Mona Post Office, on the top of the Bear Lodge Mountains, is said to have been a two-story building that looked a lot like the one in this picture. (Courtesy of the Thompson family.)

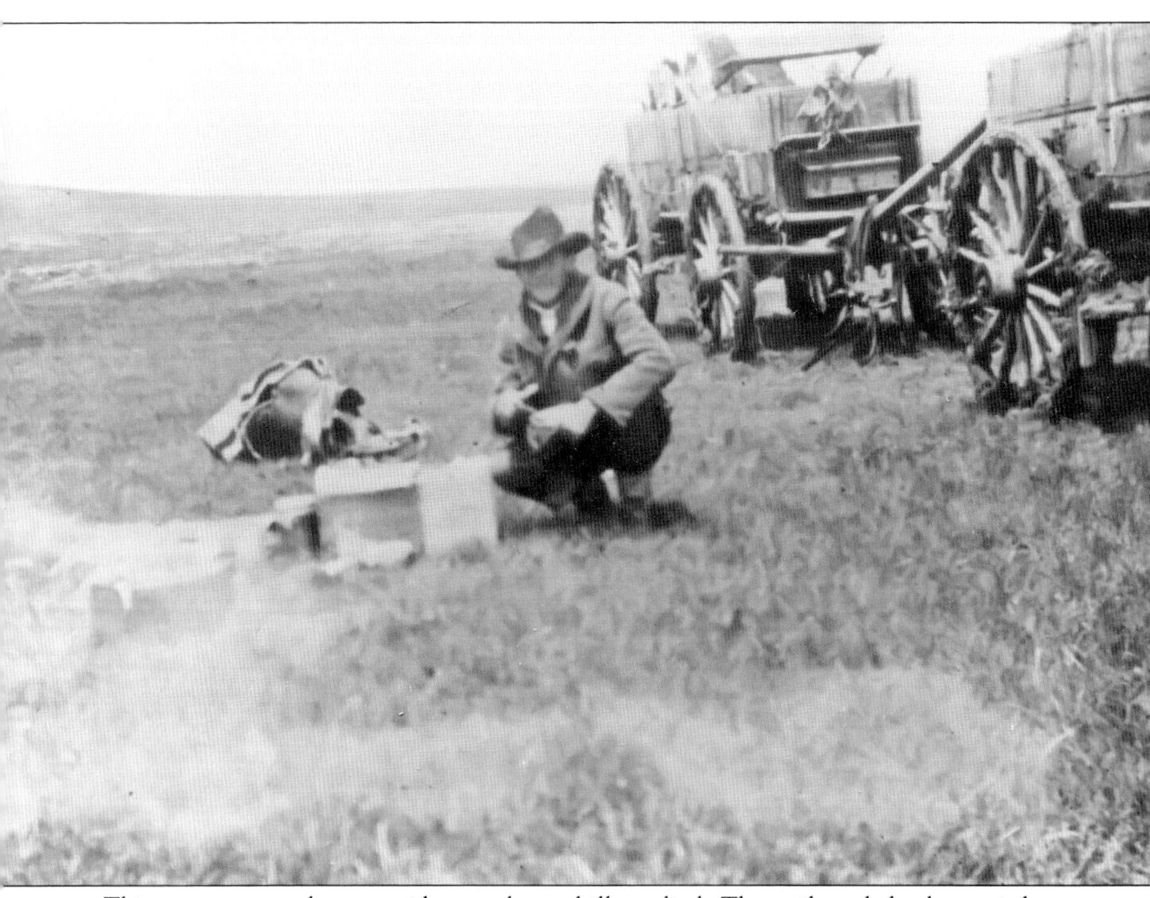

This was a very rough route, with several steep hills to climb. The mail needed to be carried across deep creeks, steep canyons, and rocky trails. A buggy was used in summer, and a sled was used in the winter months. In some places, the road washed away so badly that part of the time the mail had to be carried with a packhorse. Usually the trip could be made in one day; if the mail carrier left early in the morning, he could be back by the middle of the afternoon. In bad weather, the carrier sometimes had to return the next day. The mail carrier would often arrive at Charles Pearson's ranch in time for breakfast and then take a ranch team on to Aladdin. According to the back of this photograph, this is Joe and he is "stuck in the gumbo." Joe might make it to the ranch in time for breakfast, but it does not look good. (Courtesy of Chuck Pearson.)

Seven

The Dance Halls

Around 1910, Aladdin had a band, and so a dance hall was built. There were many dance halls throughout the neighborhood. Dances were held about once a month and were all-night affairs. People came by buggy, wagon, and horseback. The entire family would come, and no one would leave until way after midnight. There were no babysitters in those days, so where the adults went, everyone went. As the night drew on, there would be little people asleep everywhere, covered with blankets and coats.

Often, buildings were constructed just to be used as a community hall. Other dances just happened wherever there was room. Many dance halls were the second story of a barn, warehouse, or other building. Community gatherings took place in these buildings. These halls were used for dances, school plays, polling places for voting, and church. In most cases, the Reverend Tracy presided over the church services.

There were not that many other sources for entertainment at this time. People would get together for card games, birthday parties, picnics, and ball games. It did seem that something was going on every weekend. The music for the dances was mainly furnished by local musicians, and a hat would be passed around to compensate them for their efforts and to show appreciation for the good music. Albert Knowles was often one of those playing. He might have been a cowboy in his youth, but he did like to play his violin. At some time, he traded his boots for a violin. He played for quite a few dances between Mona and Aladdin. His violin is still in his family.

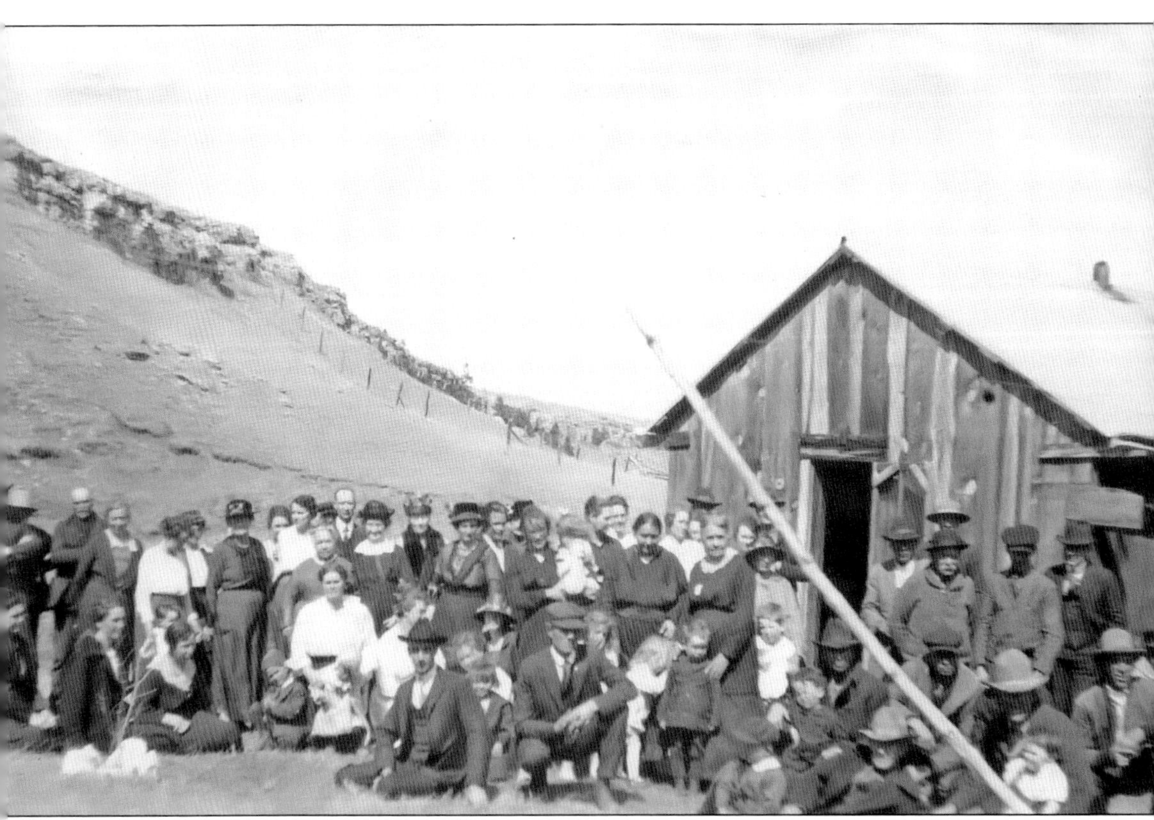

There was a dance hall in Donald. Due to the fact that Donald was a working ranch, the dances were held on the second floor of the barn. The musicians were people from around the area who could play an instrument. Keith McDonald remembers that the floors were just one layer, and a crowd on the dance floor could really get the floor jumping. Community gatherings of all kinds happened at the McDonalds' barn. It was the McDonald family who gave the name Donald to the post office and the dance hall. This is where children were baptized, couples were married, and shivarees (noisy celebrations for newly married couples) were held, along with many a barn dance on a Saturday night. During Prohibition, moonshiners made good money peddling their wares out behind the barn. This picture shows the dancers gathering outside of a popular dance hall for a moment of rest and refreshments. (Courtesy of the Thompson family.)

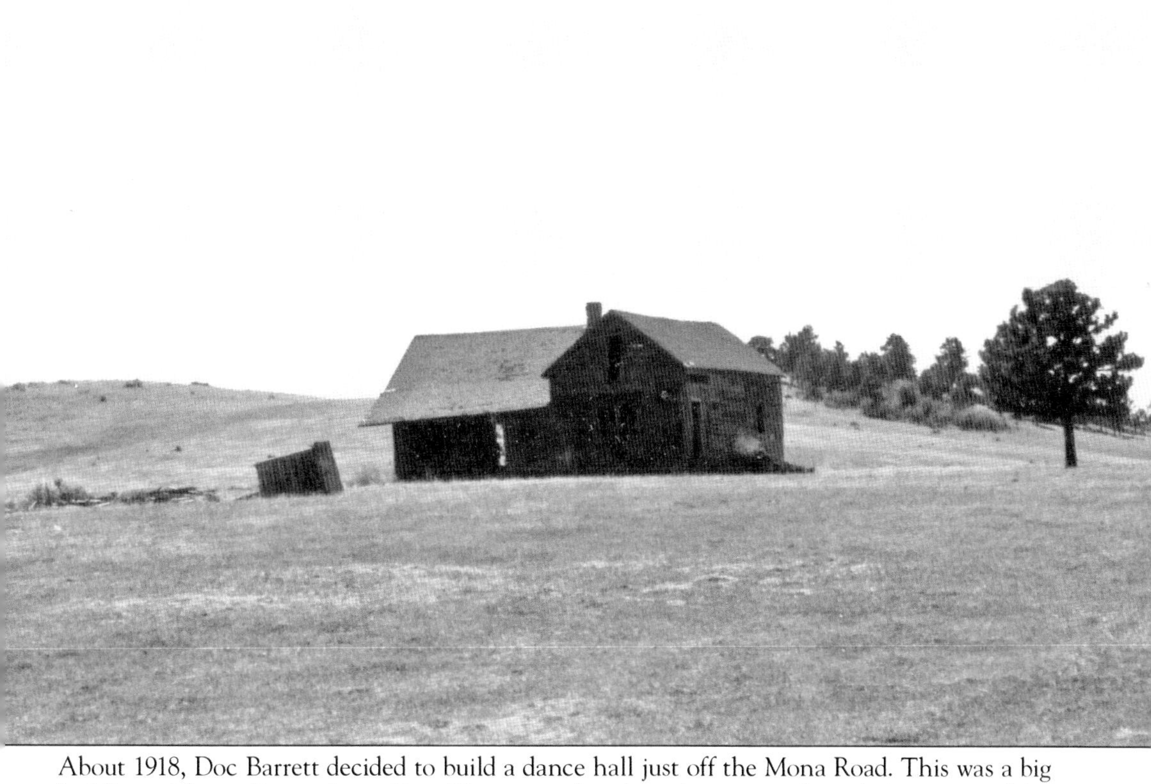

About 1918, Doc Barrett decided to build a dance hall just off the Mona Road. This was a big building with muslin on the ceiling. There were benches along one side and along part of the east end. A piano was on a raised platform in one corner and a wood-burning stove in another. There was a large bunk bed along one wall filled with straw and blankets for as many sleeping children as could be stuffed in. Some mothers would not let their children sleep there for fear of bedbugs. Candy, gum, tobacco, and cigarette papers were for sale. Coffee was 5¢ a cup; anything stronger had to be found outside. Neva Graves Davis played the piano, her brother played the violin, and sometimes Wily Massie would play the fiddle. Fred or Hal Baxter would do the calling when it was time for square dances. Young and old always had a really good time. (Courtesy of Hugh Thompson.)

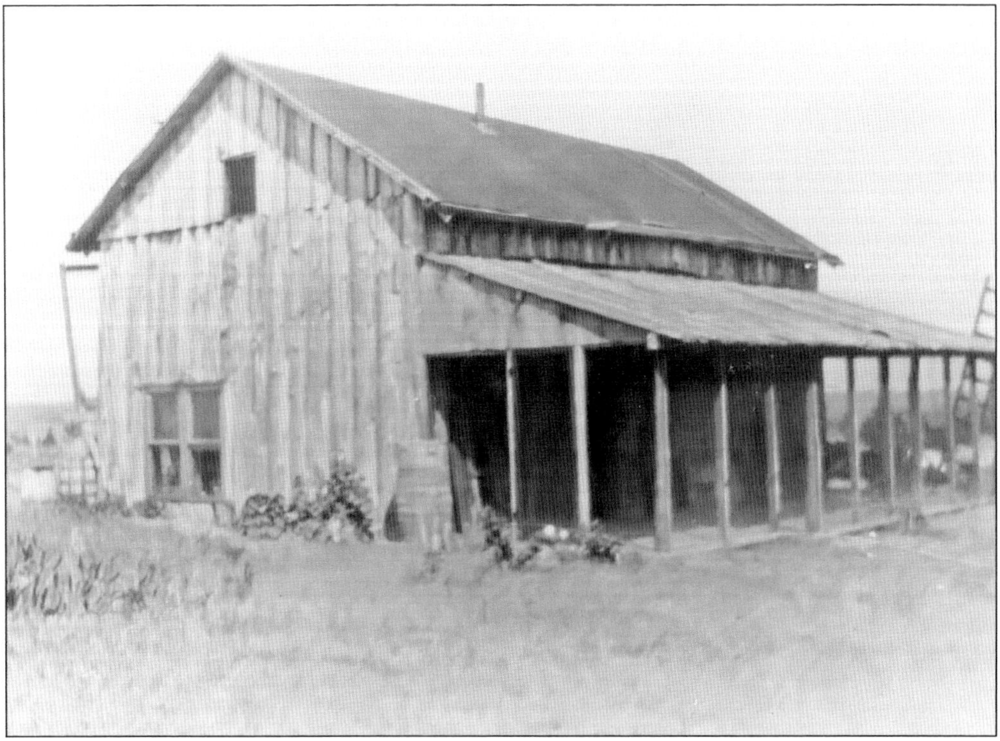

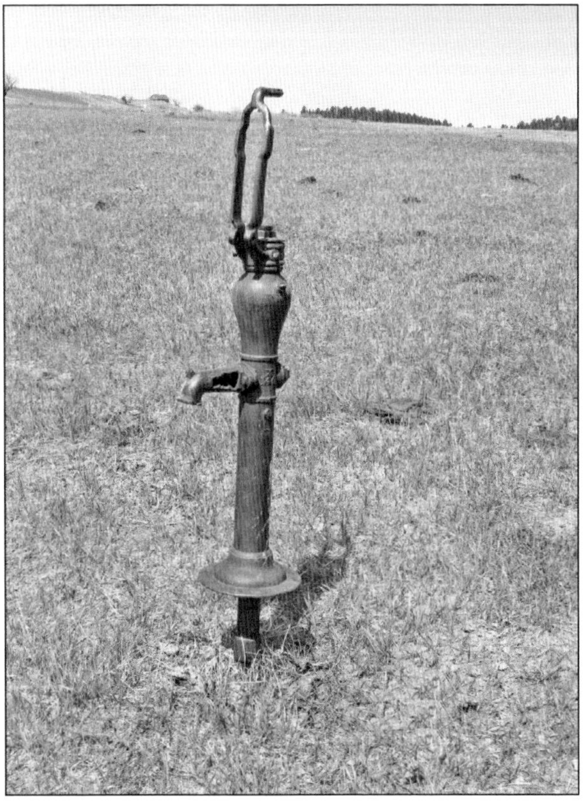

Phillips Dance Hall was about one half mile south of Four Corners. This dance hall was built by "Uncle" Herb Phillips. This picture shows that there was a good-sized porch for sitting and having an adult beverage and catching up on the news of the day before returning to the action inside. The Phillips family hosted the dances in their hall, which sat just across the Mona Road from the Mowery place. People came to dance and sing and eat together. The Phillips house burned down some years ago, and the family rebuilt farther down the road. The only reminder of the good times had at the Phillips Dance Hall is this lonely water pump that still stands guard, waiting for the music to start. (Above, courtesy of the Thompson family; left, author's collection.)

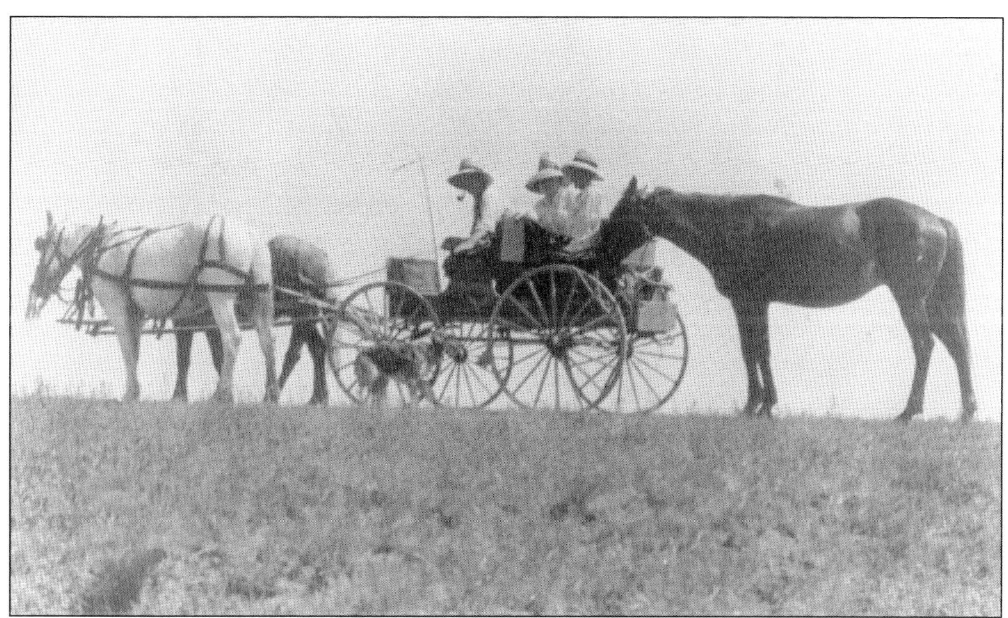

This gentleman has two pretty ladies to go to the dance with, and he is bringing an extra horse along just in case someone wants to go home early. Most of the dance halls would have a dance once a month. This could be an all-night affair. People came by buggy, wagon, and horseback, and a few even walked. Shortly after midnight, a lunch was usually served, and that would give the dancers enough energy to dance for a few more hours before they left for home. Chores had to be done no matter what time one came home. The two young men below must have missed the buggy. The horse seems ready to go, but the man with the bicycle does not look all that excited. (Both, courtesy of Chuck Pearson.)

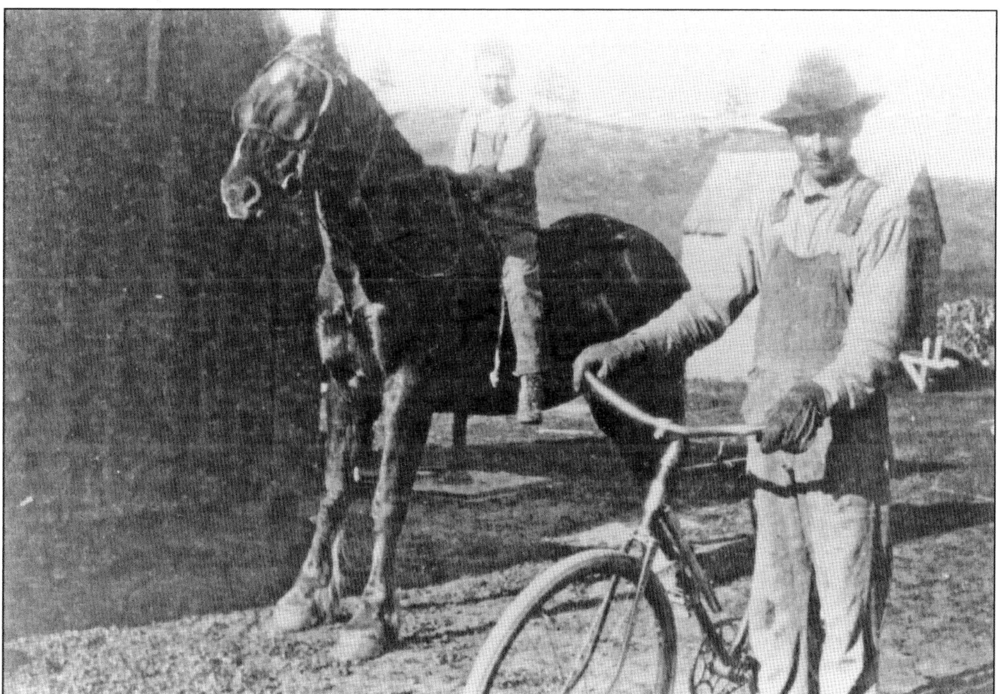

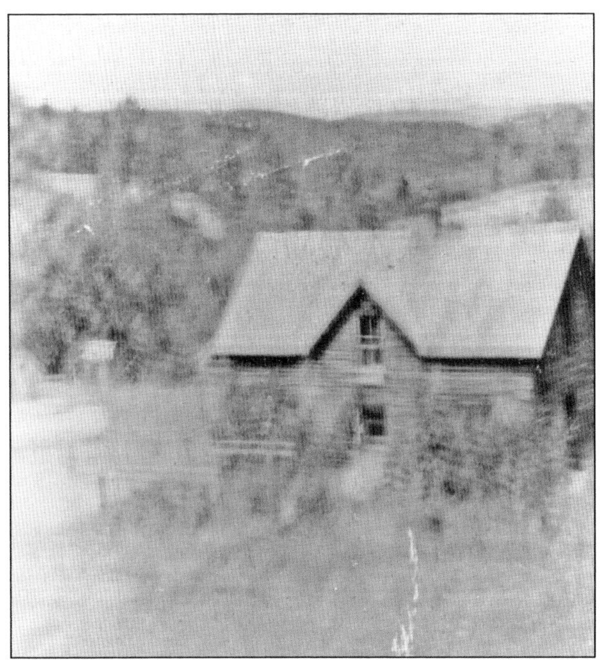

This is the Clay Massie home along the Belle Fourche River. Friends and neighbors were welcome at any time. Community gatherings, including dancing, singing, or just playing good music for each other could happen anywhere at any time. Sometimes neighbors would come to help with the haying, branding, or barn raising, and when the work was finished, it would be time to celebrate a job well done. The tables and chairs would be pushed out of the way and the dancing would begin. Visitors brought whatever they could make music on. Clay's father would play his fiddle, Baxter relatives would call square dances, Hassel Massie or the girls would play the piano, and everyone would have a good time. (Courtesy of the Thompson family.)

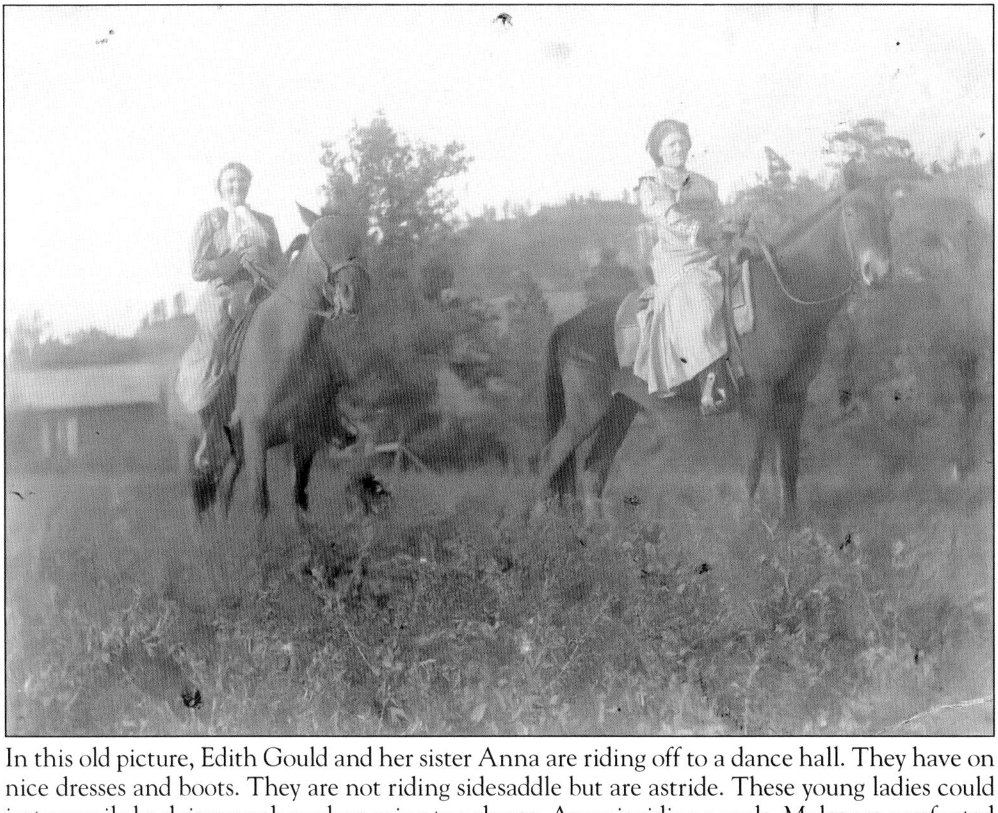

In this old picture, Edith Gould and her sister Anna are riding off to a dance hall. They have on nice dresses and boots. They are not riding sidesaddle but are astride. These young ladies could just as easily be doing ranch work as going to a dance. Anna is riding a mule. Mules are surefooted and will probably get her there and back safely. They might meet the man of their dreams at this dance, but if not, there is always the next one. (Courtesy of the Thompson family.)

Eight

Farms, Ranches, and Sawmills

Farming, ranching, and sawmills continued to be significant in the county economy long after the mines in the area ceased operation. As homesteaders came to the area, they found the moisture was greater than on the surrounding plains and that dry land farming could be more successful. But sadly, some homesteaders still could not succeed and left in despair. Early farmers cultivated wheat, oats, rye, corn, garden vegetables, and small fruit for profit. Farmers and ranchers relied on the railroad to transport their crops and livestock to market. When the railroad was abandoned, they found trucks could do the same job for them.

Texas cattle had been coming into northeast Wyoming since the late 1870s. Some of the Texas cowboys stayed and settled in Crook County. Some went to work for the large cattle companies, and others began to build their own ranching operations. Sheep followed cattle into the area, and by the turn of the century, sheep outnumbered cattle in the county. Although they met with heated words and threats, the cattle ranchers and the sheep men learned they could coexist and continue to grow. Over time, ranching and agriculture became the real successes for this part of the county. Farming and ranching continue to be significant to the economy of the county.

Logging has long been a big industry in Crook County. The heavily forested Bear Lodge Mountains became a source of timber for an increasingly important sawmill industry. Several sawmills operated in the area and made timber for the Homestake gold mines in South Dakota and for the coal mines around Aladdin. It took timber from these mills to make the railroad ties that helped advance the tracks across the northeast and southwest corners of the state as well. A lot of timber was also required for the homes, barns, and storefronts that were springing up at an amazing rate. Logging continues to be the mainstay of the Crook County economy.

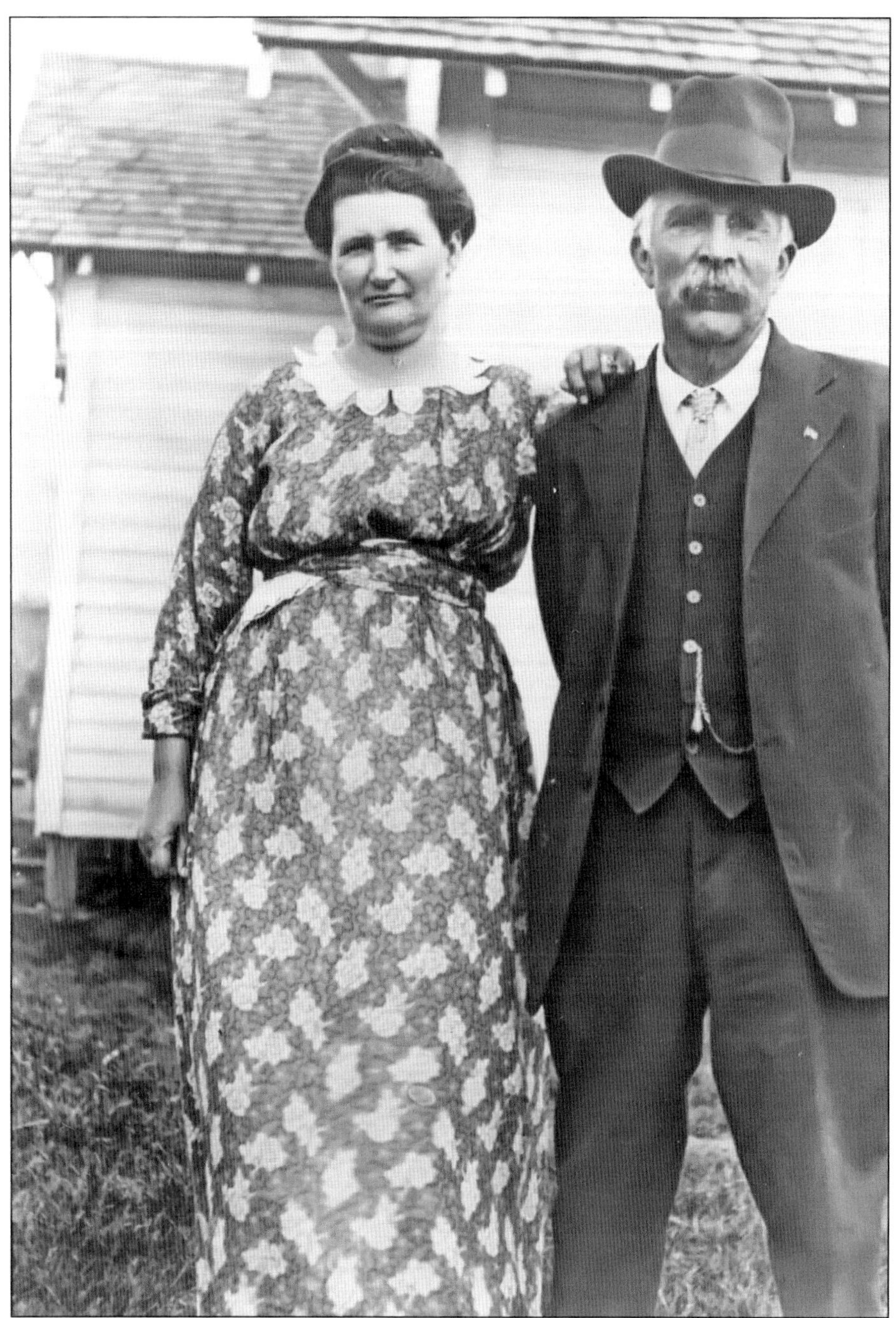

Charley and Annie Fuller came to Wyoming in 1890. Charley filed on a homestead north of Aladdin between Oak Creek and Alum Creek. In 1893, he and Annie moved onto their homestead and began their life as farmers and ranchers. Like others who filed for homesteads, they came to the area to work in the mines. They liked what they saw and decided to stay. Homestead land could be had easily; all one had to do was work hard. Charley and Annie did work hard, and their homestead grew. The 320 acres the Homestead Act offered was a good start. Those who did not realize that they could not make do on just that many acres soon moved on. Those who added to their land base survived and grew. (Courtesy of the Crook County Museum.)

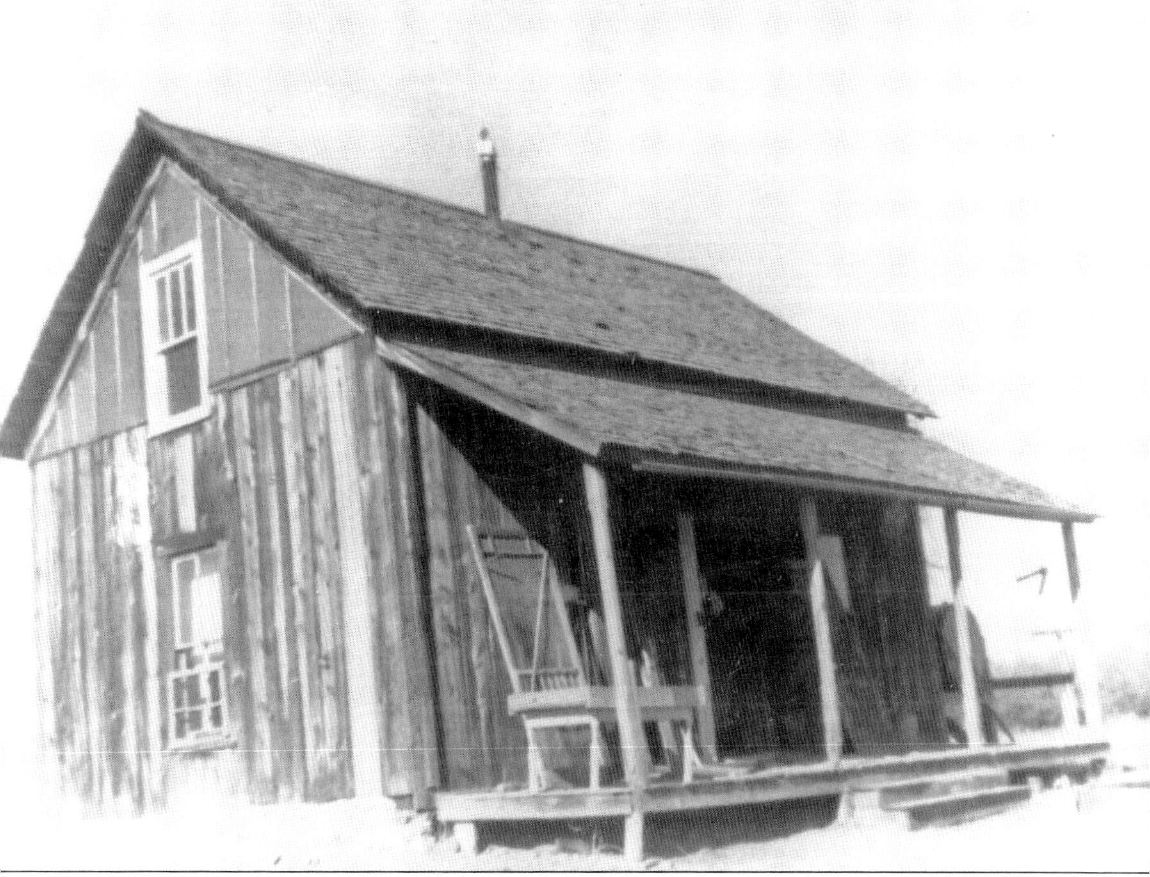

This is the homestead home of Charlie and Annie Fuller. Five of their 11 children were born in this house. Milton was born here in 1899, Ethel in 1901, Grace in 1902, Theodore in 1905, and Harriett in 1907. Warren, Ira, Effie, and Marvin were all born in Minnesota. The last two children were born in Lander, Wyoming. This house that saw a lot of hard work and children laughing still stands. It looks a little lonely and lost now but not ready to let go of all the memories. Pictures of this homestead have been used in Paul Horsted's book *Crossing the Plains with Custer,* which tells about General Custer's expedition into the Black Hills and the route he traveled that crossed the Fuller homestead. (Courtesy of Chuck Pearson.)

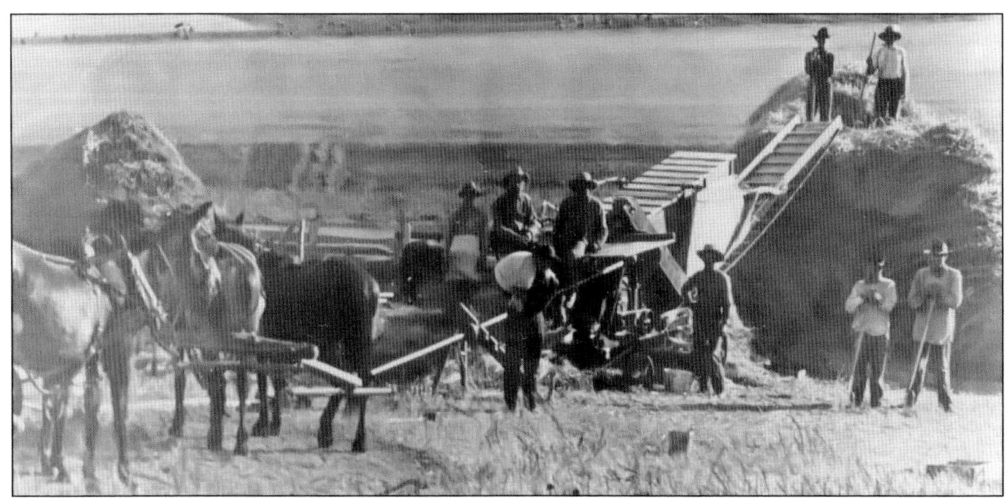

Charley Fuller worked hard at farming. It was not always easy to get crops of grain, corn, or hay through the summers. It either did not rain or it rained too much. It was either too hot or too cold. This is a picture of friends and neighbors coming to help with the haying and thrashing. The people are unidentified. His nearby neighbors at the time were Marchants, Bunnys, Baileys, and McDonalds, and they would all come to help. They would be there before the sun was full up and stay until the job was finished. When it was time for the neighbors to do the haying and thrashing, Charley and his sons would be there, and Annie would be in the kitchen helping and visiting with her neighbors. (Courtesy of Chuck Pearson.)

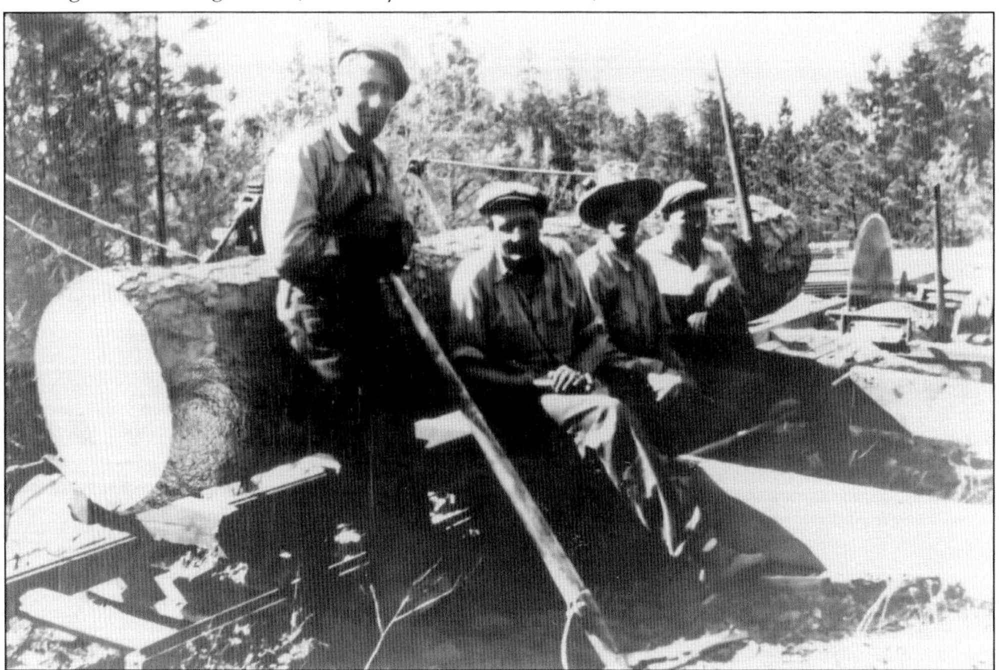

This is the Fuller sawmill. Charley Fuller's homestead had a forest of good trees and so did many of his neighbors. There was a need for the lumber these trees could provide. There were houses and businesses that needed to be built, and the gold mines in the Black Hills and Bear Lodge Mountains needed timbers to continue going further into the ground after the gold. The coal mines in the Aladdin and Hay Creek valleys needed timbers as well. (Courtesy of Chuck Pearson.)

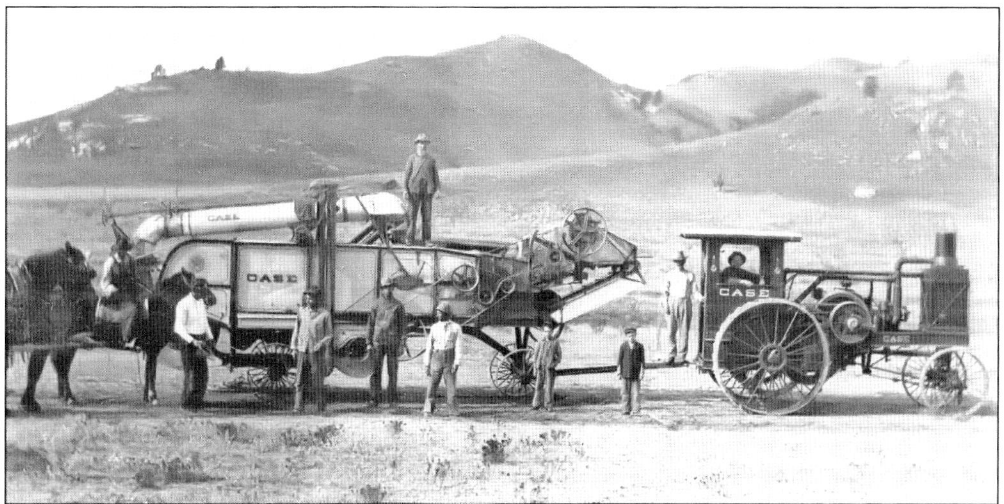

This postcard was sent to Burl Patton and reads, "here is Louis Johnsons thrashing machine. Taken down the road by Ben Weavers when they was ready to go away. Louis is the first in the picture. The expert is in the cab of the engine. This picture was taken by me, Charles Mitchell." Crews traveled from farm to farm with these huge machines that would thresh the wheat and oats, separating the grain from the straw. Crews could spend days at each farm depending on the size of the fields, working long hours in summer heat. (Courtesy of Chuck Pearson.)

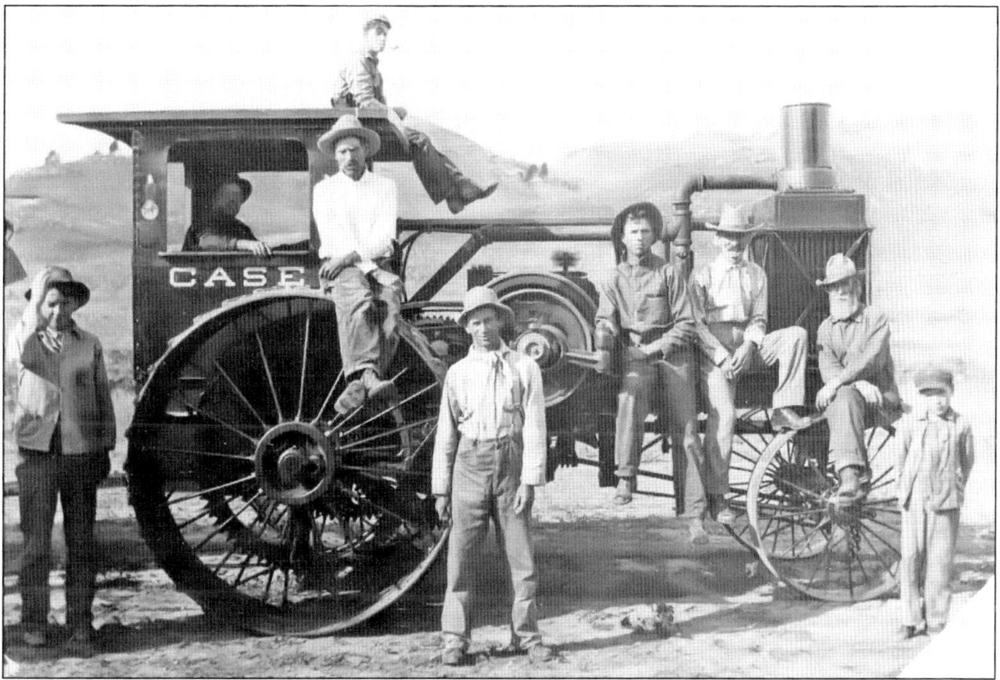

Charley Mitchell did not take this picture, because he is in it. Some of the others are John Patton, Janes Hejde, Clarence Mitchell, and Ben Weaver. It looks like they have just finished another long day. One of the major tasks each summer was and is today the harvesting of the small grains. In the days of this picture, the farmers cut the wheat or oats and tied the grain into bundles. When the wheat or oats dried, the farmer would load the bundles onto a horse-drawn rack and take them to the threshing machine. (Courtesy of Chuck Pearson.)

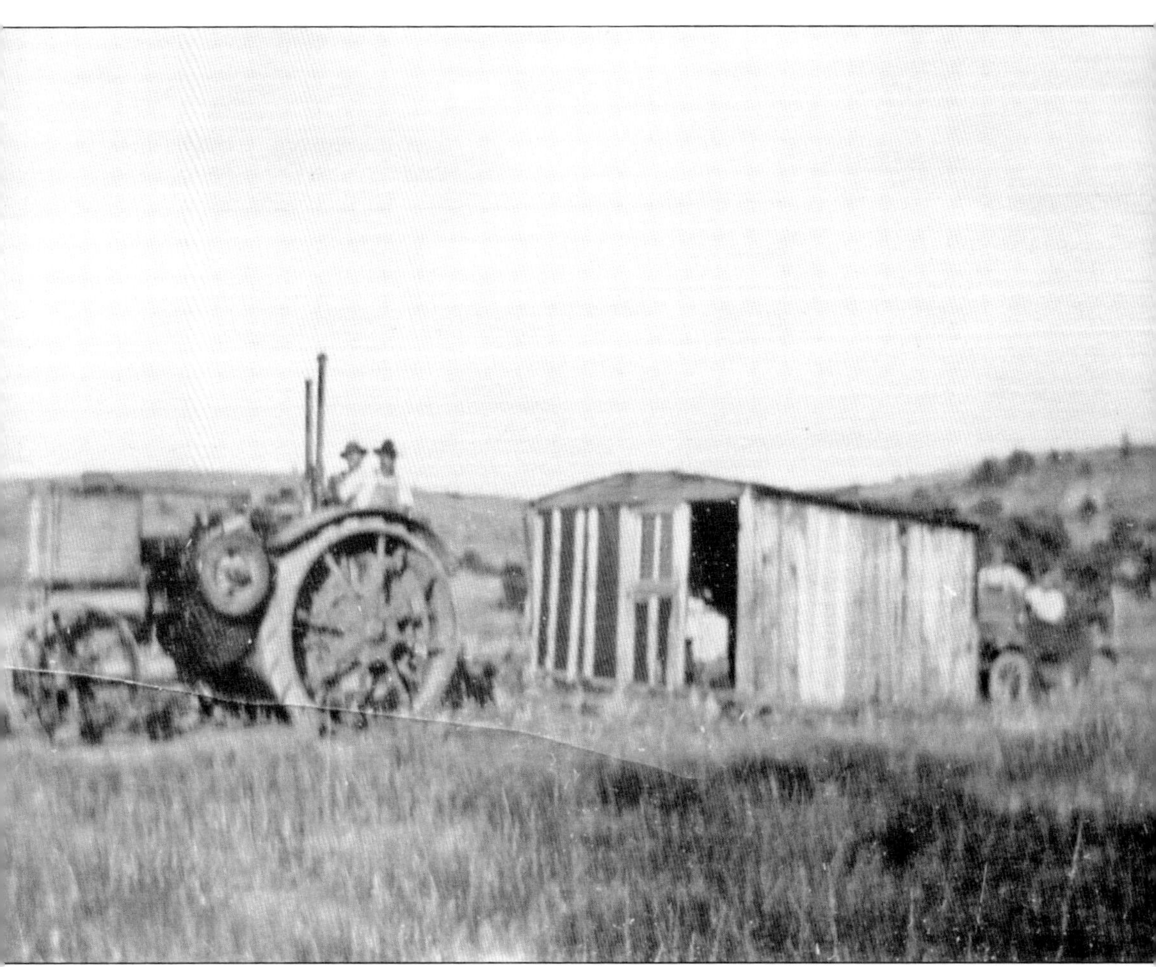

The Patton family is moving this building with a tractor that is as big as the building. This was done often. If a building was not needed or no longer used and someone else had a use for it, it was moved where it was needed. This building could be a new chicken house or pig shelter. It could be made into a machine shop and a shelter for the tractor itself. It could also be the new school. If a school was needed, there was not always time or the money to construct a brand-new building. There was always an empty building somewhere, and it would simply be moved, cleaned up, and put to work as the new school. Many homes were put together with parts and pieces of other buildings. Cindy B.'s Aladdin Café is an old gas station, moved and repurposed. (Courtesy of Chuck Pearson.)

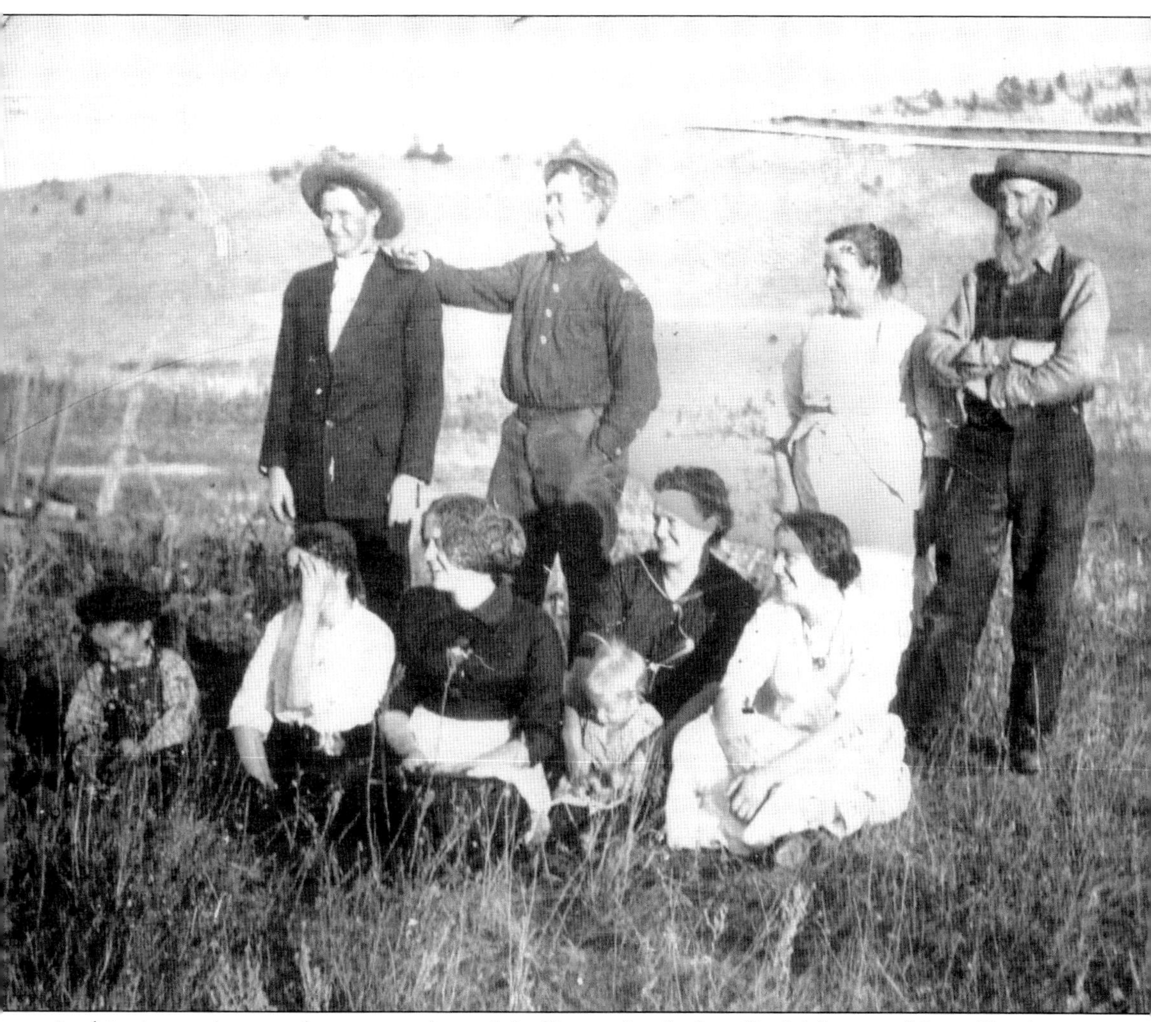

In this picture, in no order, are members of the Patton family: Jim, Burl, Mama and Papa, Frank, Zira, Lizzie, Nancy, Mary, and Margaret. Frank is the little boy, and Margaret is the baby in her mother's lap. The family has gathered for a quiet minute after a hard day's work. Threshing season was a time of hard work, of socializing with friends and neighbors, fun for the children, and wonderful food. Threshing started out really early in the morning, and by 9:00 a.m. the crew would be ready for a little lunch. By noon, they would eat a big dinner, and they would be ready to eat another lunch in the late afternoon that would hold them until everyone got home. (Courtesy of Chuck Pearson.)

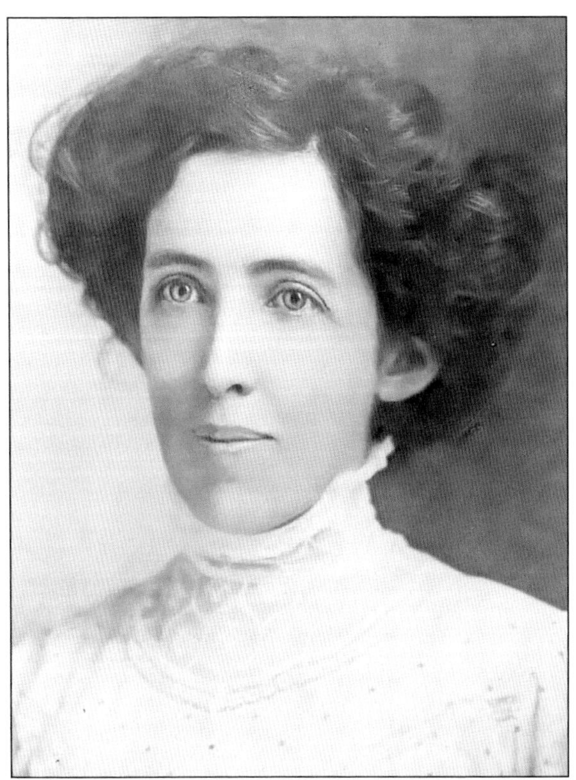

This is Katherine Morrell Aikman. Katherine was teaching at the Oak Creek School near the 2A ranch when she first met Fred Aikman. Her family had a ranch just to the north of the Aikman family ranch. Her father, Samuel Morrell, is said to have been a man of unquestionable integrity, and his advice was sought after by his neighbors and friends throughout the valley. (Courtesy of Chuck Pearson.)

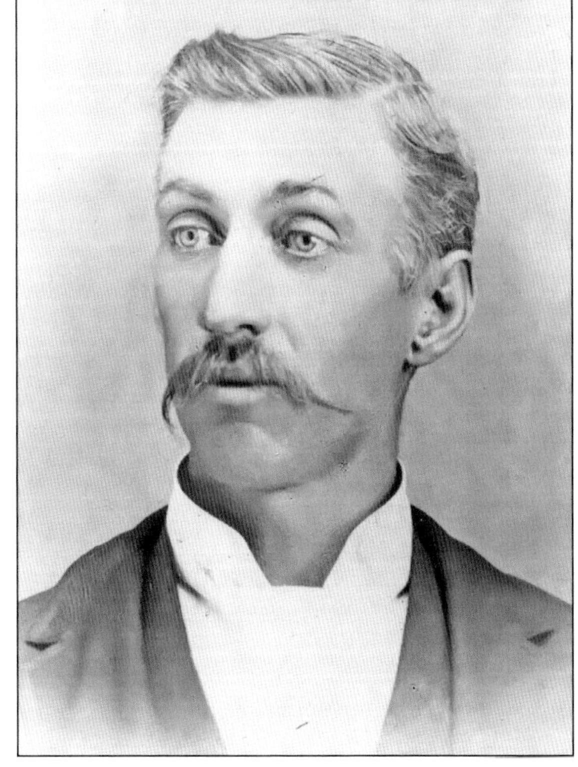

This is Fred Aikman, one of the successful early settlers in the Aladdin community. In 1884, he filed on a quarter section on the middle fork of Hay Creek, about seven miles northwest of Aladdin, and other family members also made homestead claims. These were the beginning of the Aikman ranch. Improvements were constantly being made on the ranch to provide a better living for everyone. A substantial windmill provided enough power to pump water for a garden, grind grain for livestock and chickens, and saw piles of wood for cooking, laundry, and heat. Raising and caring for sheep, hogs, milk cows, and some horses was busy and profitable for the whole family. (Courtesy of Chuck Pearson.)

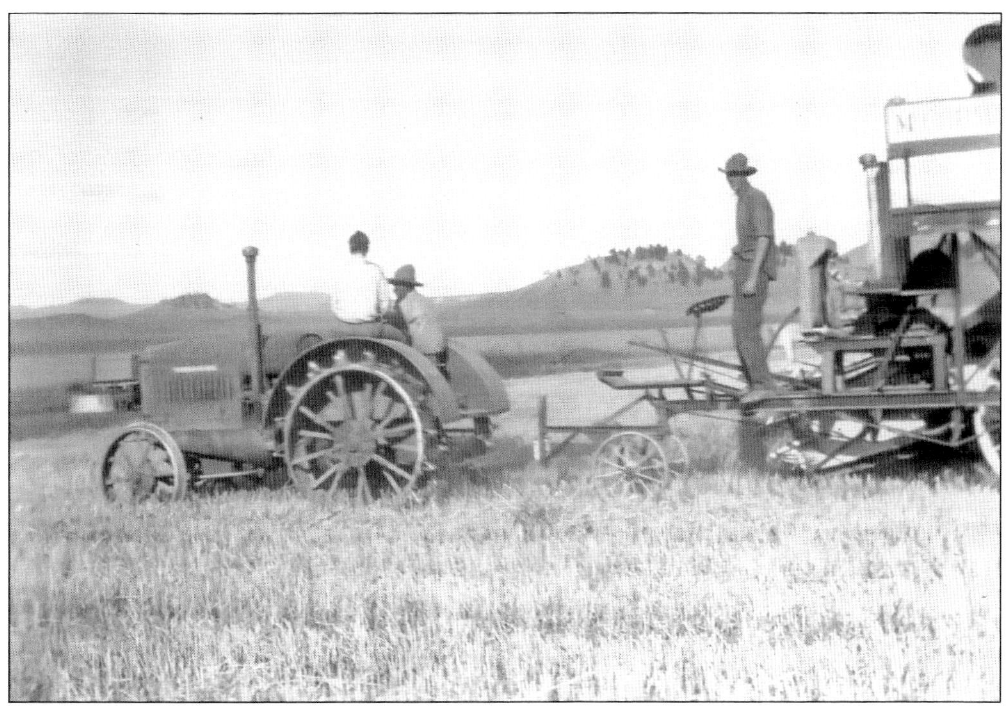

Fred Aikman was able to acquire the newest in farm equipment. He and some helpful friends try out this machine to see how it runs and just how good a job it will do in the fields, where they hope to get some work done. But these new machines did not always work the way the salesman said they would. In the picture below, the tractor seems to have gotten the best of this cowboy. It could need water, and he is doing his best to figure out how to get the water into the radiator. It is not like a horse. A horse will stop when you tell it to and drink when it is thirsty. On the other hand, this cowboy may fall, but he will not be bucked off. (Both, courtesy of Chuck Pearson.)

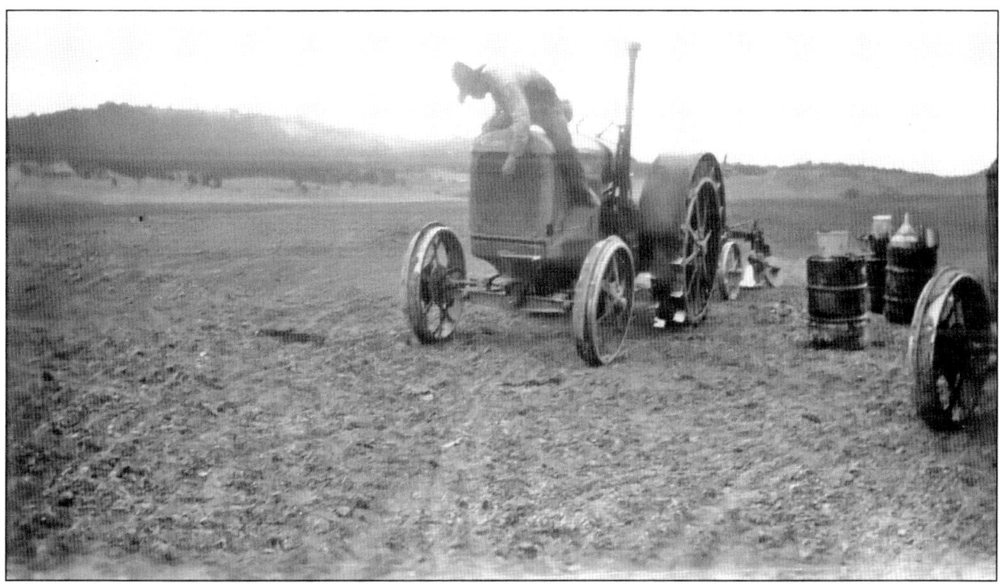

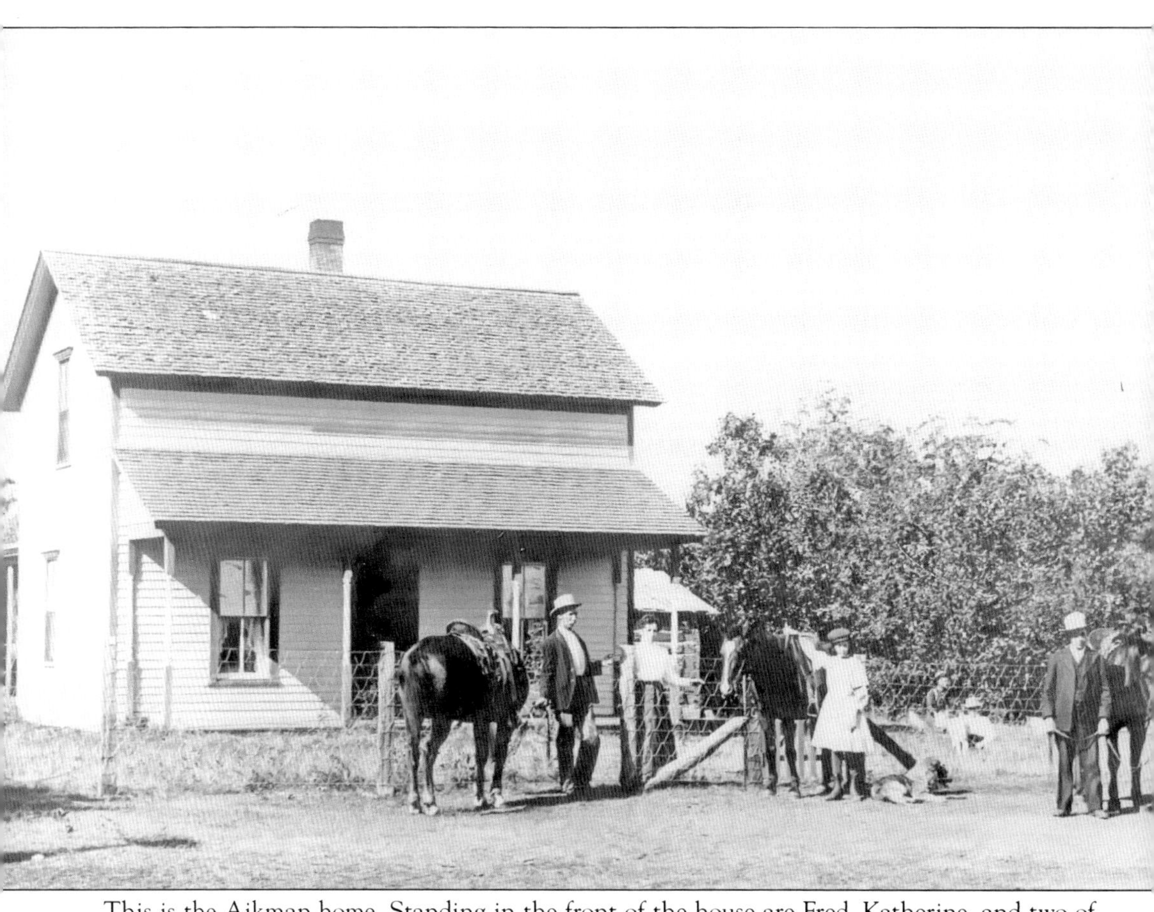

This is the Aikman home. Standing in the front of the house are Fred, Katherine, and two of their three children: Ester Helen and Sam. The Aikman ranch was sold in 1914, and the family moved to Spearfish, where the children continued their education at the Spearfish Normal School. Fred would reenter the ranching business in South Dakota using what he had learned by first ranching in Wyoming. After serving in the Army's aviation section until the Armistice in 1918, Sam would join his father on this ranch. Brother William would spend summers being a ranch hand. (Courtesy of Chuck Pearson.)

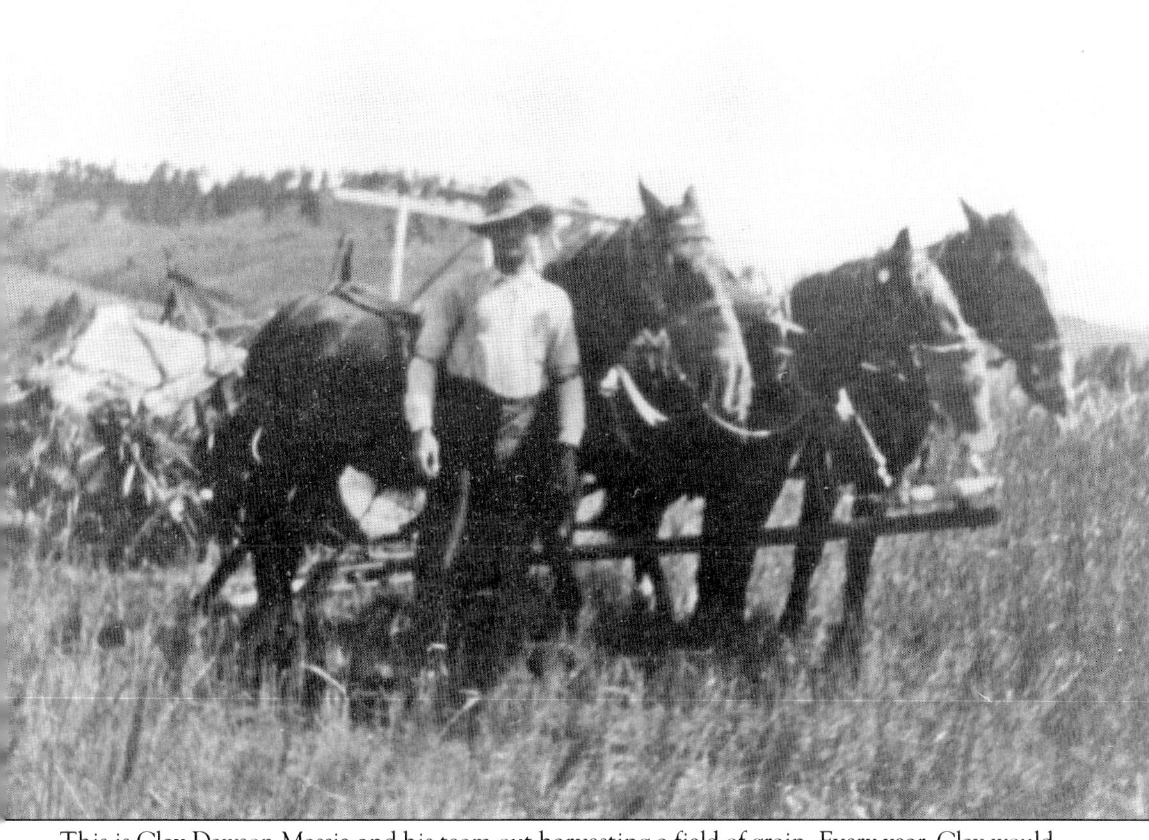

This is Clay Dawson Massie and his team out harvesting a field of grain. Every year, Clay would lament that he had never been able to grow a crop of seed alfalfa. Years later, Bill Pannell, a cousin, would laugh and say he had not been able to have a seed crop either. Clay had come to Crook County with his parents. He homesteaded near the Belle Fourche River and married Hazel Kendall. Hazel had a homestead of her own when they were married, and she was teaching, so she had a paying job. That made her quite a catch for a young farmer. She had not proved up on her piece of land when she got married, and because homesteaders must live on the land while making improvements, she lost her homestead. They raised their family on Clay's homestead but sold and moved to Sundance when Clay became Crook County clerk. They left behind a small grave on the hillside behind the house. (Courtesy of the Thompson family.)

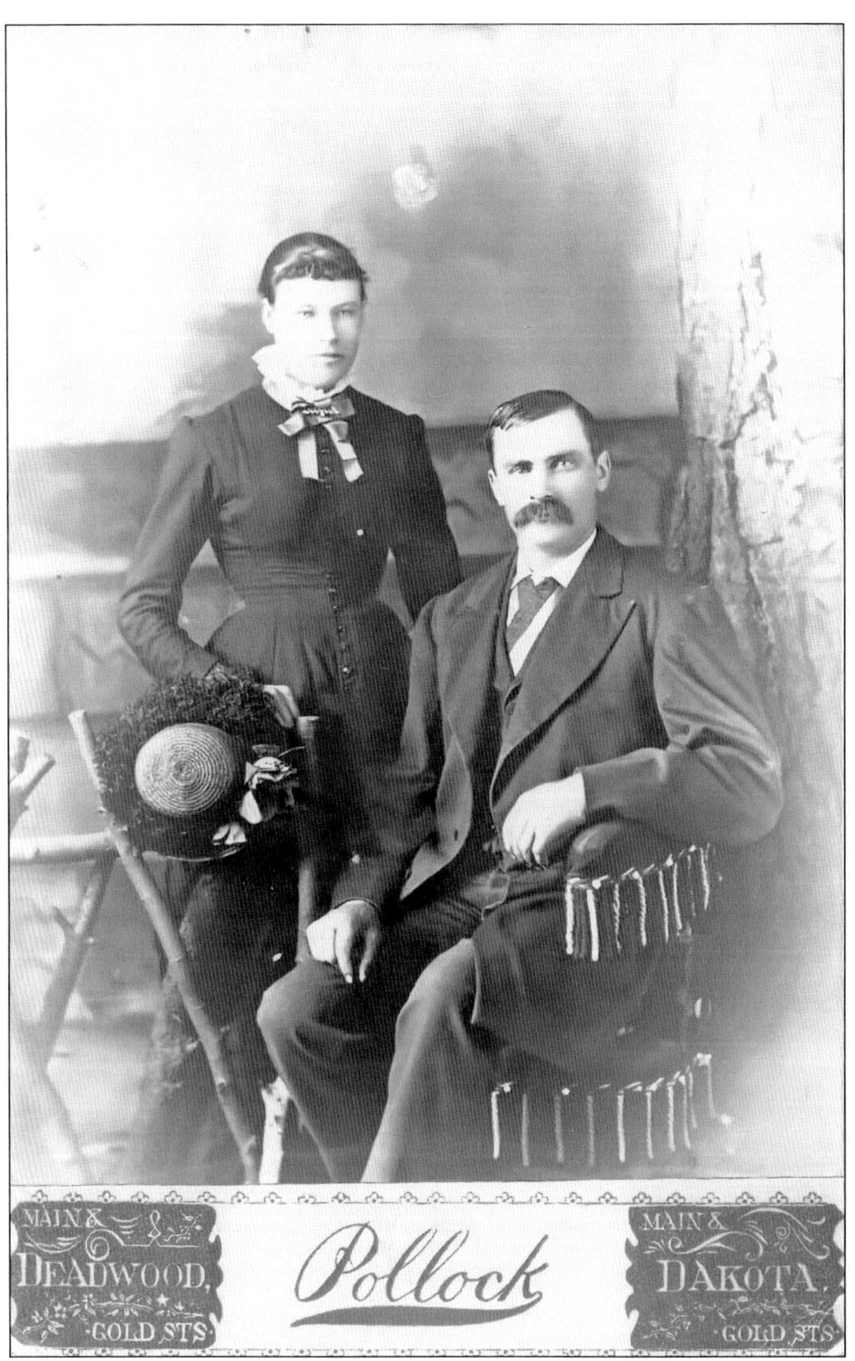

John Pearson arrived in Crook County in 1882 and settled along the south fork of Hay Creek. In April 1884, he married Augusta Johnson. At one time, Pearson owned 8,000 acres of land, with extensive holdings in South Dakota. He was a justice of the peace, and owned 10 residences and many lots. He built the Pearson Opera House in Belle Fourche. He is mentioned in *The Progressive Men of Wyoming*, which tells that John had begun a business and watched it with care, developed it with energy, and conducted it with skill, and it grew great with steady and symmetrical progress. This is a picture of John and Augusta Pearson. (Courtesy of Chuck Pearson.)

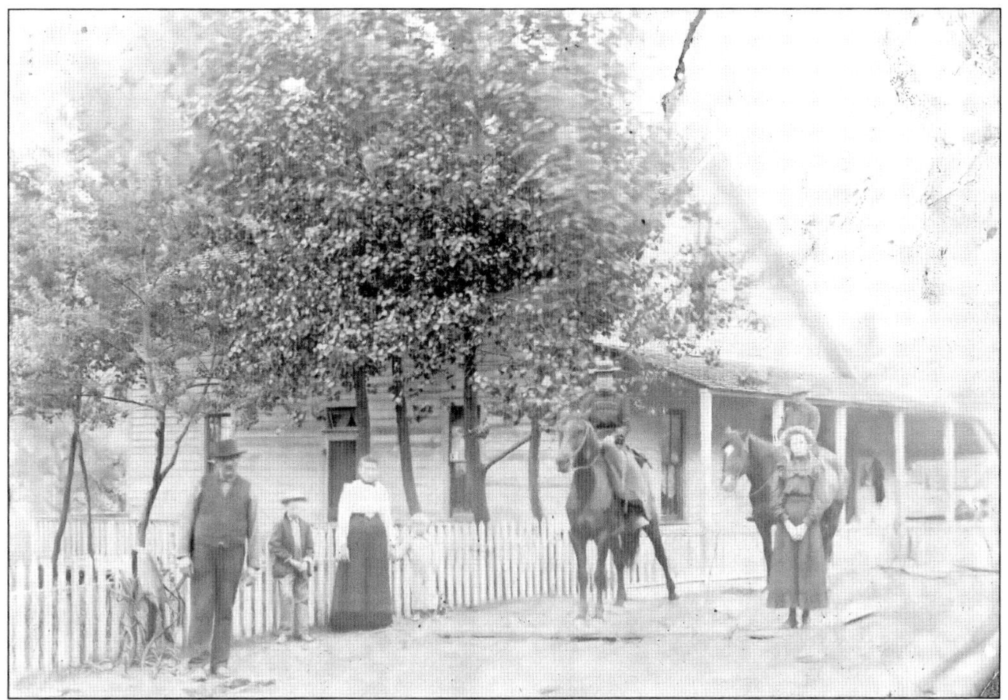

This photograph was taken in front of the Pearson house in Eothen. Pictured are, in no order, Nels, John, Mary, and Mrs. Rawlins, the cook. John established a post office in Eothen and served as postmaster for 26 years, making him at the time the oldest postmaster in the state of Wyoming. Augusta died in 1898 and is buried in the family cemetery on the ranch. (Courtesy of Chuck Pearson.)

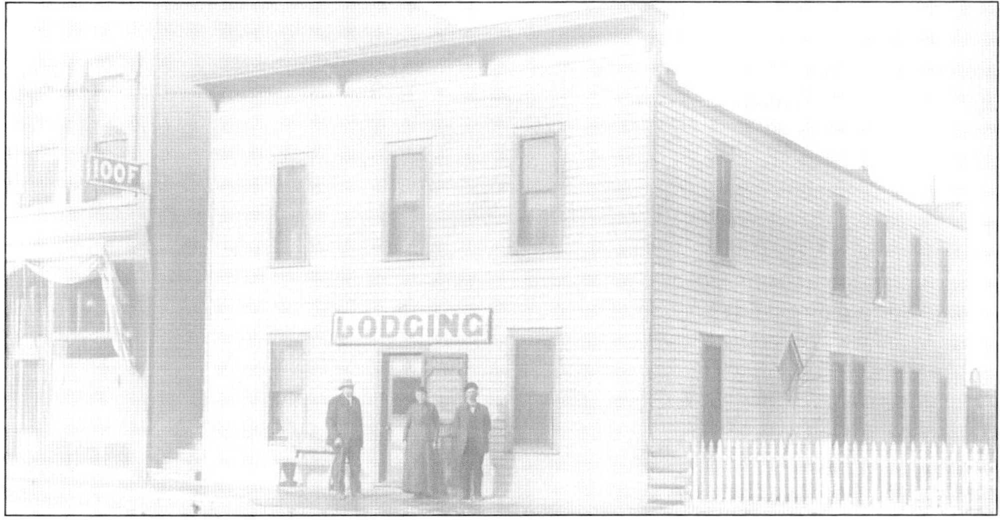

This is the lodging house that John Pearson owned. It is located on the main street of Belle Fourche. Mr. and Mrs. Campbell acted as his managers. This is just one of many businesses that John had in both Wyoming and South Dakota. In Eothen, he operated a road house for overnight guests. His large barn and corrals could accommodate many guests and their animals. John had cattle and horses, and he also had Angora goats. It has always been a good idea to have goats to eat weeds. (Courtesy of Chuck Pearson.)

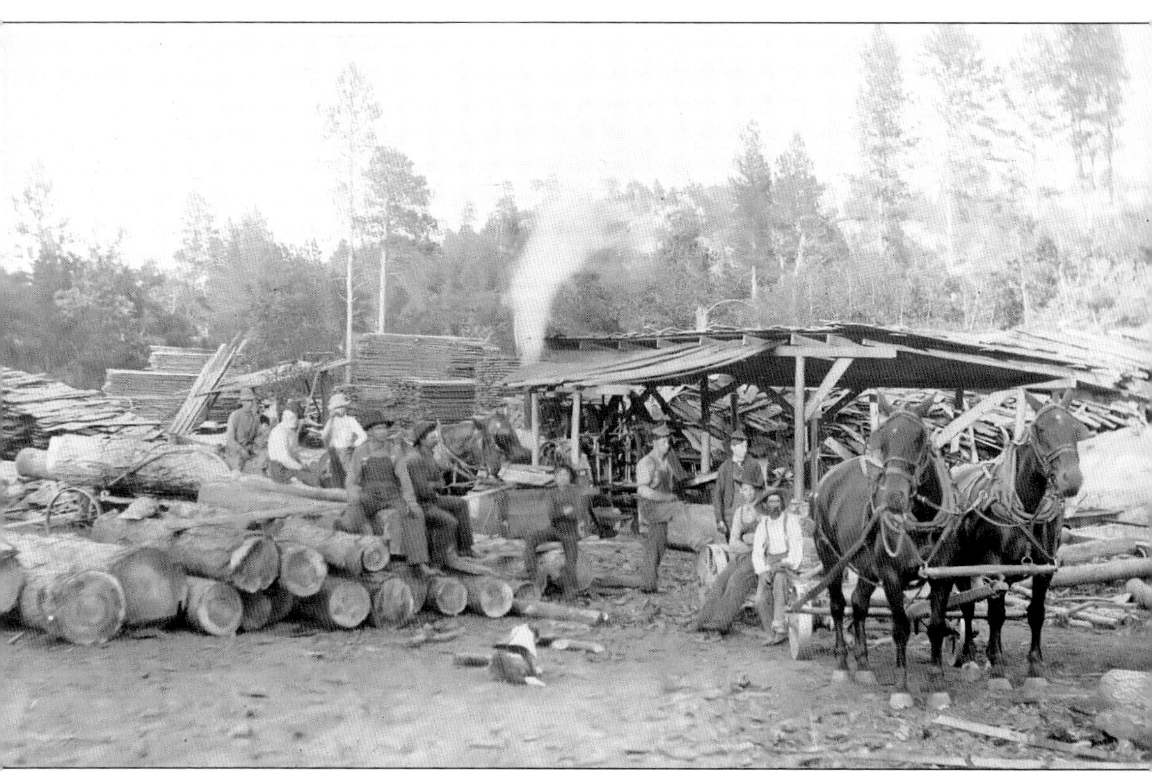

This is John Pearson's sawmill at Eothen, called the little mill. It sat close to the Bear Lodge Mountains. After the discovery of gold near Deadwood, the dense forests of the Black Hills were the primary source for the timber that was so very necessary for the development of the mine. There were sawmills like this one at Eothen popping up overnight. With all the requests for more and more timber, they were very busy. John not only furnished the mine and the railroad with the timber they needed, but the sawmill also cut the lumber needed to build his home as well as others in the Aladdin Valley. (Courtesy of Chuck Pearson.)

Nine

Friends and Neighbors

It is friends and neighbors that help everyone make it through whatever life throws at them. Living in the remote northeast corner of Crook County made that even more important. The roads were sometimes impassible, and sometimes they were little more than trails. People learned to depend on each other and to offer a helping hand whenever the need arose. Sometimes the helping hand would arrive without being asked, because it was just known that help would be needed.

Threshing teams worked together to make the work go faster. These teams of men would move from one farm to another until the grain was harvested. Everyone helped—the children hauled water, and the ladies got together to cook many meals at each home as the work moved around the neighborhood.

Barns were raised, fences built, cattle moved and branded, and schools built and moved. Families were raised among the friends and neighbors around Aladdin. Marriages happened, and friends and neighbors became family. Many people moved away, but they will always remember the people they worked and lived with.

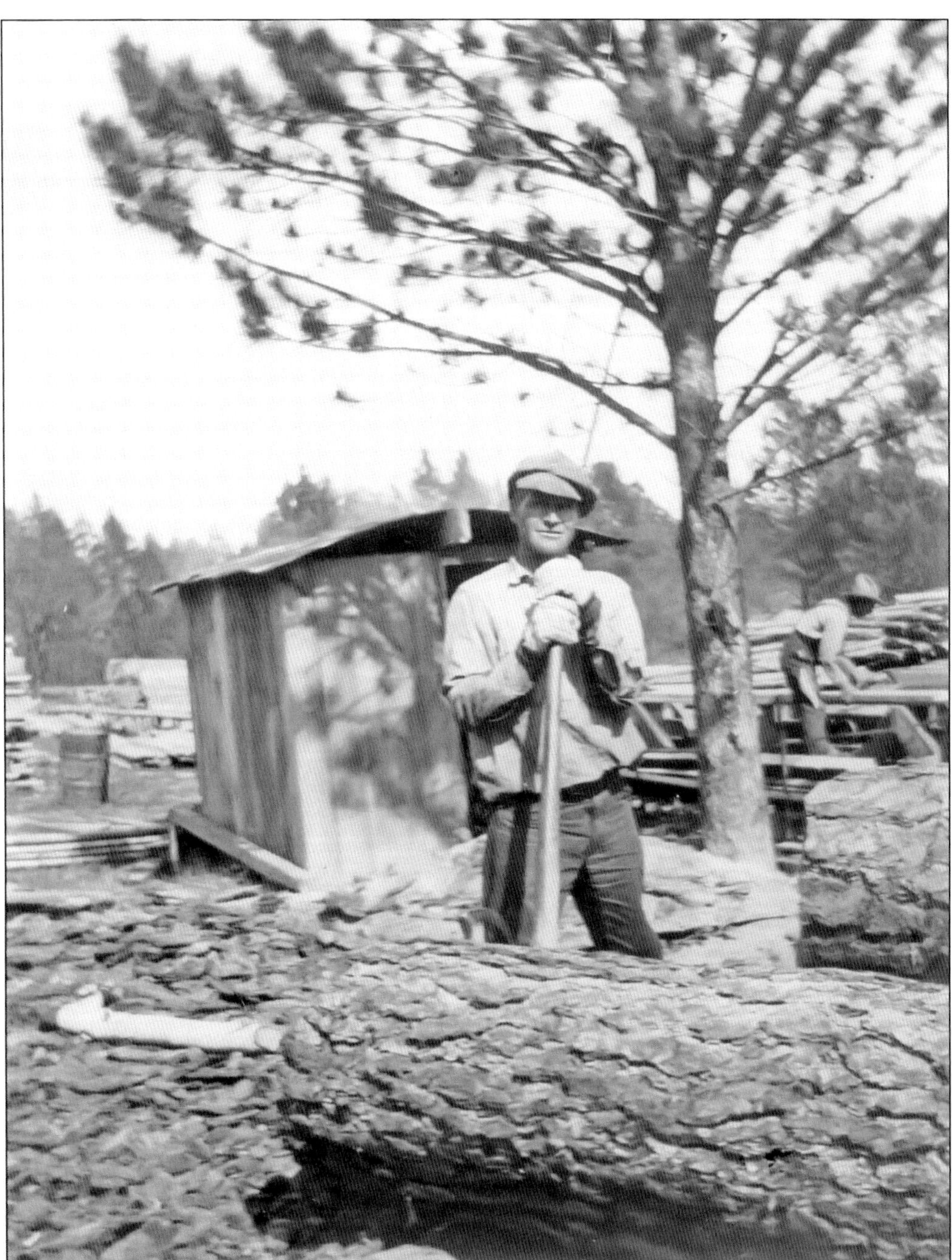

Fred Pattinson is working at the Pearson sawmill. He is cutting the timber that will become the lumber to build a new, larger house for the Pearson family. He took notice of the schoolteacher who was teaching nearby and staying with the Pearsons. Jennie and Fred were married on June 25, 1927, in an outdoor wedding under the apple trees. Fourteen months later, on August 25, 1928, Fred passed away from a heart attack. He was 40 years old. Jennie would later meet and marry Tony Kotek. They had to keep their marriage a secret for over a year because she had a teaching position in Aladdin. At this time, there was a law that married women could not teach. Jennie went on to teach school for 27 years. (Courtesy of Chuck Pearson.)

Swan Pearson came to the Black Hills and Wyoming to join his brother John Pearson. He constructed a large building in Bakertown. He lived in one half of the house and rented the other half to a family named Robinson. Later, he filed on a preemption west of the Aladdin Store. With Fritz Mortensen, he began a horse ranch, but wolves killed many of their colts. Fritz lost his life in a mine accident and was buried on the preemption. (Courtesy of Chuck Pearson.)

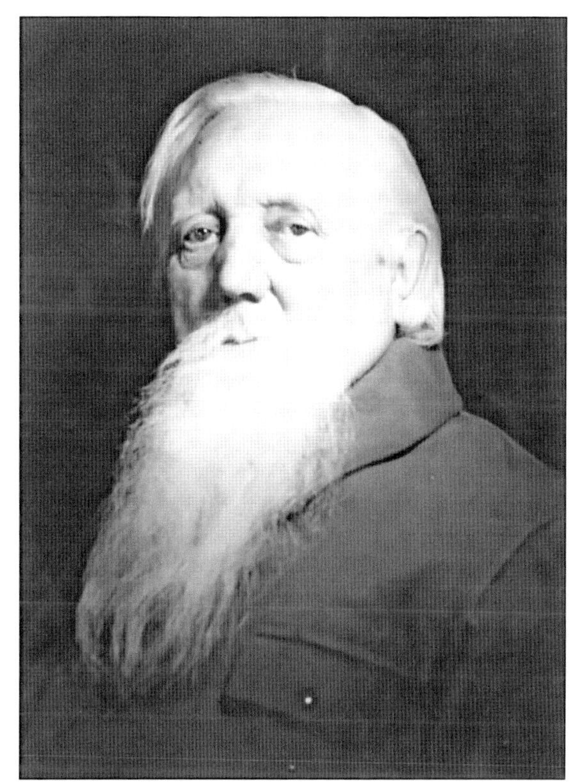

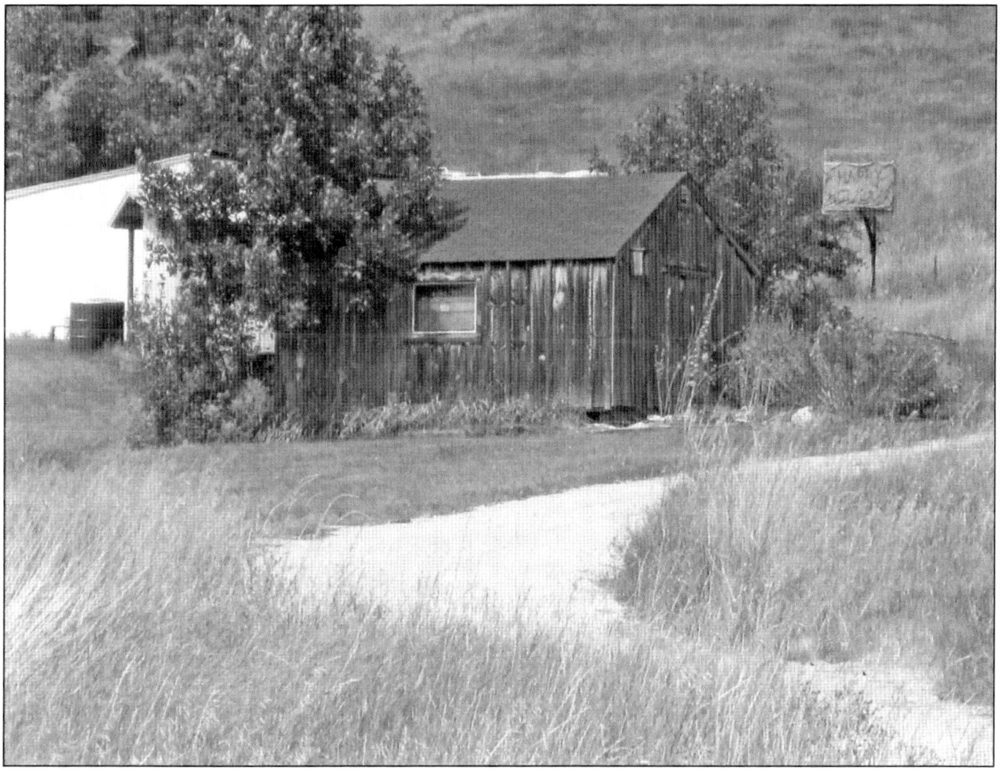

Swan never married, as an unhappy affair in his early years made him decide to remain a bachelor for the rest of his life. This was his home for his last few years. Swan walked everywhere. He walked to the store every day. When asked if he was going to the funeral of a close friend, Swan answered, "Hell no, he apparently will not be coming to mine." He passed away on July 20, 1939. (Author's collection.)

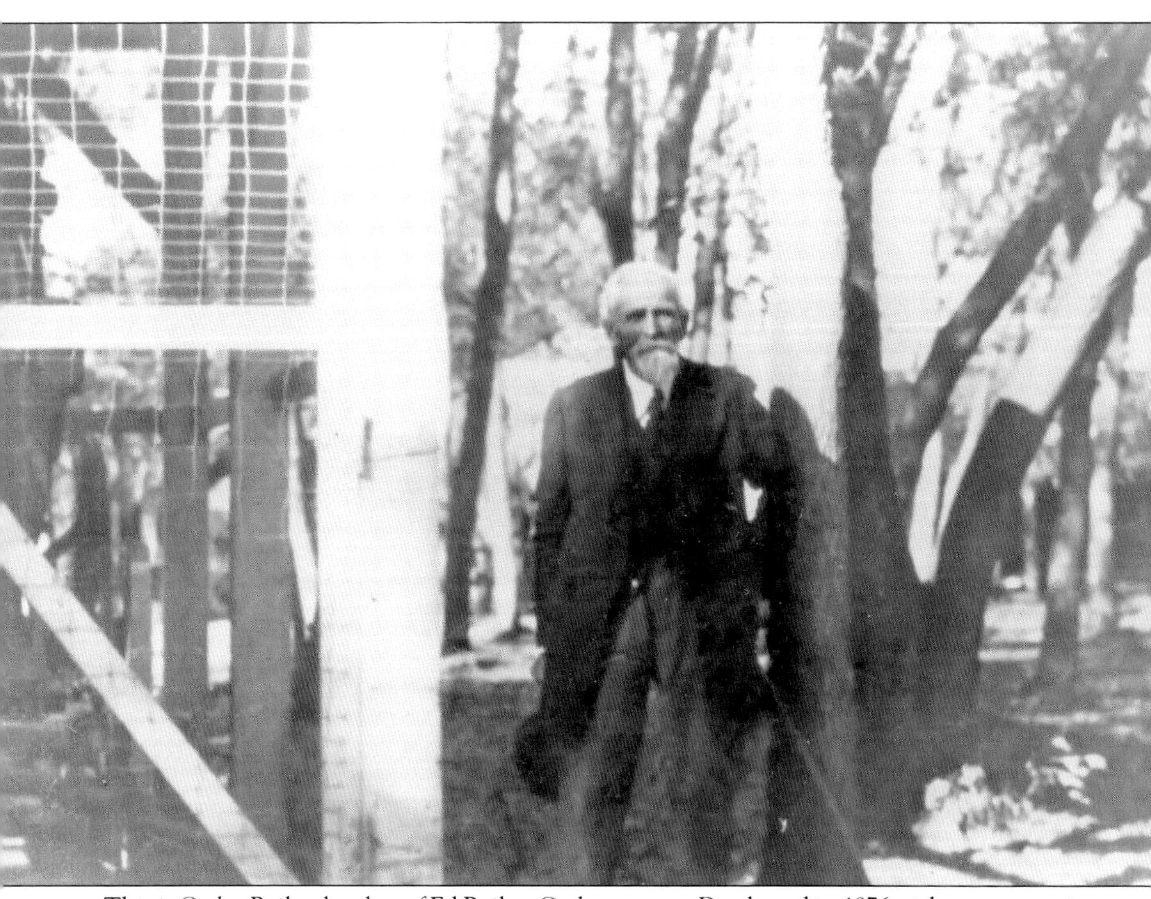

This is Carlos Bailey, brother of Ed Bailey. Carlos came to Deadwood in 1876 with a wagon train. He freighted supplies to the buffalo hunters along the Moreau and Grand Rivers in eastern South Dakota and then hauled buffalo meat back to the Black Hills, where he got 2¢ a pound from the miners. With his son Will, he homesteaded in the area of Oak Creek. When Will decided to move on to California, Carlos spent the rest of his life with his brother Ed and his wife Myrtle. At age 87, Carlos decided he had had enough of this world and walked out to the bunkhouse and chose his own way to leave it behind. (Courtesy of Chuck Pearson.)

Rosa Giachino came with her husband, Barney, and their family from Sparone, Italy. It took them 15 days to cross the ocean to New York and then take the train to Aladdin. Barney filed on 100 acres and built a two-story log house. Barney was a miner by trade and soon found work in the coal mines. Rosa milked the cows and always had chickens and a big garden. With her children, she stacked hay with a horse sweep and stacker. Daughter Gilda plowed the ground while Rosa broadcast the wheat by hand. She always had a smile on her face. (Courtesy of the Crook County Museum.)

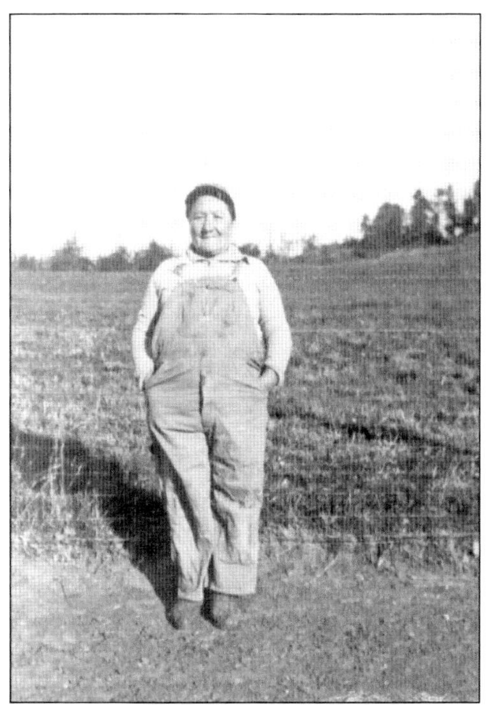

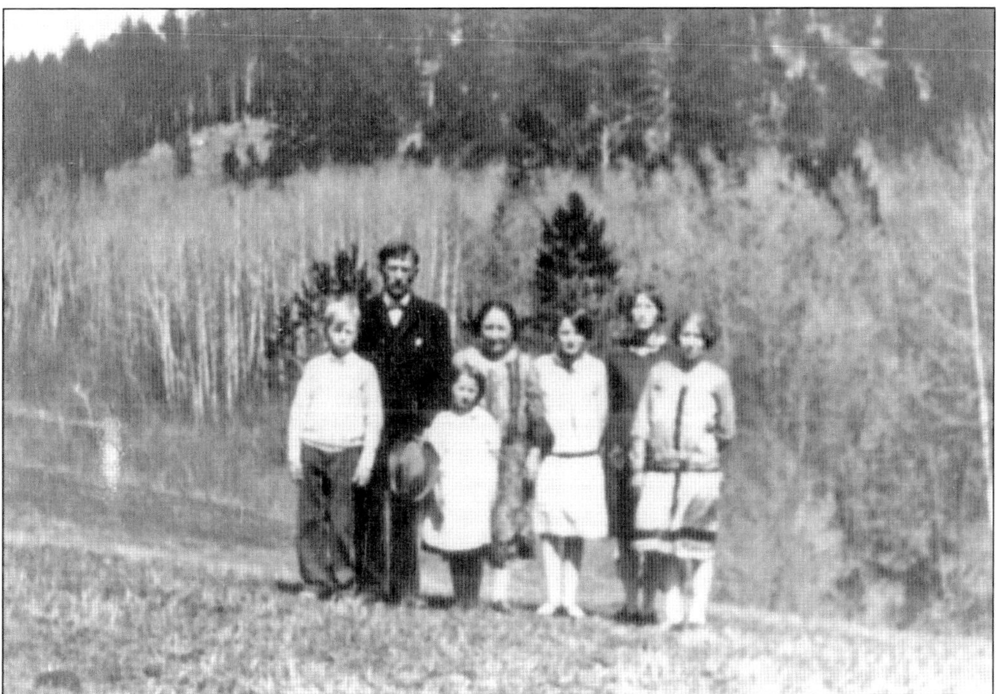

Pictured here is the Barney Giachino family. In no order are Barney, Rosa, Catherine, Gilda, Sophie, Rosalee, and Idolo. Idolo never married and lived his life on their farm. Olento died when he was only two months old. The doctor lived 30 miles away and could not get out to the family in time. The girls always said it was hard work but they were all happy. (Courtesy of the Crook County Museum.)

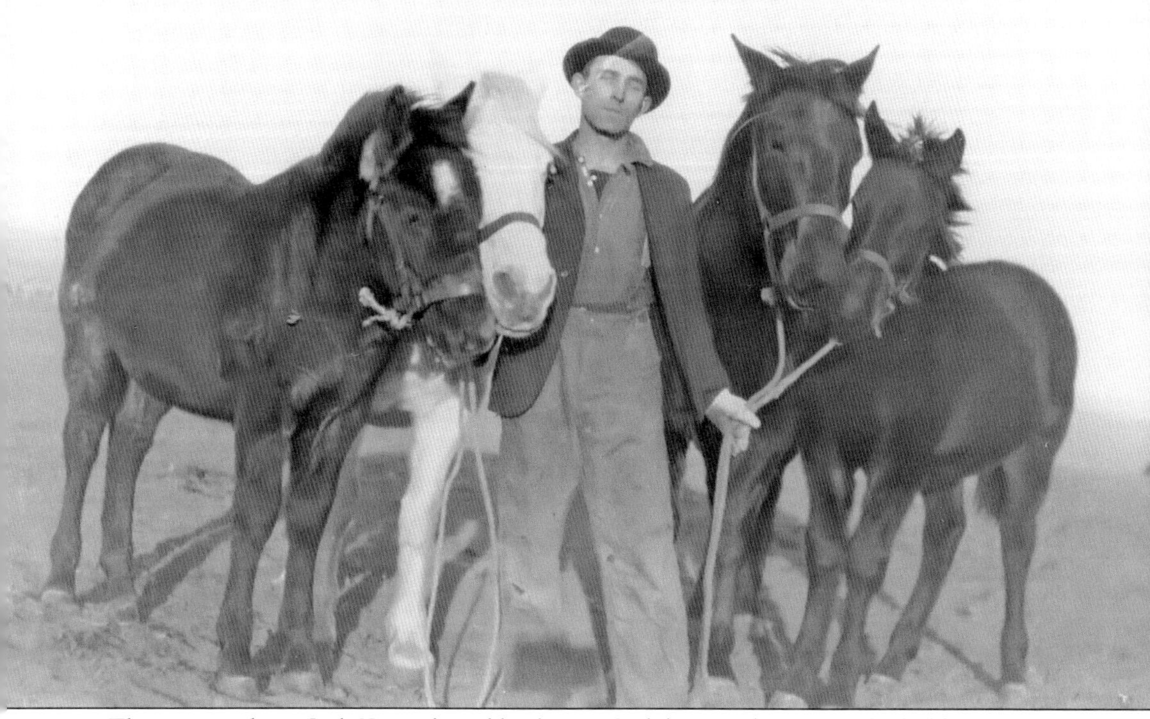

This picture shows Jack Kunerth and his horses. Jack has good reason to be holding on tight to his horses. With the Army offering good money for all the horses it could get its hands on, horse thieves were working overtime. The most notorious and boldest of these outlaws was the Axelbee gang. This gang of horse thieves had been rustling in Wyoming for several years. Ranchers were calling for a vigilante army to stop George Axelbee and his gang. The gang had a shootout at Stoneville in which a sheriff and a cowboy were killed. The vigilante cleanup resulted in the hanging of 57 men. Harry Tuttle, who did business with the gang but was not a member of it, was hanged 20 miles from Aladdin near Spearfish. This clean-up was seen as murder by some people. The good news was that remaining horse thieves and gang members became model citizens or simply left the county. (Courtesy of Chuck Pearson.)

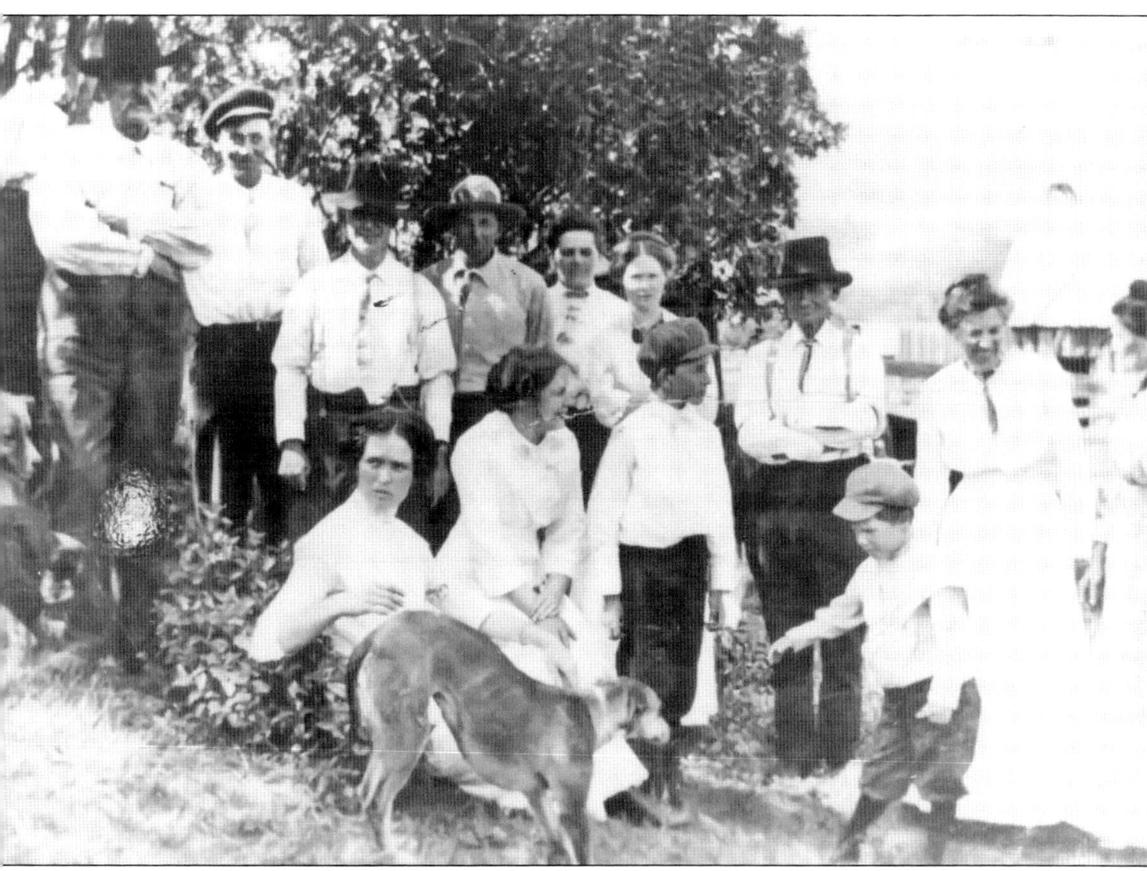

This is a picture of the Cremeens family. Having heard about Wyoming from their friends the Tracys and looking for clean air for Tony's lungs, the family decided to try the Wild West. They chartered two railroad freight cars and with all their worldly belongings headed for Aladdin. Once they arrived and unloaded both box cars, they stayed with the Tracy family until they found a piece of land near Mona that they thought suited their needs. Here are all the friends and family together again along with a few new friends. From left to right are (first row) Myrtle Tracy and Walter Tracy; (second row) J.J. Nelson, Fred Tracy, Wes Tracy, Rulana Nelson, and young Wes Tracy; (third row) Perice Mann and Ernest Cremeens; (fourth row) Harry Tracy, Tony Cremeens, Blanche Cremeens, and Minnie Tracy. (Courtesy of Chuck Pearson.)

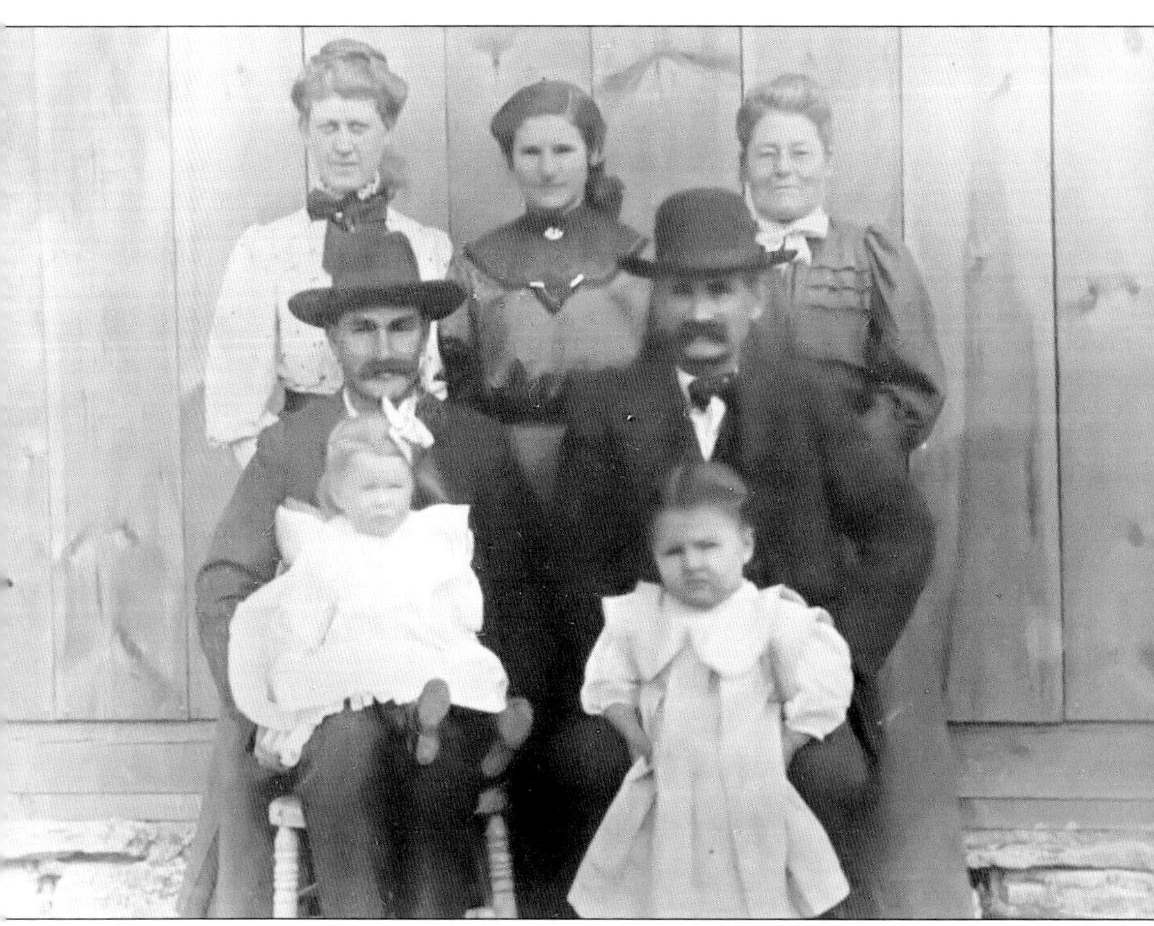

This picture of the Ellsbury family from Farrell, Wyoming, was taken in 1908 or 1909. Farrell is always listed in early post office reports as being the farthest post office not on the Aladdin route. Henry and Lizzie Ellsbury and David and Clarinda Ellsbury came to the Aladdin area in 1884. They filed on homesteads on the north part of the Redwater River 1887. In 1891, the two families moved to their homesteads and began to build a ranching partnership. From left to right are (first row) Merton Ellsbury holding his daughter Juanita and Lyman Henry Ellsbury holding his granddaughter Nettie; (second row) Ella Truax Ellsbury, wife of Merton; Marjorie Ellsbury, daughter of Lyman Henry; and Lizzie Ellsbury. (Courtesy of Chuck Pearson.)

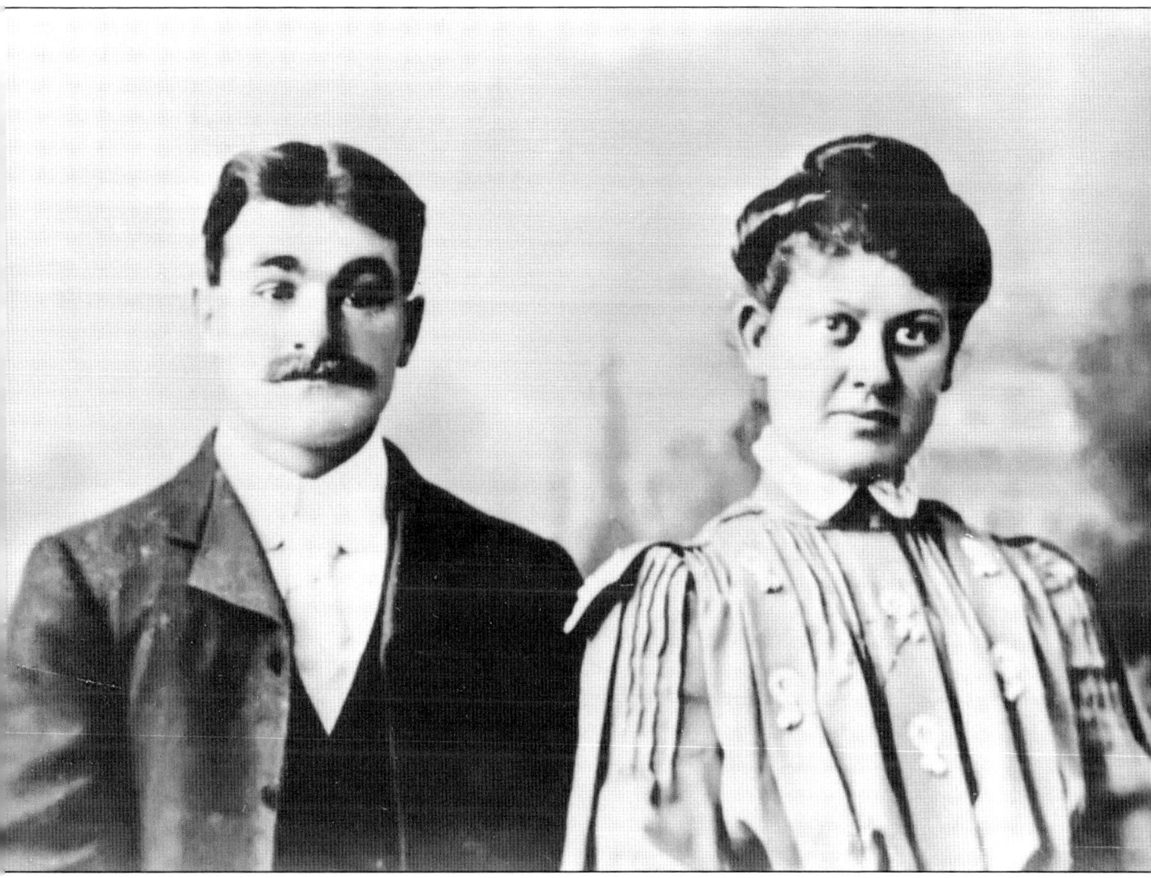

This is Merton and Ella Ellsbury. Ella came to Crook County as Ella Truax to teach school. She became certified to teach in July 1901. She met Merton when she taught summer school that year and stayed with his uncle Dave Ellsbury. School was a summer session because the snow was always too deep to have classes in the winter. In the 1902–1903 school year, she taught at the Houston Creek School. Her wages were $12 a month. On February 10, 1904, she married Merton. (Courtesy of Chuck Pearson.)

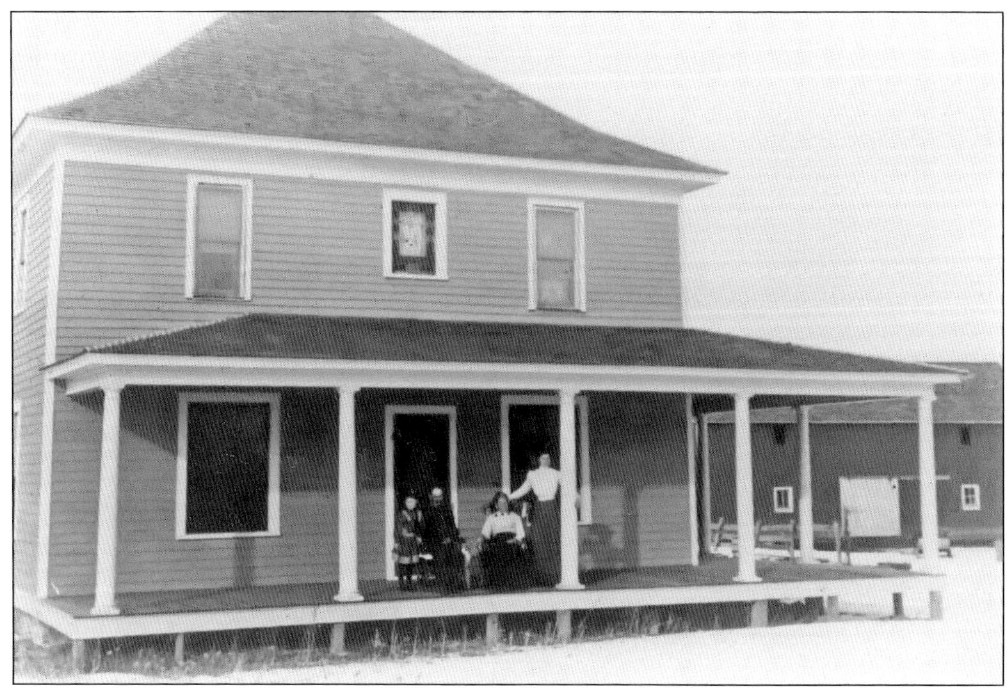

Merton worked in partnership with his father for many years. Lyman Henry Ellsbury had acted as treasurer of the school board; he was a Crook County commissioner and a state representative for one term. He then retired in 1929 to Spearfish, where he died in 1934. Merton and Ella stayed on the ranch. The Ellsbury family continues to live in this house and carry on the ranching partnerships started so long ago. (Courtesy of Chuck Pearson.)

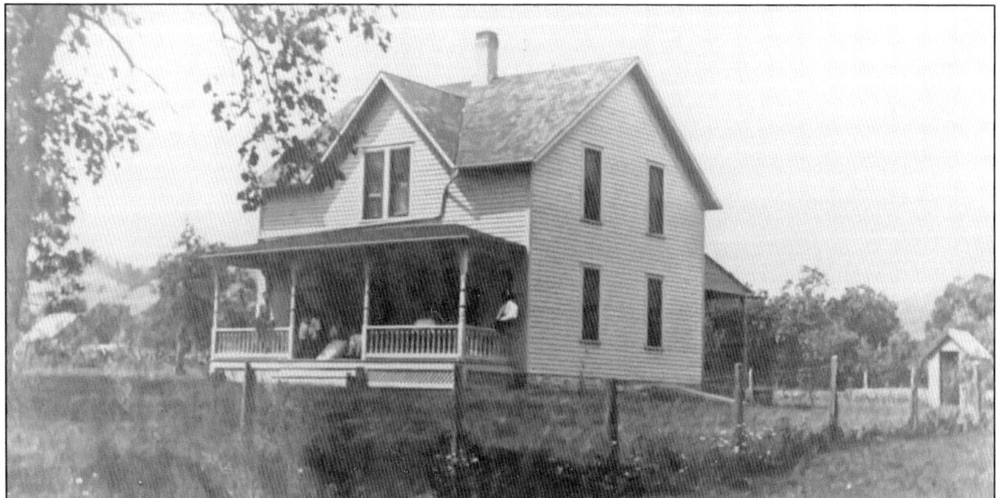

This is Dave Ellsbury's home. Ella stayed here while she was teaching at the Ellsbury School where she met Merton. Dave's son Walter was a first-grade student that year. Other children going to the Ellsbury School that year were Ned, Joe, and Jenny Lanning, Vernie Taylor, and Lottie, Henry, Leon, and Leontine Selliez. Dave and Clarinda, called Pet, would later move to North Dakota. When the Ellsbury family and the Truax families hold a reunion at the Farrell Hall, over 90 people can fill the building. The Ellsbury family continues to live in the homes built by Dave and Merton. (Courtesy of Chuck Pearson.)

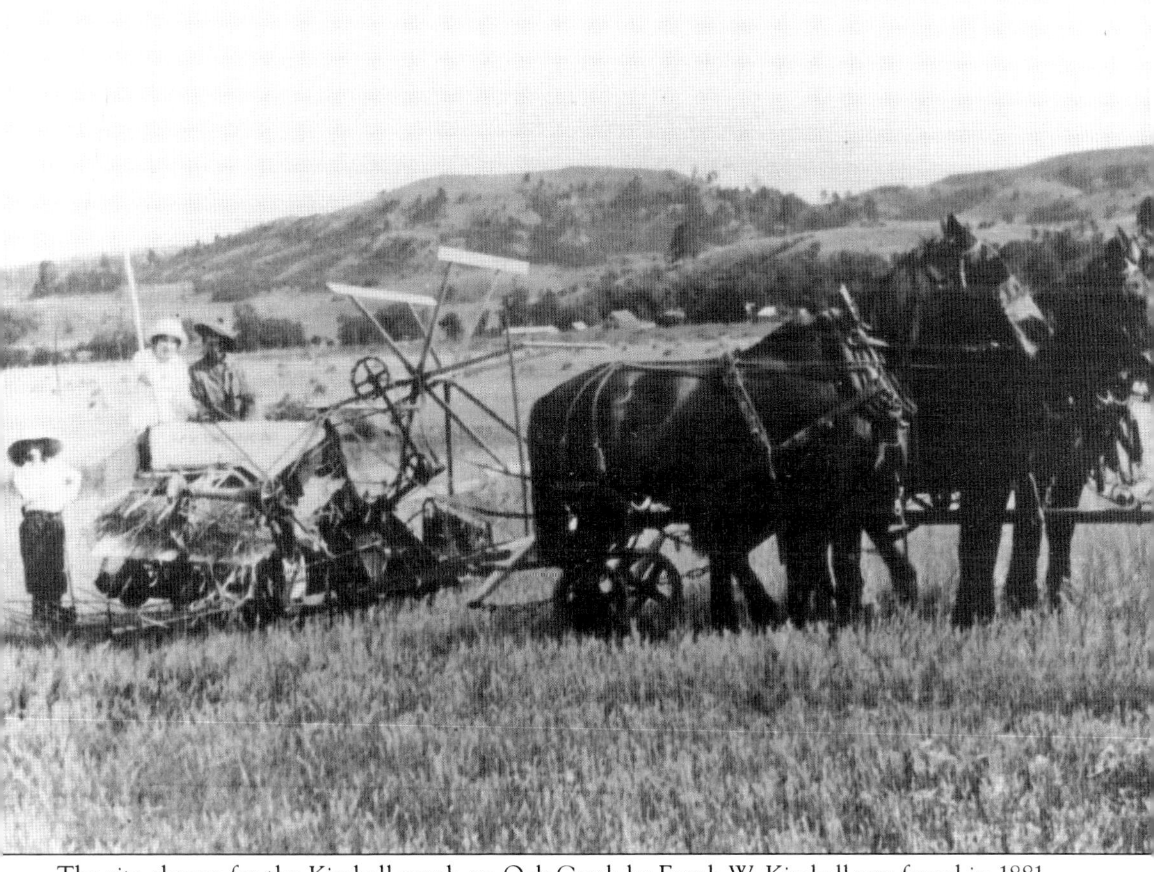

The site chosen for the Kimball ranch on Oak Creek by Frank W. Kimball was found in 1881, when he was still too young to homestead. He persuaded his parents to leave Wisconsin and file a homestead claim right next to the one he wanted for himself. He was married to Grace Darling Armstrong in Barrett by Rev. Arthur Cheeseman, a Methodist minister. Frank caught a slight case of smallpox while playing cards with some men who had been quarantined in the pest house in Aladdin. The pest house sat across the creek, and food and medicine were delivered as far as the bridge. This picture shows Frank, Grace, and son Winthrop harvesting a hay crop. (Courtesy of Chuck Pearson.)

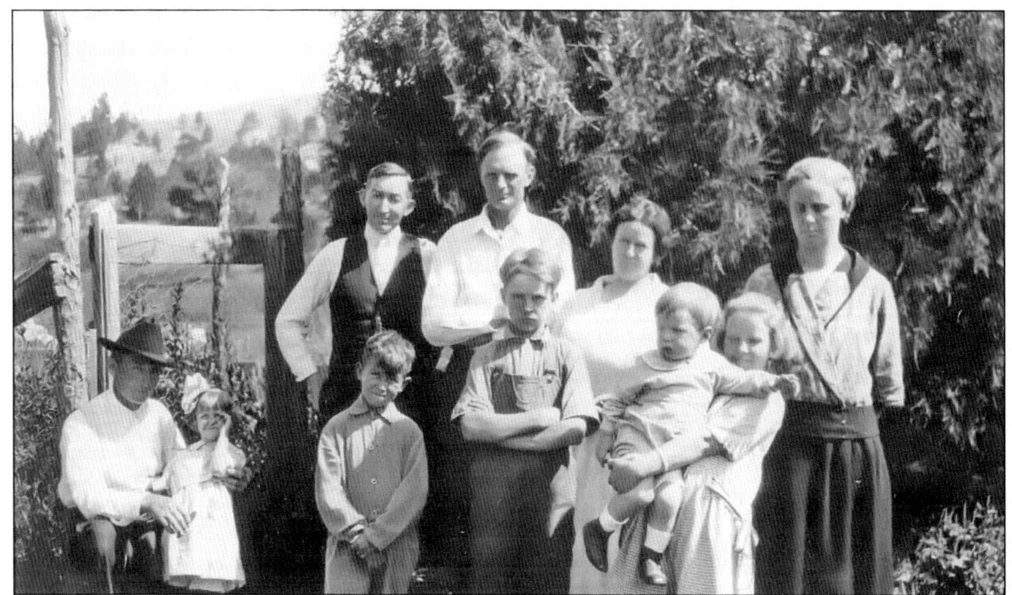

This is a photograph of family, friends, and neighbors. Sitting on the left are Matt Whalen and Virginia Aggers. The others are, in no order, John Aggers, Charles Pearson, Nancy Pearson, Margaret Whalen, Leslie Aggers, and Frank Pearson. Mary Pearson is holding John Whalen. Margaret is the sister to Charles and Frank. (Courtesy of Chuck Pearson.)

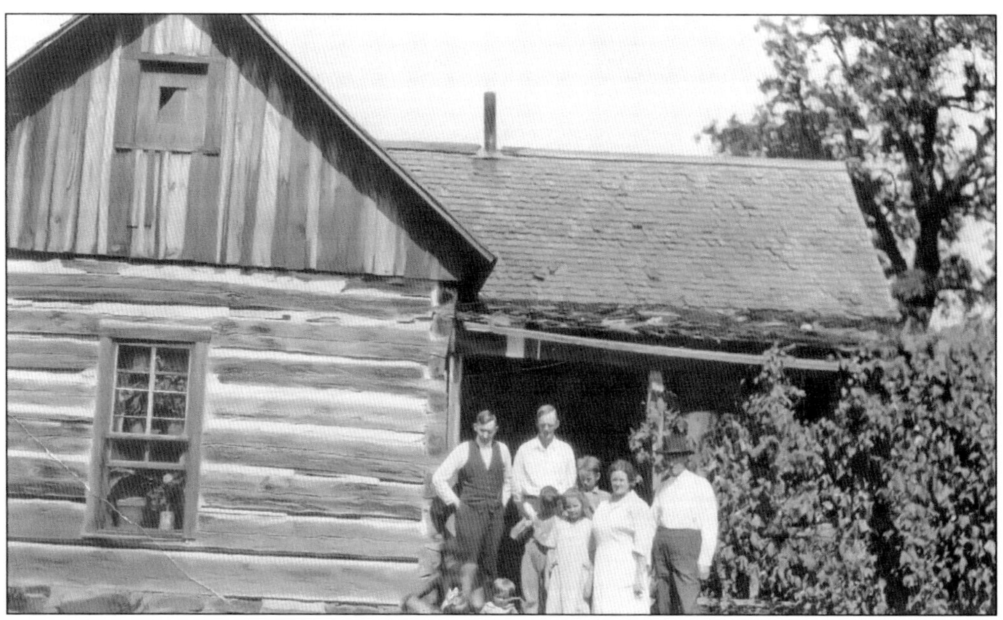

Nancy Pearson wrote on this postcard that this picture was taken at the old log house. From left to right are John Aggers, Charlie Pearson, Matt Whalen, Nancy Pearson, and Frank Pearson. This family always gathered together for work and play. (Courtesy of Chuck Pearson.)

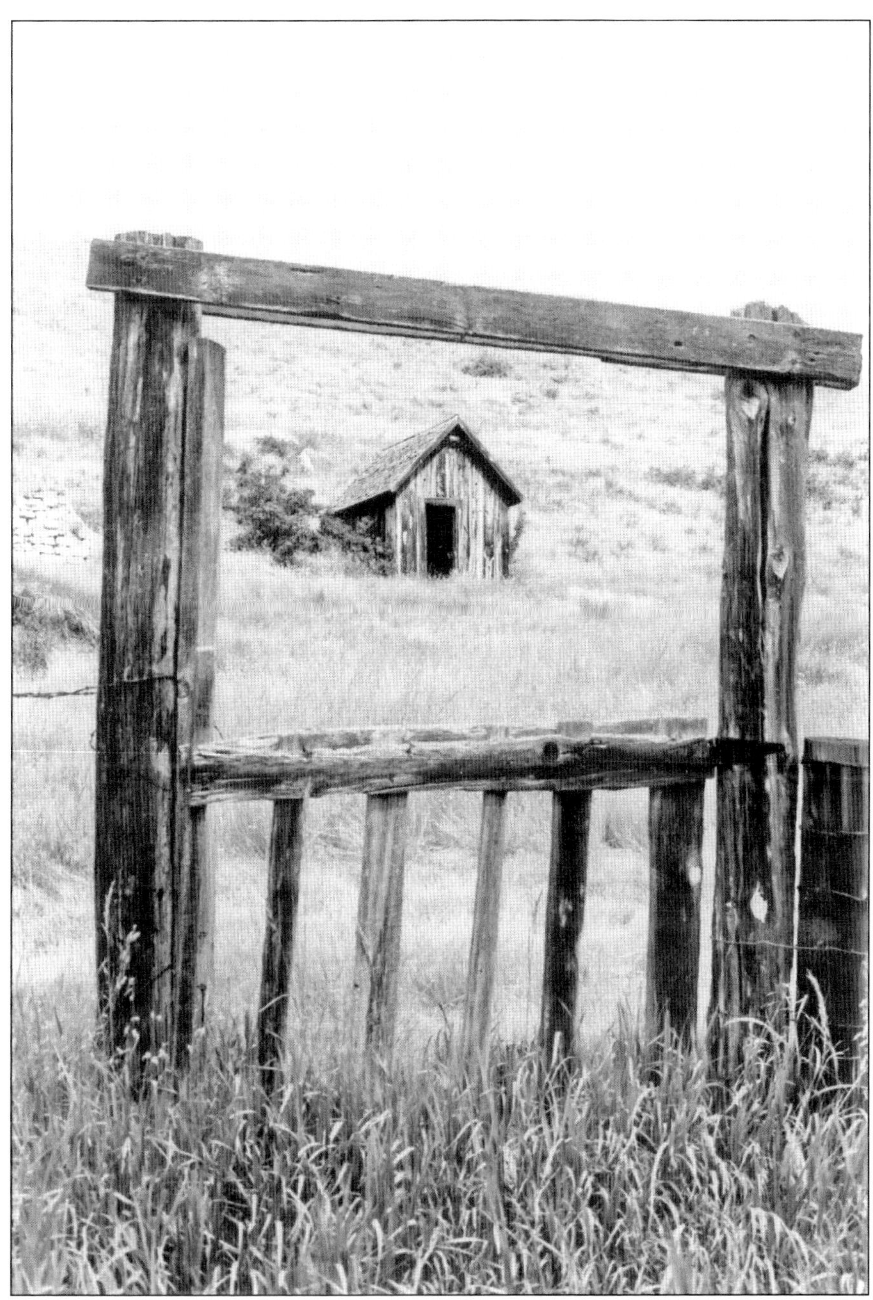

This is the homestead of Valentine Zamboni. He was called Tony by his friends. His English was not very good. When he had firewood delivered to his house, he would ask the delivery man or boys to count out what he owed them. Everybody knew how good his watermelons were. They also soon learned that he protected them with a shotgun. Tony did not trust banks. Everyone knew that his money was in tobacco tins stashed in places he thought were safe. One night, there was a bad fire. The next morning, Sheriff Amos Ewing came out to investigate. He stopped in Aladdin to ask John Whalen to come with him as a witness. When they arrived, they found Tony's body in the ashes. There was no sign of Tony's money or any of his guns. (Courtesy of Black Hills State University, Case Library, Watson Parker Collection.)

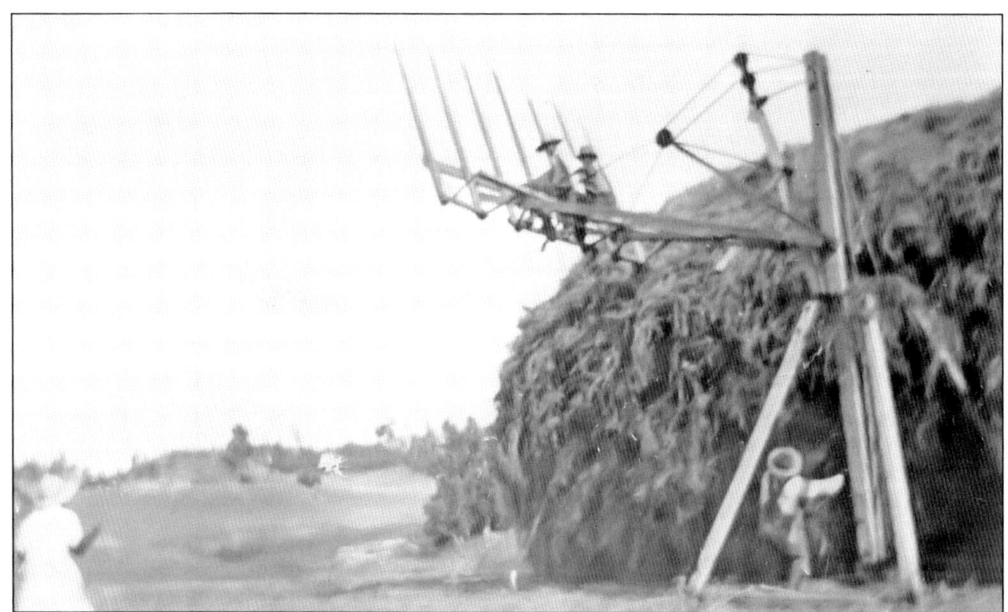

Putting up the winter's supply of hay can be a satisfying accomplishment. This must be done with care so that the stack is balanced and will not topple over. Using an overshot stacker powered by a good team of horses helps the day go smoothly. Pulling a long rope can lift the hay above the stack and dump it on the top of the stack from above. No one has to pitch the hay from the ground. Here, Rube and Jack are sitting above the haystack on the forks. Charles is guiding ropes on the ground, and Adel is standing to the left. The rope she is using to help guide the hay to the top is visible. (Courtesy of Chuck Pearson.)

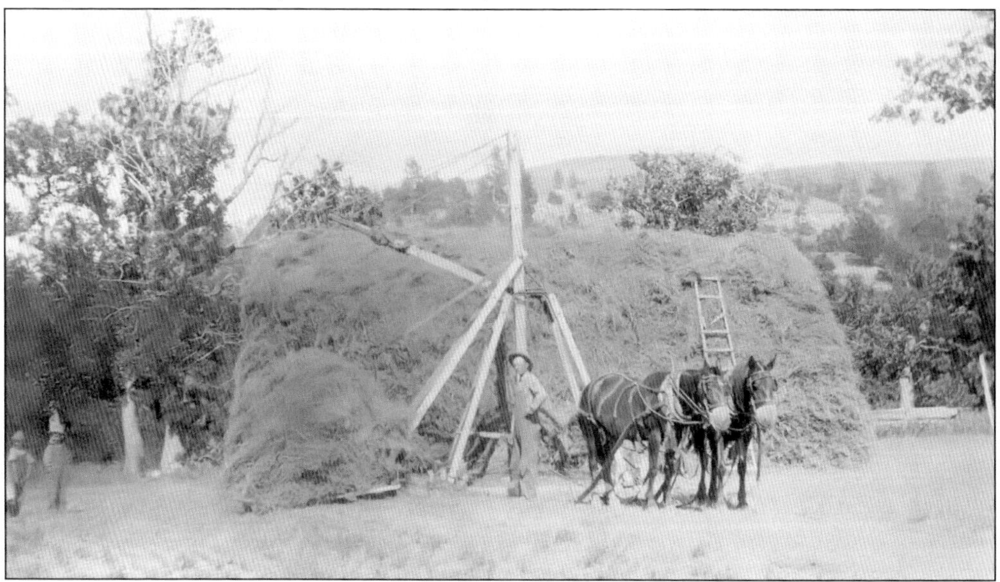

The back of this postcard tells that Charles Pearson, Prince, and Dick are stacking hay while Nancy, Frank, and Mary watch. Prince and Dick are working to pull the hay up to the top of the stack. Nancy, Frank, and Mary are staying out of the way. All kinds of creatures can come flying out as the hay is pulled up and over. Once it is stacked, sliding down the side from the top is lots of fun, but it does make a nice big mess. (Courtesy of Chuck Pearson.)

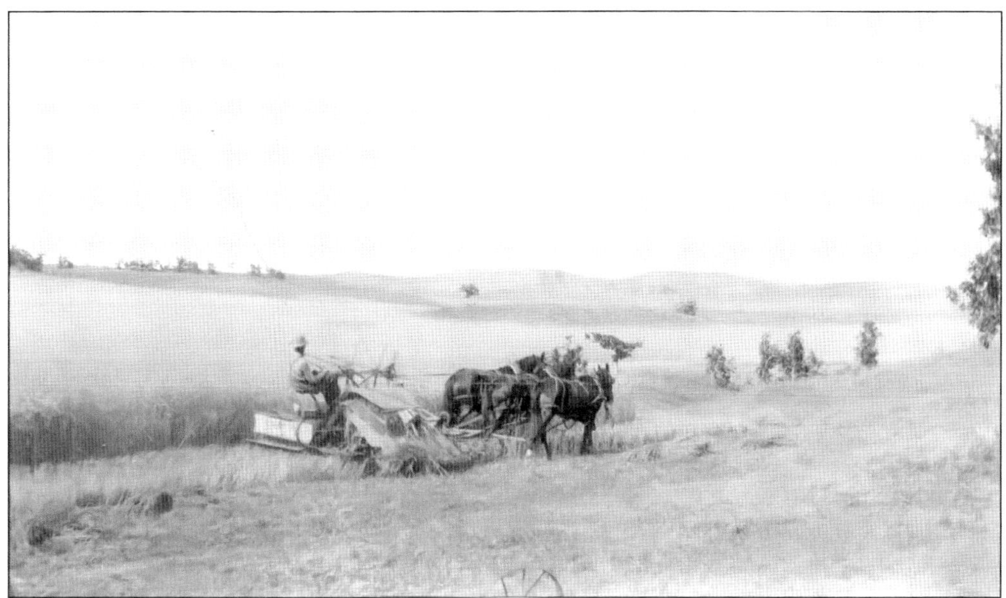

Charley Pearson is cutting rye. This is the first step in getting it ready to put up for the winter. Once it is cut, it will dry in the warm fall air for a few days, then it will be bundled and thrashed. Some farmers think threshing with a baseball bat works best. Other farmers like the help of good friends. Helping Charley on this day are his good friends Tony, Nig, and Prince. (Courtesy of Chuck Pearson.)

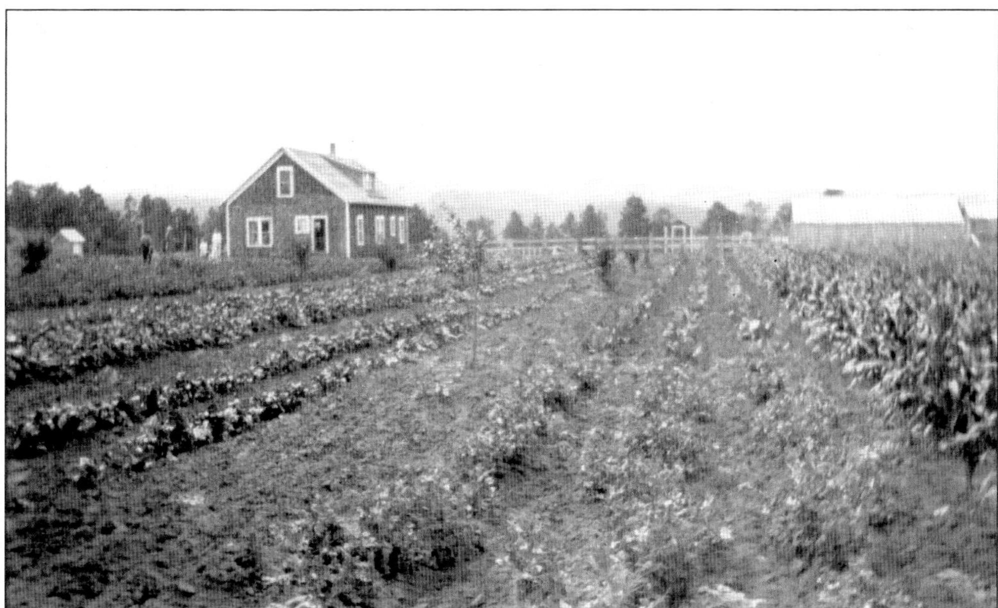

While Charley and the neighborhood men are harvesting the grain crops, the wives and children have also been doing some harvesting of their own. Nancy Pearson did not mention whose garden this is, but it looks big enough to feed a family of five or six. To get good produce out of a garden, the garden needs to be free of weeds and get a lot of water. Both of these chores were done by hand. The water was hauled by buckets from the creek or the spring, and the weeds were pulled by hand on bended knee. (Courtesy of Chuck Pearson.)

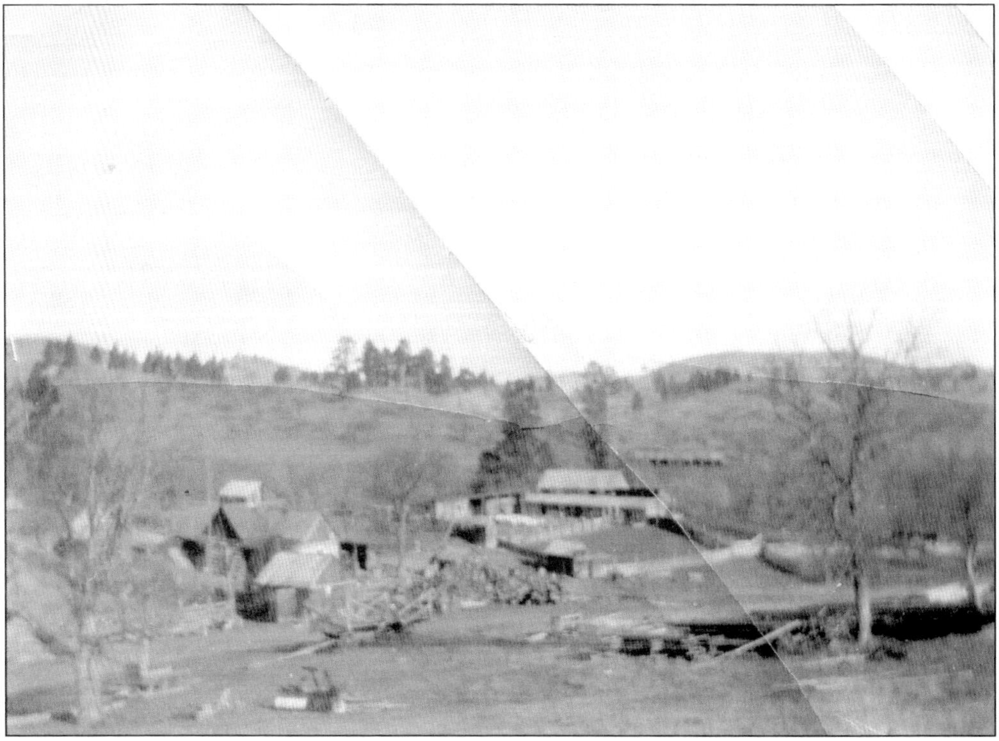

This is the Pearson homestead. To the left is the sharply pitched roof of the old log house. The barns and corrals can be seen at center. The new house that Fred Pattinson was cutting timbers for should be to the right. There are piles of lumber and logs lying about. They must not be done building. (Courtesy of Chuck Pearson.)

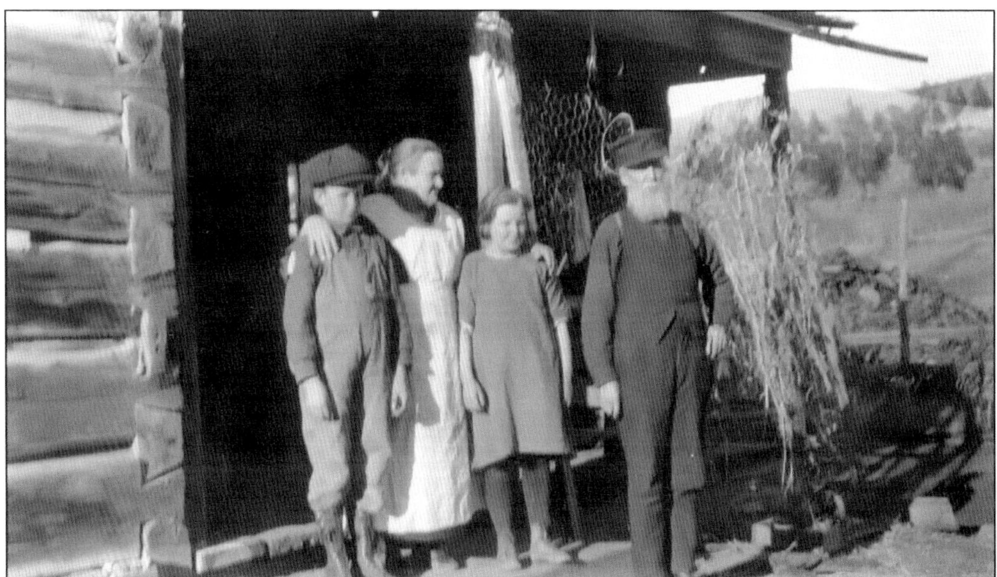

This postcard shows Mary and John Patton in the front door of their old log house with their grandchildren Frank and Mary Pearson. The square-cut ends of the logs and how well the logs fit together show that this is a well-built little cabin. (Courtesy of Chuck Pearson.)

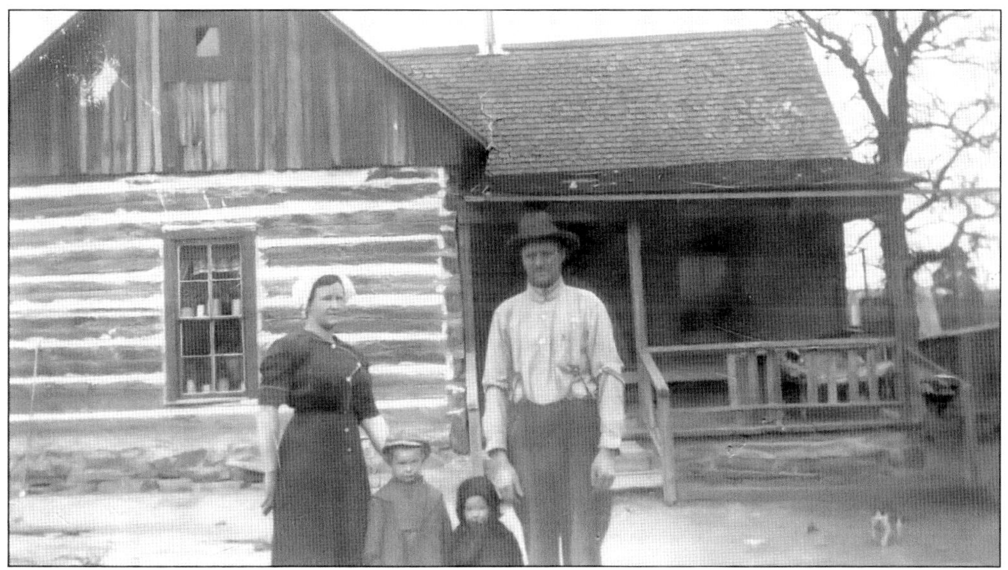

Nancy, Frank, Mary, and Charley Pearson in their everyday clothes stand in front of their old log cabin. They would live in this log house for a few more years before a bigger, more modern house was built just across the yard. (Courtesy of Chuck Pearson.)

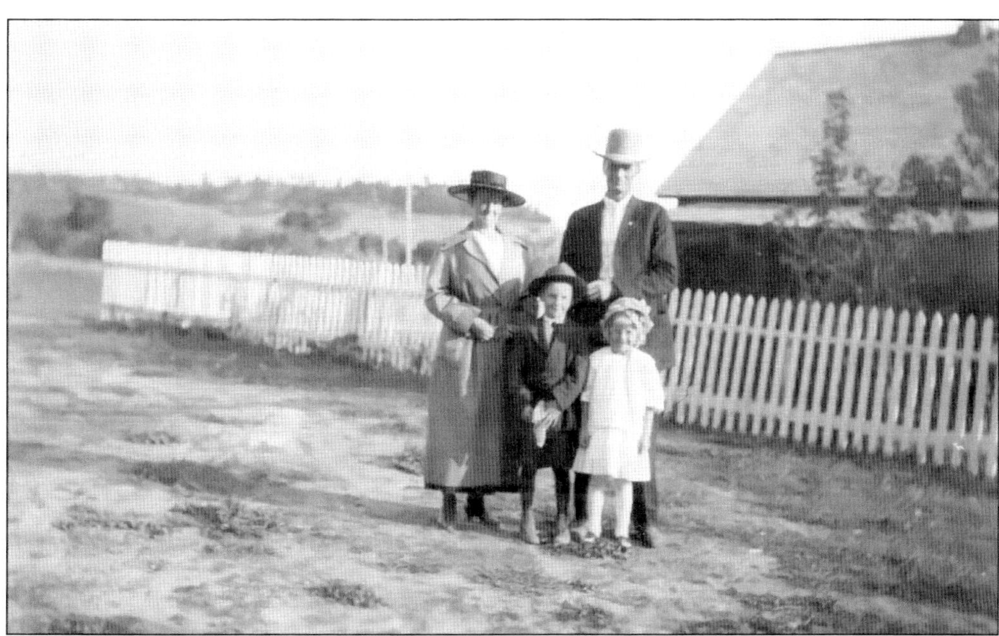

Here is the family all dressed up for Easter services. In the front row are Frank and Mary Pearson. In the back row are Nancy and Charley Pearson. Mary is all in white and looks full of spring time. Charley must have a brand new hat. Frank is still in short pants. The family is visiting their aunt and uncle Maggie and Matt Whalen at their home in Aladdin. (Courtesy of Chuck Pearson.)

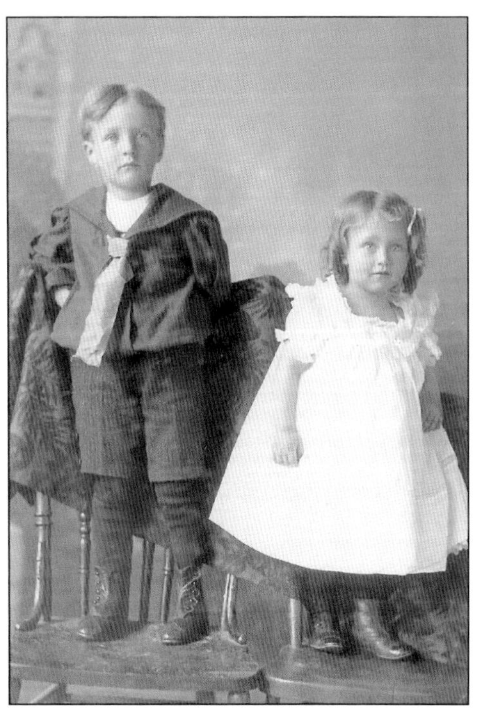

These are Amos Robinson's grandchildren. On the left is Thomas Robinson, and to the right of him, leaning away from the chair, is his sister Helen Robinson. Helen looks like she is trying to see what is in the next room or is trying to stretch the knot that has her tied to the chair to hold her still and clean. Children were often tethered to chairs, trees, or fences when pictures were being taken. (Courtesy of Tom Robinson.)

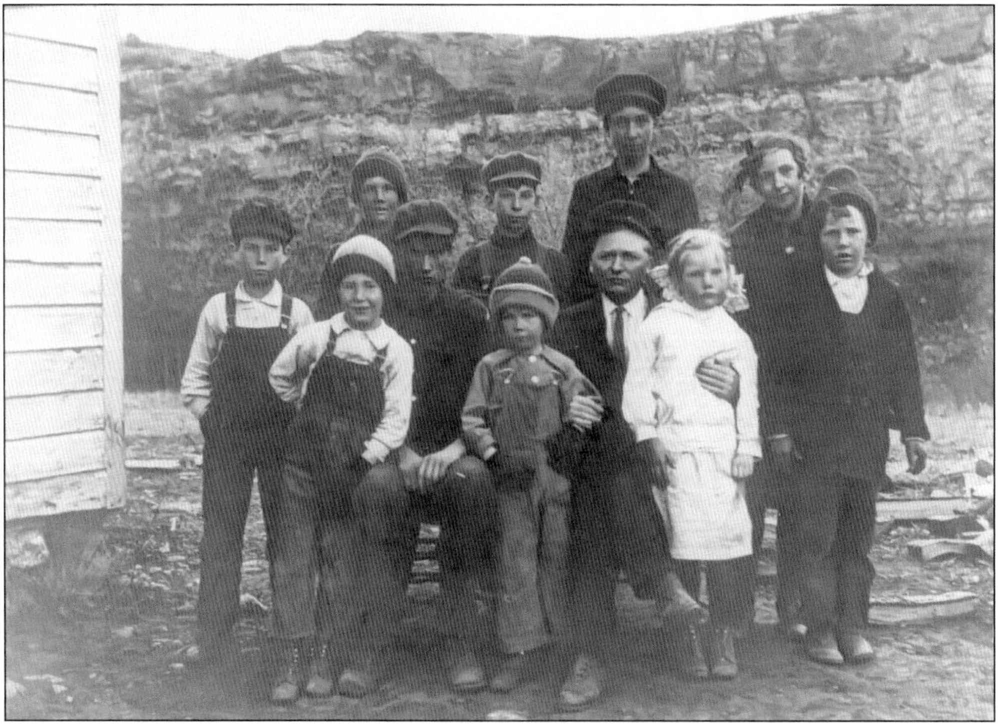

This is a picture of a school class. This is one of the few schools that had a male teacher. One wonders if he had to abide by the rule against marriage or the one about not being in an ice cream parlor. It looks like the little girl dressed in white is the only girl in school on picture day. How did she stay so clean? (Courtesy of Chuck Pearson.)

In this picture, there must be a branding or someone is moving cattle to the forest and needs a good man in the saddle. Bill Thompson and his horse Dandy have come ready to help do whatever must be done. It could have taken them the better part of the day to ride from their home along the Redwater River to Oak Creek in Crook County. Like many others, Bill's father and uncle came west to work the mines but soon found that was not for them. They found a homestead that would grow into the center of a family ranch that Bill's sons and grandsons continue to care for and appreciate. (Courtesy of the Thompson family.)

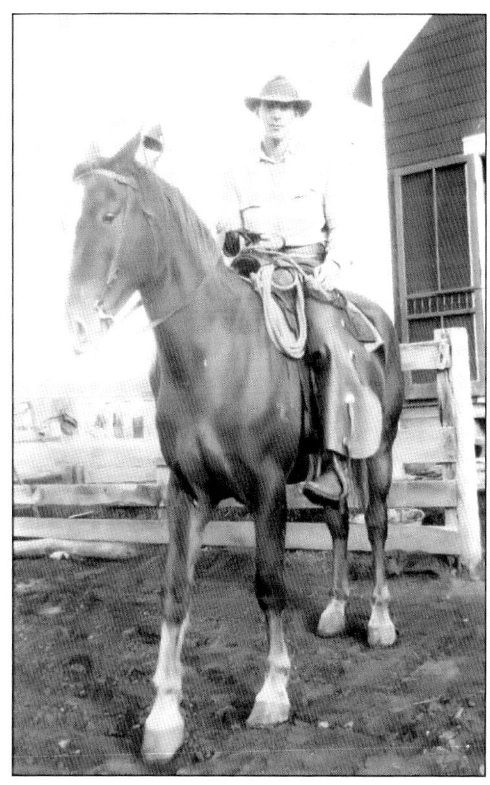

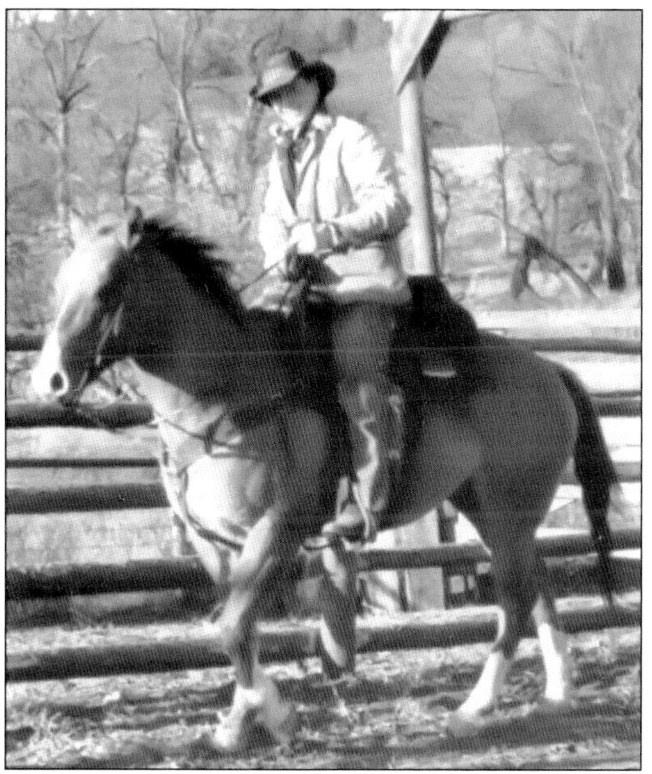

The Bunny family also came west to work the mines and soon found working the land was more to their liking. Before she married John Moline during World War II, Margaret Bunny went to California and became Aladdin's very own Rosie the Riveter. Today, the seven Molines keep their part of their mother's legacy alive and growing. This picture of a more modern cowboy shows David Moline ready to work the cattle of the X Heart ranch. These cowboys are dressed about the same despite the years. They both wear chaps that cover their legs for warmth and protection from rocks, tree branches, cattle, and even other horses. A good pair of gloves and hat will finish off their outfits no matter what the year. (Courtesy of David Moline.)